What Catalans Want
"Could Catalonia become Europe's next State?"

Interviews by Toni Strubell
Photographs by Lluís Brunet

What Catalans Want, by Toni Strubell
with Photographs by Lluís Brunet
http://www.WhatCatalansWant.cat

Published by Catalonia Press
http://www.cataloniapress.com
Ashfield, Massachusetts, USA

Copyright for text © 2011 by Toni Strubell
Copyright for photographs © 2011 by Lluís Brunet

Special thanks to Jaume Rodri for the photograph of Lluís on page 242.

Notice of Rights
All rights reserved. No part of this book may be reproduced or transmitted in any form by any means, electronic, mechanical, photocopying, recording, or otherwise, without the prior written permission of the publisher. For information on getting permission for reprints and excerpts, contact liz@elizabethcastro.com.

Notice of Liability
The information in this book is distributed on an "As Is" basis without warranty. While every precaution has been taken in the preparation of the book, the author/publisher will have no liability to any person or entity with respect to any loss or damage caused or alleged to be caused directly or indirectly by the instructions contained in this book or by the computer software and hardware products described in it.

ISBN
Print - Black and White: 978-1-61150-011-0

Print - Color: 978-1-61150-009-7
EPUB: 978-1-61150-012-7
Kindle/Mobi: 978-1-61150-013-4

Contents

Prologue: Colm Tóibín 7
Note from the Author 11

Country — 17
Carles Boix 18
Salvador Cardús 24
Eliseu Climent 30
Joan Laporta 36
Alfons López Tena 42
José Montilla 48
Jordi Pujol 54
Joan Ramon Resina 60

Economy — 67
Germà Bel 68
Joaquim Boixareu 74
Josep Mateu 80
Xavier Sala-i-Martin 86
Elisenda Paluzie 92

Memory — 99
Dr. Moisès Broggi 100
Josep Cruanyes 106
Hilari Raguer 112
Empar Salvador 118
Eugeni Casanova and
Jordi Llisterri 124

Culture — 129
Jennifer Berengueras 131
Bernat Joan 137
Jordi Portabella 143
Oleguer Presas 150
Joan Solà 156
Xavier Vinyals 162

Media — 169
Montserrat Armengou 170
Josep Gifreu 176
Pedro Morón de la Fuente 182
Vicent Partal 188
Vicent Sanchis 194

Foreign insights — 201
Helena Buffery 202
Susan DiGiacomo 208
Dr. Henry Ettinghausen 214
Alex Rietman 220
Matthew Tree 226

Notes — 233

About — 242

Prologue by
Colm Tóibín

We sit up straight and feel excited in that moment in the movie when the figure appears behind the boulder on the hill and narrows his eyes as the wagons and horses below make their journey westward through new and unmapped territory. We know now there will be action, there will be arrows and bareback-riding and a lot of shooting. The white man, moving slowly with his language and his almost innocent need to make fences, will have reason and technology on his side. The redskin will have an aboriginal relationship with the landscape; he will have a language that the microphone can barely pick up. Once the territory has been mapped by the white man, the redskin language will live on only in the names of some places; its grammar will not grace the marketplace; since it has no reason to spread, then it will slowly fade.

And so it begins, the colonial drama. As we watch this scene, some of us, with amusement, perhaps even distance and irony, we are allowed to feel that this news from elsewhere has been dramatized to entertain us; at other times, however, it feels like something whose contours and emotions we fully recognize. It is easy, then, to remember moments from the places where two languages have collided, or when one folded uneasily over another; it is easy to conjure up those gnarled landscapes of possession and dispossession in all their rich and disturbed imagery.

If later, in a moment around the campfire, one of the redskins were to sing a song about love in the language which they all share, there will be silence. They will think at first of love, and then maybe of lost love. And then maybe they will begin to contemplate other things they have lost, or might soon come to lose, which the notes of the song seem to suggest more precisely than any list they could make. Some sense of themselves, who they are, where they belong. This sense, the emotion involved, will be more pressing and powerful than maps, laws, fences, borders. For the white man on his way to victory, this idea of having a precise place to which you belong will be taken for granted. It will not need to be felt because it is not being threatened. It will seem natural, almost God-given. For others, however, it will mutate into terms with many meanings which will come to haunt the second half of the nineteenth and much of the twentieth century in Europe and elsewhere, terms such as *nationalism*, terms such as *identity*.

Take this one, for example. It was Tallinn in Estonia in 1994 and the Russians had finally gone. I was having supper with an Estonian family who were relieved at what had happened and full of hope for their country. They wanted now to connect with Scandinavia; they wanted to join the European Union. They saw Russia as an old dark place which was not progressive. They saw the Russian language as something that had been foisted on them; they didn't want to hear it again. They wanted to hear their own language, and maybe Swedish and Finnish but, more than anything, English. The fact that there were just one and a half million of them seemed only to add to their optimism, increase their happiness at the thought that they might finally be left in peace. They felt pride in themselves and who they were and what they might become.

The history of their country has echoes with the history of Catalonia. The publication of the Estonian national epic, *Kalevipoeg*, in 1862, and the organization of the first national song contest seven years later, managed to re-awaken a national spirit, a sense of a shared past moving back into the mists of time. By the 1890s this cultural force had become a political force; the movement for autonomy from Russia grew from this newly-awakened national cultural identity as much as from any set of economic arguments or needs.

The only difficult moment during the supper that evening in Tallinn came when my hosts described the large Russian population of Estonia who had suddenly found themselves in a country whose official language they did not speak. 'They still believe they are in Russia', my hosts told me. Soon, they said, these Russians would have to learn Estonian or go home, even though many of them had actually been born in Estonia. I could feel my hosts' idealism, their understanding of this as an imperative, something which must happen in a small fragile country if its entire identity was not to be lost. But I was uneasy. The idea of inclusion, the understanding that diversity and impurity have rights too, and that tolerance of others who do not fully share a nation's identity was also an imperative, would take time to seep into the body politic of Estonia.

* * * * *

This idea of a nation being created or imagined from deep roots in the past and fragile ones in the present by a group of writers and artists was something which anyone Irish is acutely conscious of. The songs written by the members of Young Ireland in the years around 1848 inspired a new national feeling:

> 'When boyhood's fire was in my blood
> I read of ancient freemen
> Of Greece and Rome who bravely stood
> Three hundred men and three men;
> And then I prayed I yet might see
> Our fetters rent in twain,
> And Ireland long a province be
> A nation once again!'

Such songs would foment a national spirit which would help, eventually, to lead to the independence of the south of Ireland in 1922 and its becoming a republic in 1948. But in these small countries of ours which have known that complex set of emotions about identity and loss of identity nothing is simple. In Ireland, in the very years when a national spirit was being created, the English language was moving slowly into a dominant position. No one has ever fully explained why Ireland did not actually become bilingual, why the Irish language began actually to disappear. Just as no one can fully explain to me the antipathy which people feel towards Catalonia in some of the places—Mallorca, say, or Valencia—where a language that sounds very like Catalan is spoken. 'It seems history is to blame', as the Englishman says in James Joyce's *Ulysses*.

* * * * * *

Thus we are not quite sure whether to laugh or cry in the exchange about language between Mrs. Rooney and Mr. Rooney in Samuel Beckett's radio play *All That Fall*. When he tells her that she sounds like she is speaking a dead language—she is speaking English—Mrs Rooney says: 'It will be dead in time, just like our own dear Gaelic, there is that to be said.' And just as the languages of the native Americans survive in the names of rivers and places, so too in Ireland it is as though two languages fought and one moved underground to become a set of signposts. The Irish names of places were adapted, as the native languages in America were, to name towns and rivers in English. In his play *Translations*, first performed in 1980, the Irish playwright Brian Friel dramatized that moment in the early nineteenth century when the English mapmakers came to make sense of the Irish landscape by changing the names of the places from Irish into English. As their Irish helper says: 'We are trying to denominate and at the same time describe that tiny area of soggy, rocky, sandy ground where that little stream enters the sea, an area known locally as Bun na hAbhann…Burnfoot! What about Burnfoot?'

These words for the names of places, as they change, mark a notable moment in the history of the colonization of Ireland, but in Friel's play they stand for something else, his drama of change explores the idea that language is not merely a tool, or a way to describe or communicate, but it is a sort of essence, something which belongs to the self, or something which causes the self to come into being, as the soul might have done in the time when we believed in the soul.

* * * * *

It is hard, in contemplating this issue of what small countries want, not to allow more images to emerge. Take this one. It was 1996 and I was sitting in a cinema in Glasgow in Scotland with a Scottish friend watching the movie *Trainspotting*. The cinema was almost full. It was all about drugs and sex and then the following piece of dialogue was spoken: 'It's shite being Scottish! We're the lowest of the low. The scum of the fucking Earth! The most wretched, miserable, servile, pathetic trash that was ever shat into civilization. Some hate the English. I don't. They're just wankers. We, on the other hand, are colonized by wankers. Can't even find a decent culture to be colonized by. We're ruled by effete assholes. It's a shite state of affairs to be in, Tommy, and all the fresh air in the world won't make any fucking difference!' I thought that this was desperately funny and began to howl with laughter. I stopped only because I was nudged by my Scottish friend into silence. I realized that there was a dead silence in the cinema. I was the only one who had laughed or make a sound. No one else thought it was funny; everyone, my Scottish friend explained, thought it was true. Its starkness as fact was a cause of shame.

* * * * *

Or take this one. It was during the war in the former Yugoslavia and I had just travelled through Croatia and Herzogovina. I had interviewed many bigoted priests and seen buildings burn. The house where I had been staying had sheds in the backyard filled with arms which would be used to attack the Muslim population of Mostar. Now I had fled the conflict and arrived in Ljubljana, the capital of Slovenia, and I was having supper with a Slovenian professor of sociology. I knew that 90% of Slovenia's 1.9 million inhabitants were ethnic Slovenians and 98% of Slovenes in what was once Yugoslavia lived in Slovenia. I was interested in what this sort of ethnic purity might do to a place, and how Slovenia had managed not to have a war, how it was already making allies in Austria and Italy with a view to getting away from its southern warring neighbours and joining the European Union. I asked the professor if he was a Slovenian nationalist? Did he feel an emotion about his country, as the Croats did about Croatia? He said that he felt no personal emotion about Slovenia as a nation. His tone was dry, matter-of-fact. He never asked such questions, he said. Rather, he continued, he did have strong views about the Slovenian economy being run from Belgrade. The idea of seceding from the federation was prompted, he told me, not by nationalist feeling, but by the desire to secure normal life. It had become an imperative to leave.

Economists, he went on, were doubtful about the advantages of secession. Half of all markets for Slovenian products would be lost. There was also another disadvantage in being such a small, independent country. He called it 'the density of political space' and it is something that people in Scotland, now that it has its own parliament, or Ireland, or Estonia, or Catalonia, know all about. In a small state, he said, everybody in the ruling class gets to know each other; there are too many friendships and thus it was hard at times to implement a rational policy. The professor himself, he said, knew more than half the ministers in the government.

I was interested in what had happened in Slovenia in the war because I felt the difference between their experience of the war would draw a line between Slovenia and Croatia which would last for a century. I asked the professor if he had been involved in the independence movement. He was in Ljubljana, he said, on the night of July 25, 1991, when independence was declared. The following night he went out to dinner with friends to celebrate. His friends, like him, were all rationalists, he said, so there were no really stirring speeches or emotional moments. He went home at two-thirty. He was woken at eight to be told to come immediately to the base from which he operated part-time as a mobilizing instructor in the local army. When he turned on the radio, he learned that Yugoslav troops were on the road. I asked him if he saw any action. Not much, he said. He found a broken-down tank with three soldiers in it.

'What did you do with the soldiers?', I asked.

He looked puzzled.

'What do you mean?', he asked.

'Did you kill them?', I asked.

'No!'

'Arrest them?'

'No, absolutely not', he replied. 'I made sure they were given coffee.'

* * * *

Or take the following moment. In 1986 I went to the home of Alan Black in Bessbrook in County Armagh in Northern Ireland. He was a Northern Irish Protestant and I was a Southern Irish Catholic. A decade earlier, when he was coming home from work with eleven of his workmates, the van was stopped by what they had thought at first was the British army. Ten of them were Protestants like him, but one was a Catholic who was told to identify himself and then step aside. And then, in one of the worst sectarian attacks in the history of Northern Ireland, the eleven Protestants were shot. Ten of them died. Alan Black survived.

We sat in his front room and watched a documentary which had been made about these killings. And Alan Black seemed upset not only by the anniversary itself and the memory of how his friends had died but also because one of the English Sunday newspapers had arrived and interviewed him about the Anglo-Irish Agreement, signed by Mrs. Thatcher and the Irish Prime Minister the previous year, which gave the Dublin government a say in the running of Northern Ireland. It was as though being a victim, or the survivor or an atrocity, gave him a special right to speak, and he deplored that.

Like most Protestants in Northern Ireland, however, he was against the Agreement. He did not believe that the Dublin government had any right to be involved in the governance of Northern Ireland. I was interested in what he had to say. Up to then I had believed such opposition irrational, something which arose from pure bigotry as much as anything else. Up to then I had only once or twice sat in the home of a Northern Protestant on such easy and familiar terms. The partition of Ireland had kept us apart. I listened carefully as Alan Black turned to me and said that, as a Protestant, he was against all forms of arbitrary authority, not only in religious but in civil affairs. That was the basis of his citizenship. And that was, he implied, why people like him in Northern Ireland did not want a united Ireland. They saw the Republic of Ireland as a Catholic state, and they saw Catholicism as a form of arbitrary authority. And now the Anglo-Irish Agreement was allowing a government for which he could not vote, which was not accountable to him, have some power in his country. He thought this was wrong.

What was strange was that I had never heard this argument before being presented as normal, rational. I found myself nodding in agreement, but I was not sure. The Agreement had for the first time recognized the allegiances of Northern Irish Catholics as being valid. In places where there are competing questions and arguments over nations, identities, allegiances and borders, nothing is ever simple. It is often easier to be puzzled than sure. As one of the characters says in Brian Friel's *Translations*: 'Confusion is not an ignoble condition.'

* * * * *

And finally this, the matter of Catalonia, and what Catalans want. On April 27, 1988, I went to Montserrat for the feast day of the Virgin. Later, when the ceremonies were over I decided to walk back down the mountain. Soon, I was offered a lift by an elderly couple. They both were from Madrid and spoke in Spanish. They had come especially for the feast of the Virgin, they said, but they did not want to stay any longer, they did not like what they saw. The mountain was beautiful and they had enjoyed the journey. The problem was the language; they couldn't understand a word of the Mass, nor a word of the sermon. And they were in their own country, they emphasized. And to make matters worse, the wife had tried to buy some holy pictures with prayers printed on them but they had them only in Catalan, and she had left without buying anything.

Was everything like that now, they asked me. It was, I said. There was a television station in Catalan, many radio stations, two newspapers, signs in shops, lessons in school, lectures in the university. All in Catalan. In Barcelona, I said, the street names were in Catalan only. The husband said that he was first in Barcelona in 1939 and it was a great city. He had never imagined that this could happen, he said. Why do they want to have everything in Catalan, they asked. She didn't understand, the wife said, why they couldn't just use Catalan among themselves, but surely for big occasions, like the feast day of Montserrat, they could use Spanish, which was the language everyone understood.

* * * * *

That same week an exhibition opened in the Plaça del Rei in Barcelona, in the Sala Tinell and the Church of Santa Àgata, called *Tàpies, els anys 80*, which was sponsored by the Barcelona City Council. Antoni Tàpies's work, in all its mixture of wildness and restraint, in all its imaginative freedom, in the mixture of private and public references within its imagery, represented something essential for Catalans. The pictorial surfaces were suggestive, open-ended, at times playful but also filled with a sort of solemnity. In any argument about Catalan identity or nationhood, or the Catalan spirit, or the future of Catalonia, a tour of these new works by Tàpies would make arguments or lists of grievances or demands sound hollow. This is what art and music and literature can do in fragile societies, they can come to matter more because they hit the nervous system, the core of self, the place where identity is at its most raw and open.

One of the essays in the catalogue for that show read: 'Tàpies's Catalan identity has been viewed as a constant in his career that gave unity and continuity to his art... Many motifs appearing in the work of Tàpies have been recognized as references to his Catalan roots, but his Catalan identity has also been explained on a deeper technical and formal level. The significance of craftsmanship in his work, especially his profound knowledge of the materials he employs, has been associated with Catalonia's traditional craftsmanship. Ultimately, Tàpies's intellectual attitude towards mysticism, the esoteric and the magical has been explained through his Catalan identity.'

Looking at his work makes it easier to understand that the business of what we want in the world is complex and not always rational, even if it can be made to seem so at times. Identity comes from something deep and strange, and the idea of language, in all its complexity, lives at the mysterious core of what it is to be alive in the world, as Caliban had occasion to explain to Prospero in his famous cry in Shakespeare's *The Tempest*:

> 'You taught me language; and my profit on 't
> is, I know how to curse. The red plague rid you
> For learning me your language!'

This relationship between Caliban and Prospero has many forms through history, most of them protean and unstable, filled with ironies and strange twists. The idea, for example, of the small country or nation becoming or remaining more prosperous than the place which came to take it over, or becoming more rational, more peace-loving and progressive, has echoes in the recent history of Estonia, Slovenia and Catalonia. The idea, too, that nothing is simple within this world filled with constitutional compromises, remaining grievances, conflicting loyalties, competing identities, uneasy allegiances, uncertain borders and unpredictable outcomes can be used to explain what is happening now in Catalonia, the Basque Country, Ireland and Scotland and also in places such as Quebec and Kurdistan. But it might also be true to say that this idea of identity under pressure, in one form or another, has been present in history since time began. In its own way, it represents a secret history of Europe, to name just one place. It is unlikely to go away.

Introduction

What Catalans Want

What Catalans Want is a book that takes a concerted look at Catalonia at a moment when the country's political future as a Spanish autonomous region has been called into question for the first time since this formula came into being in 1980. It does so by talking to representative personalities from all walks of life who provide clues about the recent developments in the country. The book appears in the wake of two major events. On the one hand the Spanish Constitutional Court's ruling of June 28, 2010, which severely limits the Catalan Statute of Autonomy approved by both the Catalan and Spanish Parliaments in 2005 and 2006. And secondly, the impressive demonstration of July 10, 2010, in which over a million Catalans took to the streets to protest against this ruling in a rally which marched under the banner, 'We are a nation. We decide.'

The aim of this book is not so much to conduct a survey regarding the country's possible independence but rather to uncover what it is that makes so many of the inhabitants of this small western European country begin to feel as uncomfortable about forming part of Spain as they are comfortable about being members of Europe. The people interviewed in search of answers to these questions include the current and last presidents of Catalonia, the last president of triumphant FC Barcelona, six professors from major European and American universities, three leading economists, one leading jurist, two leading businessmen and five media experts and journalists, among others. Four of the interviewed are foreign residents in Catalonia, while another teaches Catalan in Ireland. Defying all categories is remarkable Moisès Broggi, the 102-year-old war surgeon who served with the International Brigades in the Spanish Civil War.

One key issue is the growing 'disaffection' that former Catalan President Montilla recently admitted many Catalans feel with regard to Spain *(see page 48)*. This is occurring at a time when identity issues have also been raised in countries such as Scotland, Quebec, East Timor, Montenegro, Tibet or Flanders. Other topics raised in the book include language, economy, business, religion, sports, immigration, culture, transport, historical memory, new technologies, infrastructures and the mass media. Two interviews look into bullfighting in Catalonia, an issue that hit the headlines worldwide on July 28, 2010, when the Catalan Parliament took the historic decision to abolish this practice in Catalonia, much to the irritation of most Spanish media.

Although it is often hard for journalists and international observers to forecast those points on the globe where apparently innocuous events may one day become newsworthy, for the last few years there has been good reason to believe that Catalonia could be one such place. This may come as a surprise to those who see the country as stable, pro-European, and relatively prosperous, which, of course, it is. It may also unsettle those who tend to associate these kinds of developments with ex-Communist or Third World countries. Nevertheless, there is little doubt that democratic Europe would be ill-advised to overlook what is going on in Catalonia as historically it has done with conflicts affecting other areas of the continent. No one who has kept an eye on the media in recent years can have failed to notice that something is not right in the relationship between Catalonia and Spain. In July 2010, this question even led to a question being asked by over a dozen MPs from six different groups in the British House of Commons[1]. Although it may cause concern, dismay even, to those who may see this kind of dispute as 'something Europe should have put behind it', there is a very real sense among Catalans of all circumstances that the arrangements made following Franco's death to acknowledge Catalan rights and identity have not been lastingly respected.

Not surprisingly, therefore, the 'Catalan issue' has made international headlines on several occasions. The major European and American media gave front-page coverage to the unofficial referendums on independence that have been held in over half of Catalonia's towns since September, 2009. In late June 2010 there was also ample media coverage for the aforementioned Constitutional Court ruling against the Catalan Statute and the July 10th rally, which the ex-vice president of the Liberal International, Mr. Emil Kirjas, described as 'the biggest expression in favour of self-determination to have been carried out in the last twenty years in Europe'. Admittedly, European and American tourists pouring into cosmopolitan Barcelona will have almost certainly remained happily oblivious to these developments even as they were taking place. Wasn't this also true for visitors to the 1984 Sarajevo Olympics?

Parallel to this, a considerable number of intellectuals hitherto seemingly uncommitted to Catalan nationalism have come out in favour of self-determination, even independence. This is the case of the respected Barcelona notary and *La Vanguardia* columnist, Sr. Juan José López-Burniol, who stated in January 2010 that relations between Catalonia and Spain had gone 'beyond the point of no return'. Other well-known pro-Socialists, such as the journalist Josep Ramoneda or philosopher Xavier Rubert de Ventós, have publicly admitted that, if given the chance, they would vote in favour of independence. Former president Pujol, though by no means an overt proponent of independence, also showed support for the local independence referendums, as have the country's major trade unions and thousands of popular clubs and associations, including Pakistani residents' associations. To break all clichés, there are even instances of Andalusian Flamenco clubs that danced for free at meetings in favour of these polls. In the same vein, on November 26, 2009, twelve Catalan newspapers[2] jointly published an editorial, which, though not independentist,[3] had the unambiguous title 'Catalonia's dignity' and warned of the possibility that Spain's Supreme Court might limit Catalonia's national rights, as indeed occurred seven months later. This in turn sparked the hysterical reaction of most of the Madrid press. In addition, it should not be forgotten that in 2006 and 2007 two more massive demonstrations had been held in Barcelona in favour of the country's 'right to decide'.[4] Who would have imagined such developments at the start of the New Millennium?

One may well ask why all this turmoil is occurring at this precise moment. One major reason is clearly the parliamentary debate over the new Catalan Statute and the aggressive opposition shown by a significant proportion of Spanish society to it. As of 2005, the Catalan Parliament exercised its right to revise the original 1979 Statute, with a view to achieving a greater degree of home rule. The new Statute was voted in by almost 90% percent of the Catalan Parliament, and granted the Catalan government new powers aimed at normalizing the Catalan language[5] and gaining more legal and financial instruments than it had controlled in the past. It also defined the country as a Nation, in line with historical tradition. Despite some pruning and the consequent loss of some Catalan support for the bill during a series of parliamentary debates in Madrid,[6] the Statute passed into law in 2006. However, it was challenged in the

Constitutional Court, which four years later ordered the cancellation of the 15 articles that contained the basic improvements the Catalan parties had so eagerly sought at the outset. This led to a crisis in which, although it had already come into force, the new Catalan Statute was severely mutilated on the grounds of its alleged incompatibility with the Spanish Constitution. What further irritated many Catalans was the fact that the Conference of Spanish Bishops ostensibly joined forces with the Spanish right, by drawing up a document that specifically considered Spanish unity a 'moral asset'.

To make matters worse, the Constitutional Court responsible for deciding on the legitimacy of the Statute degenerated into a battleground between 'progressive' and 'conservative' judges. The result was that, some four years after the Statute had gained political approval, the Court had still not made a ruling on its validity. In addition, what discerning Catalans perceived as the arbitrary disqualification of some of the Court's more progressive members coincided with the excessively extended terms of office offered to some of their conservative opponents in the Court. All these elements combined to create a situation of heightened tension. Catalonia's mistrust of the Spanish Supreme Court and the widespread perception that it lacked legitimacy rivalled the intensity with which the mainstream media in Madrid fanned the controversy over the harsh sentence against the Statute that was rumoured to be in the offing. The rift between Catalonia and Spain had never been greater in living memory, a sensation that was further underscored when the harshness of the Court's ruling was confirmed. The result of this whole process was that many Catalans became increasingly convinced that their country had no real place in present-day Spain. Certainly not if any degree of dignity were to be preserved. It was therefore not surprising that a survey published in Barcelona's conservative *La Vanguardia* in July 2010 should have showed that almost 48% percent of Catalans supported independence, some 10% more than those opposed to it. When compared with surveys held even five years earlier, the growth of support for independence can be said to have been spectacular.

Apart from the Statute crisis itself, several other factors also contributed to the growing rift between Spaniards and Catalans. Perhaps the most important of these was the financial plundering that many Catalans feel themselves to be the victims of.[7] It is now common knowledge that Catalonia contributes as much as 10% percent of its GDP in unreturned taxes to Spain, a figure that has even led some economists to speculate how the Catalan economy is able to survive at all. To add insult to injury, the public verification of this degree of plunder contrasts with firmly entrenched attitudes in many parts of Spain, where Catalans are commonly portrayed as selfish subsidy-hoggers. It is the sort of cliché that the publication of official figures would surely dispel in other latitudes, but which sadly persists unscathed in present-day Spain.

One final factor that upsets many more politically-aware Catalans is Spain's continuing unwillingness to heal old wounds from the Civil War. It offends many that the death penalties against Catalan president Lluís Companys (1933-1940)—along with those of tens of thousands of fellow Republicans—have not been legally annulled, despite the promise made by current Prime Minister José Luis Rodríguez Zapatero to do so during his 2004 election campaign. Parallel to this is the painful fact that prominent Spanish judge Baltasar Garzón was suspended from office for taking steps to investigate Franco's crimes, a measure which is particularly unacceptable for those demanding higher democratic standards in Spain. In addition, the fact that in recent times King Juan Carlos has failed to show any degree of commitment to Catalan feeling on these and other issues cannot be overlooked as a reason for the significant drop in popularity the monarch has suffered among Catalans.[8] This is yet another of the questions that *What Catalans Want* explores, in an attempt to analyse the fascinating yet sometimes imperceptible changes occurring in Catalonia today.

Note from the Author

Producing this book has been possible thanks to the invaluable cooperation of a number of people and organisations. To name the principal ones, I must start with my mother Amèlia Trueta and Liz Castro, without whom the whole project would have been a wash-out, and Colm Tóibín, for his excellent prologue. Lluís Brunet—my excellent photographer—and I are also very grateful to all those interviewed. We are also particularly appreciative of the aid and encouragement offered in difficult moments by Paul Preston of London School of Economics and Tony Grahame, of Sussex Academic Press. The following groups have also helped us greatly: Òmnium Cultural, Col.lectiu Emma, the Catalunya Estat foundation, the monthly *Catalonia Today* and *I'm Catalan, I love freedom*.

Toni Strubell
Sant Feliu de Guíxols
July, 2011

Country

Carles Boix
Concern for Catalonia at Princeton

Carles Boix belongs to a generation of young Catalan academics working at leading US universities.[1] He obtained his doctorate at Harvard in 1995 and lectured at the University of Chicago from 1999 to 2006. Currently he is Professor of Politics and Public Affairs at Princeton, where he conducts research and lectures on political economy and comparative politics. His book Political Parties, Growth and Equality *(Cambridge University Press, 1998) won him the William Riker prize for the best book on political economy, awarded by the American Political Science Association in 1999. His* Democracy and Redistribution *(Cambridge University Press, 2003) won the same prize again in 2004, as well as the Mattei Dogan prize for the best book on comparative research. He has also acted as editor of the* Oxford Handbook of Comparative Politics *(Oxford University Press, 2007) and as an adviser to the World Bank and the International Development Bank.*

Despite his intellectual achievements, Boix doesn't see his job as one ensconced in the classic ivory tower. He is very much a committed intellectual. His stimulating articles in the Catalan daily Avui *and on the popular Catalan web page* El Singular Digital *(www.elsingulardigital.cat) make him a point of reference on political issues for Catalan readers. Ever concerned about the future of Catalonia, he has repeatedly insisted on the strong need for political regeneration in the country.*

As an expert on political affairs, what is your opinion regarding the Spanish Constitutional Court's ruling against the Catalan Statute on June 28, 2010?

I think it clarifies a great many things. It restricts Catalan home rule to the status quo, and in certain ways may even be seen to limit it further. It is the final blow to the federalist bid to try and make Catalonia move forward and guarantee for itself an area of safety for its powers and jurisdiction. As I wrote in *Avui*,[2] the sentence rules out the possibility of our country recovering financially. On a more introspective level, it also obliges federalists to choose. Some of them are opting for Catalan sovereignty; others insist that federalism is still possible in Spain. For me they're banging their heads against the wall.

Was the response to this sentence as you expected?

The July 10th demonstration was a splendid and festive affair. It has really marked a new rallying point for the country. It also shifted the necessary pressure onto our politicians. It was unexpected in the sense that we were always being told that our concerns were not focussed on this issue and that our nation was practically inexistent. Now it's quite clear that is not the case. So all this has to be adequately channelled. I prefer to think CiU,[3] the moderate nationalists, will have got the message. And perhaps a credible pro-independence force may yet take root.

You mention the march's success was surprising, even to its organisers.[4] For some Catalans, though, isn't there sometimes a sense of embarrassment at being identified as 'Catalanists'?

Yes, I'd say that's true of lots of Catalans. I think it's because they are often haunted by a sense of false cosmopolitanism. Catalans love their country but they all too often seem afraid to admit it. They seem to be embarrassed about being seen to be concerned about the 'eternally unsolved' Catalan issue. When living or travelling abroad, you might think that this sense of unease would diminish. But, funnily enough, it often does not. You become increasingly interested and involved in your own country, and you find your thoughts constantly turning back home.

And yet critics suggest that travelling helps 'heal' what they see as absurd nationalist feelings…

It's funny you should say that. The other day my wife and I were reading a poem by Kavafis on the journey to Ithaka.[5] It says that, when you come back to your particular Ithaka—whatever it might be—you'll be wiser and you'll understand what those other Ithakas mean. I think getting to know other countries enriches you, but the most important thing is to have an Ithaka of your own. So I don't think travelling 'heals' you, as cosmopolitans like to make out. I reckon the line Catalans have on this one is wrong. The French, the English, and the Americans never need to 'heal' themselves of their national identity. It comes naturally to them and they don't give it a second thought. When some talk of the need to 'heal' ourselves, what they really mean is that we haven't yet solved the question of our national identity. Not that we are ill because we have one! Really, I don't think Catalans need to 'heal' themselves of anything in particular.

Some Catalans paint a pessimistic view of the country's future and point to the need to adopt a 'now or never' attitude…

Yes. This wave of pessimism has cropped up quite recently. It may largely be put down to immigration, I think. It would be helpful if non-Catalans thought about the way we've evolved. Catalonia has been very successful, from an economic and cultural point of view, over the past couple of centuries. The Barcelona phenomenon, with its worldwide appeal, is a success story that needs to be seen in the context of an Iberian Peninsula that's far from successful. During the last two hundred years Catalonia has been the economic and industrial vanguard of Spain. That encouraged substantial migration from the poorest regions of Spain. Those arriving in Catalonia were assimilated into the country in quite a similar way as occurred to immigrants in France, where approximately one third of the population—including Nicolas Sarkozy—are direct descendants of foreigners. Catalonia too has a magnetic effect. In 1920 immigration was largely Spanish-speaking. But by the second generation, their offspring had generally been assimilated, both socially

and linguistically. This was largely made possible by the fact that Catalans are very rarely racist. They practice a cultural and civic brand of nationalism quite divorced from the ethnic line that prevails in other places. In contrast, during the 1880s the founder of Basque nationalism actually criticized the Catalans for encouraging immigrants to learn their language!

So what is the problem today?

Our current problem—if it may be defined as such—started in the 1950s, when large-scale Spanish immigration doubled Catalonia's population. It was a time when all the practical mechanisms for promoting functional assimilation were outlawed by the Franco dictatorship. From the start, the regime was brutal in its repression of the Catalan language, to a degree—one may add—that Hitler never was with Polish during the Nazi occupation of Poland. In the 50s and 60s, the situation was made even worse by radio and television, which were exclusively in Spanish and were absolutely Spanish in content and ideology. The only thing working in favour of national integration was the presence of a powerful, left wing, anti-Francoist underground movement that was always openly favourable to Catalan culture. The country achieved democracy in 1975 with two reasonably porous linguistic communities and with political parties that shared a broad consensus about the need to recover home rule.

The problem is that in the last ten or fifteen years there has been a new wave of immigration, and the country has grown from six million to seven and a half million inhabitants in a very short time. Understandably enough, that makes some Catalans worried about the future of their language and culture. While their concern has no racial component, it has started to make people question our national character, because this is basically what has made us so economically successful and creative over the past 150 years. In this context we find ourselves wondering what we ought to be doing, just as might occur in other countries in our situation. Although the Spanish State has granted us a certain degree of autonomy, it doesn't do much to help when it comes to this sort of issue, because it has never accepted the need to build a State along the lines of the Swiss model, for example. And that is what has created this state of unease in Catalonia, because a lot of people feel they've been pushed up against a wall.

In countries like the United States integration is made possible by the 'melting pot" effect'. Does this not occur in Catalonia?

In the USA the melting pot effect is decisive. It's based on two factors: firstly, the values of freedom and opportunity that inform the American Constitution. And then there's the so-called 'American Dream', which enables social and economic advancement. One can draw parallels between this and what is called the 'social lifting' effect in Catalonia. That is, the chance the country gives newcomers to improve their status and that of their families. This has worked very well in the USA. There is not only a constitutional awareness of the need for integration but also a context of economic success. That has helped immigrants identify with their new community. People may use their old language within the family, but the *lingua franca* they communicate in socially is English.

In Catalonia there has been a similar degree of immigration. But the country is not an independent State! It only has limited resources to encourage integration, such as the education system—which is certainly an important one—and the promise of social and economic advancement. The question is whether or not the people who are coming into the country identify their own future paths with the country they are settling in. Here there are two discourses scuffling to get the immigrants' attention: that of Catalonia herself and that of Spain. My feeling is that it depends a lot on the people involved. I see some immigrant groups who are very willing to understand Catalonia and identify with it, whereas others have got a view of the world that makes it very hard for them to integrate. Some only acknowledge State-based allegiances. Many Latin Americans, for example, see Spain—and not Catalonia—as their major reference…

Is the problem one of political power?

Basically it is. The problem of the Statute of Autonomy can perhaps be best understood if we remember something that the politician Francesc Cambó[6] said back in 1918, when it seemed that Spain was willing to offer Catalonia some degree of devolution to prevent a break-up similar to that of the Austro-Hungarian Empire: 'I'd rather have complete power over one particular area of government than shared power over many.' That is one of the major problems that Catalonia has been faced with in recent times. We have recovered very few exclusive areas of jurisdiction—far fewer than people think or than we have traditionally aspired to. Sharing areas of jurisdiction means being the junior partner with the State: you hardly ever get your way. In normal federal States it's quite different. In Spain some people talk about federation. But they tend not to understand that a true federation is based on the guarantee that no Land, State, or Canton will be in a minority position all the time, nor permanently forced to foot the common bill or justify everything it does. And yet, in Spain, Catalonia is always in a minority position. There is no guarantee that in any dispute she will be treated fairly and in a way free of majority imposition. The basic requirements for any federal kind of working order just aren't on the cards.

So what should the answer be?

Well, if the federal State is ruled out, another possible option for ensuring rights for minorities would be for them to be granted exclusive powers in particular policy areas. Having exclusive jurisdictions would require the central State and the autonomous region to treat each other as equal partners. In short, Catalonia must have a bilateral relationship with Madrid for Catalans to be happy about being a part of Spain. Otherwise, as has happened up to now, whenever there is an absolute majority in parliament, the Spanish government ends up steamrolling over key Catalan interests. That has been Catalonia's major problem for the last thirty years. In my opinion, the new Statute of Autonomy, even if it had not been so severely cut back, would not have solved things. Think of the following example. In the discussion over the Statute, some parliamentarians suggested that the new law ought to contain a reference to the historic rights of the Catalan nation. They said it should acknowledge the laws that governed Catalonia until they were abolished by force in 1714. Now, that reference was vetoed by the Socialist Party, even though it defines itself as 'Catalanist'. Those who vetoed the reference interpreted those historic rights as some kind of antiquated Burkean vestige. They were wrong, since it was intended as a way of guaranteeing the protection of exclusive rights over certain policy areas, such as, for example, immigration. The real problem, though, is that all this seems to be unacceptable for Spain, and that is what has put Catalanism in a difficult position and made people take a more radical approach. If not even federalism is possible, then people opt for new options.

How would you define the recent evolution of the Catalanist movement?

I think Catalanism has changed because the world has changed. In the last 30 or 40 years we have witnessed key political and economic changes in Europe. The EU has turned the whole continent into an open market, globalizing all Europe, so to speak. It has also pacified Europe.

Our great grandparents always had to travel to Madrid to bargain over tariffs and economic policy. Given the international set-up of the period, they were closely tied to Spain at a time when Spain was rife with social conflict, authoritarianism, and pure force. But now, we can govern ourselves—in theory at least—in what is a peaceful and open continent. Madrid is less relevant as a centre for solving the problems of Catalonia. That explains why so many people are now in favour of independence, although many of them only see these developments in an intuitive manner. Every day, there are more and more businessmen who realize that their businesses have gone almost entirely international. Many of them now see Spain no longer means much to them from a business point of view.

Salvador Cardús
A reference point for public opinion

Salvador Cardús i Ros (b. Terrassa, 1954) is a household name for those who follow the media in Catalonia. 'Have you read Cardús' latest article?' is a question that has formed part of Catalan small talk for two decades. In hard-fought TV and radio debates he will push home arguments that often leave his opponents reeling. This was the case, I remember, when once confronted with a Madrid-based journalist who went on and on about Catalan being an 'imposed' language, Cardús' sharp memory for the facts and the impressive list of laws and situations with which he proved Spanish was indeed the only language imposed on anyone, completely toppled any form of opposition.

Cardús writes almost weekly both for Avui *and* La Vanguardia[1] *and regularly appears in Catalan TV debates. Cardús has a Ph.D. in Economics, though he now teaches Sociology at the Autonomous University of Barcelona's School of Political Science and Sociology. During the 1993-94 academic year he was Visiting Fellow at Fitzwilliam College, Cambridge. He is also an active member of the Anglo-Catalan Association, founded in 1954, a key organization in the relationship between Catalans and the English academic world.*

Dr. Cardús' main research areas are the sociology of religion, the mass media, and nationalism. His published works include books on education, the sociology of the younger age groups, and, more recently, nationalism and the role of journalism in Catalan politics. He has collaborated in major jointly-authored publications like La política cultural europea [European Political Culture] *(1990) and* Formas modernas de religión [Modern Religious Forms] *(1994) and is a regular contributor to national and international sociology journals. He helped set up the educational journal* Crònica d'Ensenyament [Chronicles of Education] *(1987-88) and, from 1989 to 1991, he held the post of deputy editor of the most important Catalan language daily newspaper of the time,* Avui. *A selection of his articles in the press appeared in the volume* Algú sap cap a on anem? [Does Anyone Know Where We're Going?] *(1992) and his essays on religious affairs have been published in* Concili amb folre i manilles: L'Església catalana a través del seu concili [Ecumenical Councils à la Catalonia: The Catalan Church through its Council] (1995). *He has also worked for television as a consultant for different series such as* Ciutadans [Citizens] *(1994),* Les coses com són [The Way Things Are] *(1995) and* Vides privades [Private Lives] *(1996-98), produced by Televisió de Catalunya.*

What is your opinion of the Spanish Constitutional Court's ruling against the Catalan Statute of Autonomy?

Whatever else may be said, I think it would be a mistake to see the sentence as a mere whim of the Constitutional Court. Firstly, because it is based on doctrine that is coherent with a Constitution which, as no-one can forget, sets down clear limits on Catalonia's options for self-government. It also responds to a political climate that is widespread in Spain in which one of the objectives is to put an end to the development of regional autonomy. It is no coincidence that, in his final evaluation of the Statute episode—in July 2010—Prime Minister Zapatero should have talked in terms of a 'mission successfully fulfilled'. All this means the ruling must be taken very seriously. Especially for the political message it implies. They are telling us, loud and clear, that as far as Madrid is concerned, the process of devolution is over.

What do you make of Catalan response to the ruling?

I think Catalans have received that message loud and clear. The political situation leaves little room for doubt: either the conditions laid down in the Statute ruling are accepted—that is, bowing down to the joint political dictates of the PP and PSOE[2] —or a process of democratic confrontation must begin in order to challenge the rules set down in the 1978 Constitution. One may either see this process as one which seeks more home rule or, more bluntly, as one openly favouring independence. The vast demonstration of July 10th, along with surveys published in two of Barcelona's more moderate papers (*El Periódico* and *La Vanguardia*)—the latter speaking of approximately 48% support for independence in Catalonia—suggest that the second option has made huge progress in the last few years. Our future is wide open.

Some years ago, Catalonia seemed to be a more or less contented region of Spain. Today that image has been broken.

Before Catalonia trusted in her own strength and had prospects of progress and prosperity for the future. Catalans thought they would be able to increase their degree of self-government within Spain. If other conditions had been made possible in our political relationship with Spain and if the idea of a plurinational State—one showing respect for its diversity—had prospered, then a majority of Catalans might have ended up going along with that model of home rule. But many Catalans have gradually come to the conclusion that the leeway Spain offers for self-government is very narrow indeed. Madrid has lost its confidence in the idea of regional self-government and cut down on it considerably. This was what first became apparent with the LOHPA affair[3]—as early in the day as 1982—although this tendency became even more aggressive after Aznar's 2000 landslide victory.[4] The experience of the reform of the Statute, with the farcical Constitutional Court sentence of June 28, 2010, has forced many Catalans to see the light. But awareness of the fatality of this situation has also been heightened by the fact that the fiscal plundering which Catalonia suffers at the hands of Spain[5] has been made known to all. We live in a situation in which we are denied the guarantee that our daily work will contribute in any way to our prosperity.

You recently said that Catalan independentism has 'come out of the closet'. What exactly do you mean by that?

The phrase 'come out of the closet' has become popular recently to describe people who, after years of concealing their homosexuality, lose their inhibitions and openly admit their sexuality. In our country there were many independentists who did not own up to this part of themselves, while others were afraid to confess to it in public. But the time has come to put an end to this and for people to speak up. This is the process we are undergoing. It explains why independentism is growing. It's not so much a question of 'new' independentists—though these are also popping up all over the place—but ones who before had been afraid to show themselves as such and confess to it openly. Independentism has now become normal ideological currency. The independence debate has become normal.

Don't you think that massive immigration from Spain in the last century has made Catalan independence a chimera?

No, I don't. The most recent wave of immigration cannot be said to have more emotional ties with the State than it does with the country that gave it jobs and a chance to prosper. Maybe it's necessary to overcome many immigrants' indifference. But this problem holds true both for Catalonia and for Spain. As regards the immigrants of the 50s—we're talking about people who came here sixty years ago—I fear we are faced with a myth that has been manufactured and used with the aim of justifying colonial dependence on Spain. It has been used—and still is—as the big argument, the big scarecrow to put fear into our hearts. They talk of the 'upheaval' of civil unity, the 'rupture' of social cohesion... If in sixty years this cohesion has not been achieved, it can hardly be the fault of the independentists, I say. Isn't it the fault of the unionists that have leaded its wings down for so long? In fact, I think the degree of social cohesion we have in Catalonia is similar to that of other modern societies. To aspire to a greater level of homogenization just isn't reasonable. No advanced country—not even the United States—seems to want to give away its independence to favour greater social cohesion, faced with a population of diverse origins. Everyone knows that the opposite is true: independence would favour the social coherence and the civil and political unity of Catalan society, as it does in any other country. What divides us is the ongoing colonial situation we have to bear.

What's your opinion of the local independence referendums held since autumn 2009? Aren't they just a romantic gesture?

Whatever else they are, they are a movement that makes a major contribution to spreading the debate on independence. They contribute to making the idea popular at the same time as they take away some of the drama. Quite another matter is the wishful thinking some of those favourable to independence may indulge in! This may be risky, because it could make one lose track of reality. To my mind, there is some rushing and too little strategic vision involved.

However, in the very spontaneity of the process we may find positive aspects, such as the fact that hitherto unknown actors have popped up in the public eye. So people who would probably never have had a prominent profile in a more contrived context, have become committed activists for the independence movement. I'm referring to people of a very high personal and professional status who have decided, maybe for the first time in their lives, to commit themselves politically to their country. Let's hope all the effort and enthusiasm it has taken will be well channelled and lasting. In this movement, I dare say we shall come up with the leaders who will take the country forward to independence in the future.

What role has the official Church played with regard to the Catalonia/Spain debate?

I regret to say it has been almost totally absent from it. What we now call the 'official Church' depends on—and is subservient to—the dictates of the *Conferencia Episcopal Española* (Spanish Bishops' Conference). The grassroots work and effort to accommodate Catalan realities—'incardination' in ecclesiastical terms—carried out in the heart of the country by bishops such as Guix, Deig, Camprodon, or Torrella, as Pont i Gol had done before, has all vanished into thin air. We don't even know what key centre and points of reference in the Catalan church, such as Montserrat, Poblet or the Caputxins de Sarrià, think about this subject. The Tarraconense Concilium we had all hoped would lead the Catalan church as of 1995 is now just a ghostly memory.[6] It was the symbol of a Church that could have come into being, but which has failed to do so.

Spanish politicians and jurists say that the only sovereign nation is Spain, and that Catalonia is not legally a nation. Can this be changed?

From a Constitutional point of view, they're dead right. Here a lot of confusion has been created to try and justify all kinds of political ambiguities, such as those that speak of 'asymmetrical federalism' or 'plurinationalism', concepts that really have no place in the current Constitution. There are also those who speak of a formula based on 'shared sovereignty', an idea that no-one seems to know just how to accommodate into the current constitutional framework. All in all, these are just juridically barren political terms. As regards the independence of Catalonia, it goes without saying that the only way it will be attained will be through a clean break with Spanish constitutional order. And this must obviously be achieved in an entirely democratic way. But there must be a break. One cannot unlock a cage from the inside. And less so within the constitutional labyrinth we now live in.

You have written at length about the Catalan media. Do you think they will one day be willing to move in the direction of an independent Catalonia?

The Catalan media are diverse and represent different interests. The private and larger ones, logically, stand for the current status quo and do not favour developments aimed at emancipating Catalonia. Public media, due to their very nature, must observe the current legal order. We cannot expect them to anticipate things nor take up positions over and above their own legal status. Indeed, we must be grateful that they inform the public of the steps the country is taking towards its freedom. There are small private media that are more sensitive to the will of the people. But they tend to be less influential. Nevertheless, today's communication systems offer other free and alternative resources. Digital papers, blogs, YouTube, social networks such as Facebook or Twitter, and all the possibilities that the Internet offers. These are especially important among the younger age groups, though not exclusively so. Apart from the traditional media, there are many other means of communication that can push in the direction of a free Catalonia. When we come nearer to our goal, I feel sure the traditional media will chip in too.

What's your opinion of the three-party government of Catalonia or *Tripartit* that has run the country in the 2003-2010 period?

It is an experience that has been spoiled by the lack of what I call proper 'coalition culture'. It has also suffered from the mediocrity of some of its leaders and from appalling episodes of sectarianism in which its members have often preferred to kill the golden goose rather than lose out on party interests. They have often given priority to these interests over the need to govern the country soundly. Neither under the presidency of 'whimsical' Pasqual Maragall (2003-2006) nor under that of 'sensible' José Montilla (2006-2010; see page 48) has it been possible to offer people the confidence and rigour that was needed when the going got politically and economically rough. And this is what we are experiencing right now, in mid-2010.[7]

Eliseu Climent
Valencians: Catalans from "Down Under"

It's not easy to understand the cultural and political Catalanist movement in Valencia today without reference to the jack-of-all-trades figure of Eliseu Climent. This dynamic lawyer and cultural activist can be described as the champion of off-beat cultural phenomena south of the Ebre. "Off-beat", that is, only in the sense that, given the current political make-up of Valencia, the struggle for the acceptance of Catalan culture as the legitimate local variety is very much an uphill slog. The all-powerful local Partido Popular, in the saddle since 1995, is openly hostile to anything Catalan and counters all such initiatives head-on.

Making up for the Valencian Administration's lack of interest in the language is hard going. Valencia has a markedly lower level of schooling in the local language than any of Spain's other bilingual regions. It's also the one that invests least in promoting the local language in the mass media. The Valencian opposition newspaper Levante-EM *recently published a report which reveals that the Valencian Generalitat spends approximately 58 times less on this need than the Catalan Government, 47 times less than the Basques and even 3 times less than Asturias, a region where the local language (Asturian or Bable) isn't even official! The Partido Popular has done its best to have the language of Valencia relegated to the rank of folkloric appendage. With that record, it's little wonder that the language is hardly used at all in the Valencian Parliament and Administration. What's more, the Generalitat government is crusading to have the booster stations relaying the only 100% Catalan language TV station (TV3) closed down by the law courts. Some estimates reckon that there are currently 200,000 fewer speakers of Catalan in Valencia today than there were when Franco died. In no other autonomous community has a similar drop in numbers of local language-speakers been registered in the same period.*

*As a pro-Catalan cultural activist, Eliseu Climent is the ideological heir of Joan Fuster (1922-1992), an intellectual and journalist who became a cult figure for those defending a Catalan identity for Valencia late in the Franco dictatorship. In 1962 Fuster wrote a book—*Nosaltres, els valencians *[We, the Valencians]—that defined the events, indecisions, and problems that he saw as keys to the configuration of Valencia. Fuster renamed the region País Valencià (Country of Valencia), a term that infuriates the Partido Popular and all those intent on obliterating the region's Catalan traits (but have no qualms about importing Castilian ones wholesale). In his book, Fuster examined the clichés that abound about Valencia and insisted on a common political identity with the Catalans as the only possible way of ensuring the region's survival. Fuster's and Climent's efforts to strengthen Catalan identity in Valencia have produced the impressive Octubre Cultural Centre in downtown Valencia,[1] the weekly current affairs magazine* El Temps *and the hugely dynamic association Acció Cultural del País Valencià (Cultural Action of the Country of Valencia), which has recently collected half a million signatures in favour of preventing the ban on the reception of Catalan TV in Valencia.*

Do Catalans and Valencians feel like they're part of the same country?

Deep down, most people realize we're much the same people. But we've suffered for a long time from the existence of internal frontiers. Historical developments, unification under the Spanish realm and the weight of the administration are all factors that have created barriers between our regions. But I feel they are more imaginary and psychological than real. It isn't unlike the rift that exists today between the cities of Alacant[2] and Valencia. Does that mean we aren't one people? I don't think so. Does it mean our identity doesn't need reinforcing? No, it certainly doesn't. The founder of the Catalan countries, King Jaume I, was a monarch with many qualities. But he was no prophet! By splitting up his realm between his two sons, he gave rise to this strange syndrome of division that still exists between Catalans, Valencians and Majorcans, despite our common history and culture. It was a split that was to be disastrous for our country. Of course, constantly being on the losing side throughout history hasn't exactly helped.

Which of the historical developments that you mention was most harmful in your opinion?

Without a doubt, the military defeats suffered in 1707 and 1714.[3] Since then, shrewd Spanish rulers seem to have made a concerted effort to highlight all our local differences in a strategy designed to separate us! A good example of this is the current Spanish Constitution, which cunningly forbids the federation of autonomous regions, a step that was clearly aimed at us. Who else? The fact is that we are one people. To speak for myself, I must say I feel just as much at home in Elna (in French-administered Roussillon) as I do in Alcoi (in southern Valencia).

How do you rate the attitude of the Valencian government towards the language and culture of Valencia?

I'm afraid the consequences of their constant attacks on our culture are quite damaging. I think that if this were happening further away—in Tibet, Kurdistan or Bosnia, say—journalists would probably be swarming like flies over the issue, rightly judging it to be a case of cultural genocide. I often wonder if our plight is simply invisible to them. On another level, Valencian culture—be it music, literature or drama—is hardly ever featured on the official Valencian TV, Canal 9. And yet, in spite of all the obstacles they put in our way, I'm proud to say that constant mobilization and a climate of increasing social consciousness don't allow them to always get away with it. Although the first PP president of Valencia, Sr. Zaplana had two major anti-Catalan obsessions in mind when he took power in 1995,[4] he wasn't able to carry them out. An intensive campaign on our part made him give in and we won. He didn't dare alter the education system or the administrative areas within the region, and that's because we've got a country behind us, or at least part of one. We aren't as powerful as we'd like to be, sure enough, but we hold our own! In the future we may well have our chances. So we must be ready when those moments come.

Isn't it confusing that the language is often called "Valencian" in the south, and "Catalan" in Catalonia proper?

I don't think there's anything wrong with calling it Valencian in colloquial terms. But you can't escape the fact that the scientific name of the language is Catalan. Even the Spanish law courts agree with us on that. People don't generally go around talking about "Algarvese," "East Anglian" or "Salamancan," do they, because the languages involved are Portuguese, English and Spanish. So why Valencian? Oddly enough, the people who most turn their noses up when we use the term "Catalan" are usually the most solidly Spanish-speaking! Whatever the case, the terminology problems we have are those that typically affect stateless languages deprived of sufficient political backing. The bottom line is that it's a question of power. So for us the name of the language is essential.

How would you compare the role played by Barcelona and Valencia with regards to the territories they are capitals of?

It's logical that there should be differences. Firstly, because Barcelona is in the north, which is significant in itself. And secondly, because it has succeeded in

becoming the capital of a nation. Even though it's often excessively closed in on itself—Lleida and Tortosa are right to complain about this—it's a leading world city. Whatever one may think, there's a sneaking admiration for Barcelona in Valencia. All right, it's a form of admiration that tends to slip into envy and rivalry. But it's interesting to see that in an opinion poll published three or four years ago in Elx, 93% of those interviewed declared Barcelona to be their "ideal city".

And not Madrid, as clichés might lead one to expect…?

No. Which reminds me. When the Coup d'État occurred on February 23, 1981, General Milans del Bosch brought his tanks out onto the streets of Alcoi. I happened to be there in the City Hall with all the city councillors—including some right-wing ones—and we couldn't leave the building. So the Council's Emergency Committee decided to phone the Catalan Generalitat to find out what to do. No other institutions or party headquarters were consulted. Only the Catalan Government! So it can't be denied that, deep down, Barcelona still enjoys prestige, acting, as it does, as a kind of reference point.

Is pro-Spanish feeling stronger in Valencia than in Catalonia?

Maybe. But that's hardly surprising. One thing you have to remember is the role played by the Church. Whereas in Catalonia it's provided vital support for Catalan identity, in Valencia it has largely backed Castilian assimilation. The War of Spanish Succession in the 18th century was also important in this respect, because the reprisals meted out in Valencia were ferocious. For example, our legal system was completely done away with, something which didn't occur in Catalonia, the Balearic Islands, or even Aragon. I think the repression was tougher in Valencia because the rebellion here was more active than elsewhere. Research by Castelló University has recently revealed that 30,000 Valencians died in the wake of the battle of Almansa in 1707. To that you have to add exile on a huge scale. Valencia was shattered and, with the aid of a very Castile-oriented Church and aristocracy, it soon became a colony. The role of our bourgeoisie also differs from Catalonia's. Unlike ours, from the 18th century onwards, Catalonia's middle class was very active creating national industries. In the late 19th century, it created political parties—such as the *Lliga*—to try and stand up to Madrid. In Valencia, where interests were vested in free trade, no local party was created. In addition, one shouldn't forget the intense campaign by Madrid to Castilianize Valencia as a barrier against the spread of Catalan influence—a campaign that found plenty of local collaborators, not least in the Franco period.

The Spanish State seems to be obsessed with keeping the Catalans and the Valencians apart…

That's what the historian Vicens Vives argued. He held that in Madrid they were adamant in opposing any attempt to reunify the Catalan-speaking countries. And that's still very much the case. They're afraid that reunification would shake the very pillars of the State. I remember hearing one Spanish Army general say: "Who cares about ETA? The real danger for Spain is the Catalan language." That's why they feel it's essential to make this part of the realm as Spanish as possible. The full brunt of the state machinery is regularly deployed in this exercise. Still, I've always thought that in many ways the "Spanish flavour" that Valencia is said to have is little more than a sugary façade. Every year, at the launch of the city's famous *Falles* festival, the Spanish national anthem is always met with loud whistling and booing. Deep down, the embers of consciousness must still be fizzling [laughs].

You founded the very successful association Acció Cultural del País Valencià [Cultural Action of the Country of Valencia) and the splendid Octubre Cultural Centre. What were your objectives?

To make people recover their self-awareness—now that we've rid ourselves of our old inhibitions. To counter the desperate passivity that often prevents Valencians from making progress, a syndrome which over the years has become embedded in our society, almost imperceptibly at times. For instance, before the Octubre complex was opened, lots of people—especially Catalans—said they thought it was a crazy idea. "You'll be bombed out," they said. "They'll have the place closed down in next to no time!" But the amazing thing is that absolutely nothing like that has happened! It just goes to show that the fears that had paralysed us for so long were quite unfounded. We just opened the doors, and in poured the people. The experiment worked! It also persuaded a lot of people in Valencia that Valencian Catalanists don't have horns or wield a devil's fork. So I think we've helped to rid the national issue of some of its sores and stigmas. At the Octubre Centre we do everything in Catalan, or else with simultaneous translation, and that's it. No hassle! For things to work, sometimes you just need to knuckle down and get started.

The struggle against the closure of Catalan TV in Valencia has also been one of your major issues in recent times, hasn't it?

Yes, that's right. Over twenty years ago we collected funds to set up booster stations all around the country for people to be able to watch quality TV in their own language. Some programs attracted more than a million viewers! We paid for the stations by way of popular subscription. It helped to link up our people to the rest of our national space. We've always found it hard to keep up communications. But it's now, in the era of globalization, that we're getting the most ferocious attacks. The current Valencian government is having all the booster stations closed down. On top of that we've been given huge fines that no cultural entity could ever hope to pay. It isn't just an attack against freedom of expression but against the European Charter, a document which protects the right of minority languages to maintain communication spaces beyond their strictly administrative frontiers. What we now want is a State decree to recognise those rights. To get that, we've had to carry out a vast campaign to collect over half a million signatures in support of what's called a "Popular Legislative Initiative (PLI)" which is to be debated in the Spanish Parliament. We collected all the signatures in four months, a major achievement by any standards.

Do you think the different Catalan-speaking regions will ever recover their sense of togetherness?

That's the task we now have before us. We must try and remove boundaries that exist between us and what they stand for. In the times we now live in, confronted as we are with globalization and challenges of all shapes and sizes—from immigration to the enlargement of the European Union—we can't settle for old administrative structures based on division. In that sense I heartily applaud the recent concern, jointly expressed by Catalan and Valencian business leaders, regarding the State's utter disregard for the future of the Mediterranean transport corridor, where the shortcomings of the traditional rail freight route and the old roads have been pointed to in no uncertain terms by experts in various fields. We must learn from the past and look ahead. I remember some words uttered in Valencia by President Jordi Pujol in 1992, when he attended a tribute to Joan Fuster: "Valencians, Catalans and Majorcans. Separately we can probably survive. But together, we would do so much better." If that was important in 1992, now it has become imperative. If we don't join together, this country simply won't wake up.

Joan Laporta
FC Barcelona's triumphant President

Joan Laporta—'Jan' to his friends—is one of the best-known Catalans in the world. He has undoubtedly been the most successful president in the history of FC Barcelona (2003–10). During Laporta's seven-year presidency, Barça won two of their three Champions League trophies (2006, 2009), their only FIFA Club World Cup (2009) and four Spanish League titles (2004–5, 2005–6, 2008–9 and 2009–2010). The amazing 2009–2010 season, referred to by some as Barça's Annus Mirabilis, is said to have been the best season ever accomplished by a top-level team in Europe. In fact it has been called an 'unbeatable' record, since Barça won every single title it was in contention for that year: the Spanish Cup, Spanish League, European Supercup, Spanish Supercup, Champions League and FIFA Club World Cup. A remarkable achievement by any standard, especially if we bear in mind that it was coach Josep Guardiola's first season at the helm of a first division team!

As regards Joan Laporta's presidency of the club, the paradox about the record-breaking 2009–10 season was that it came in the wake of his trickiest period as president, after two league flops in the 2006–7 and 2007–8 seasons. The well-funded campaign of opposition to him actually called a motion of censure against him, which narrowly missed forcing his resignation. Though it's hard to explain exactly why Laporta was subjected to the censure motion, the fact is that the media had for some time been portraying him as an off-beat and erratic club president. They showed no mercy when judging his occasional slip-ups and eccentricities, which often went no further than anecdotes that heartier English club chairmen might actually brag about. Ex-Avui newspaper editor and current Barça TV director Vicent Sanchis[1] has his own theories about the attacks against Laporta: 'Envy is one of the major vices of our country. And he's got too many things going for him. He's young. He's attractive. He's successful with Barça. And with the girls. Lots of people just can't forgive him for all that.' Certainly, the establishment has it in for him, seeing him as a threat to the status quo, especially after it was rumoured that he wanted a future in politics, a prospect that was confirmed with the creation of his own party—Democràcia Catalana [Catalan Democrats]—in early July 2010 and its participation in a broader pro-independence coalition, Solidaritat Catalana per la Independència [Catalan Solidarity for Independence] in the November 2010 elections for the Catalan parliament. Be that as it may, Catalan supporters are much given to lynching those glorified the day before, especially when 'the ball doesn't make it into the net', as the saying goes. But when all is said and done, Laporta is the man who turned a traditional 'losers' club' into the most powerful and victorious team in the world in the new millennium.

Some observers say that you've been the greatest president in the history of FC Barcelona. Would you go along with that?

The greatest president we've had was undoubtedly Joan Gamper,[2] because he founded our club and also saved it from disappearing on a couple of dicey occasions. And he was also a first-team player. His spirit is the ideal I've always aimed for. My colleagues and I have merely tried to follow in his footsteps. It is true that, in terms of titles, these seven years have been the best, and 2009–10 has been the best season in the club's history, with a haul of six cups, a feat that may never be beaten. I think the secret of our success is the staff I've been lucky enough to have alongside me. Having Txiki Begiristain as director of sport is one of the best decisions I've ever made. Likewise, having Frank Rijkaard and Josep Guardiola as coaches has been vital. Pep, in just one season, achieved the impossible. But none of this could have happened without the players themselves, the major actors in this success story. The club's management board also had an important role to play during these seven years in which, despite the pressure we've been under, FC Barcelona has been deemed to be the best club in the world.

Is it true that FC Barcelona's commitment to the Catalanist cause has never been as 'visible' as it is today?

That's why I decided to stand for the Presidency. I was brought up in a family tradition of allegiance to FC Barcelona and Catalanism. I think being president of the club is a way of defending the rights and liberties of our country, and I said so when I stood for office, so no-one should be surprised that I've managed the club in an unashamedly Catalanist way. I'm proud of the work that's been done on this front. We have not only achieved the best Barça in history from a sporting point of view, but also the most internationally acclaimed Barça. Unlike those who say Barça must only be a club, we have been faithful to the notion that it is 'more than a club', which has been Barça's official motto for decades. That slogan does not just reflect the club's identity from a sporting point of view, but also from the point of view of our country's culture and our idea of solidarity. It has been our guiding principle in good times and bad. I know some people can't forgive me for expressing my Catalanism openly, but I think opposition has come from sectors that practice intolerance and don't want to risk losing their privileges. Some people are also afraid that that kind of stance could support the idea that what Catalonia needs, once and for all, is a state of its own. I'm pleased that we've been able to defend our country and its culture. And when I say defend, I mean putting the Catalan flag on our shirt, favouring the consumption of Catalan products labelled in our language, and going as Catalans to the United Nations to sign the Global Alliance agreement with UNICEF. I think we've taken a bold step to put Barça directly in contact with the world, without having to pay the toll of going through Spain, so to speak. When taking decisions, we've always borne in mind what the effect might be on the country. For many years our country has been on the back foot. We thought it was high time we stopped playing on the defensive.

Are you taken seriously when you insist that you preside over a Catalan, rather than a Spanish, club?

Wherever we go, no matter what international forums we're present at, we always do so as Catalans, without any inhibitions. We make an effort to explain who we are, rather than insisting on what we are not, and we do so in a positive and natural way. In many international situations we feel our position is perfectly well understood. People are curious about an issue that always seems to be present—albeit informally—at the venues of bodies such as FIFA or UEFA, the European Clubs Association, and when we play Champions League matches. Our official emblems are the club badge and the Catalan flag. When playing away at official UEFA matches, we often have to struggle to get clubs to use Catalan on their loudspeaker systems. We have to tell them our club language is Catalan. This sometimes causes problems. But our insistence leads to comments and raises interest. It offers us the chance to explain that the Spanish State is one thing and the Catalan nation another. Catalonia lacks full national rights that,

obviously, we don't wish to surrender. This may seem a romantic idea to some. But if we're to be considered normal Europeans, we too must be entitled to exercise our right to self-determination. And that is something we can justify by pointing out that we've got a thousand years of history and age-old institutions behind us, as well as our own language. Indeed, as the cellist Pau Casals used to claim, the first parliament in Europe was Catalan. This is something that the English-speaking world takes great interest in, and not only in countries like Scotland, with which we have a lot in common, but in the whole of Great Britain. Centuries of political culture and democratic tradition make Britons respect what Catalonia represents.

In Derry too we've played matches at which the Catalan flag and national anthem were present, as they were on our last visit to Manchester. In the United States, on our pre-season tours, we are also fully accepted as Catalans. However, I realize that, although a lot of people sympathize with us, in the end it all leads to nothing. The interest we arouse—as so often with things quaint or odd—fizzles out when problems are left unsolved. For example, the international recognition of Catalan national teams will only be possible when we have a state of our own. I want my sons to live in the world as Catalans in the most natural way possible. I want my father's dream to come true for my children. I hope that we too can see that day! So I intend to do as much as I can to bring it about.

How do you view the development of Catalanism over the past few years?

Our country is waking up. I think that has a lot to do with the fact that Spain doesn't solve our problems, and that makes people angry. Over the last few months I've been trying to see if the reaction of Catalan society to recent events might contribute towards the creation of a Catalan State. I think it's time we took that step with courage and determination. Things seem to be on the move. People are increasingly aware that, although the Catalanist movement has largely continued to exist thanks to the efforts of grassroots organizations, there may be limits to what they can achieve.

If Catalonia were independent, wouldn't Barça supporters miss the matches against their eternal rival, Real Madrid?

That's a question we could talk about once Catalonia becomes a free State. There are a number of possible formulas. After all, Monaco FC plays in the French League. I think the market is bound to have a say in the matter. And I'm sure the Spanish will be keen that we stay in the Spanish League. There are lots of historical links with Spain. Maybe an Iberian League might be the answer, including the Portuguese teams. But I insist, those questions are secondary at the moment, and I think the priority is for Catalonia to obtain a State of its own as soon as possible.

How is it that Josep Sunyol, the Barça president shot by Francoists in 1936, was not honoured until 1996? Doesn't that clash with the club's Catalanist record?

That sort of incongruence is precisely one of the reasons that made a group of Barça supporters—to which I belonged—see the need to try and change things, and made us decide to stand for the presidency. In the nineties, the country was progressing along democratic lines, and yet we could see that the Catalanist spirit was getting thinner and thinner at Barça. The memory of our Martyr President—Josep Sunyol i Garriga—and of our founder, Joan Gamper, tended to be swept under the carpet. I think people were afraid to talk about our history. In Sunyol's case, the fact that he was probably shot for being a Republican and the President of Barça when he fell into fascist hands in August 1936, seemed to be taboo. In his column '*Esport i Ciutadania*',[3] in the thirties, Sunyol used to explain what sport meant to the country and how it could serve to develop people's sense of citizenship. He showed what Barça meant to the Catalans. We were concerned that the management seemed determined to conceal this and other significant facets of our club's history. From the moment we reached the presidency, we made a concerted effort to proclaim our history. Recently we've followed with great interest the initiative of the *Sàpiens* history magazine to try and discover, with the aid of cutting-edge technology, exactly where Sunyol might lie buried in the mountains north of Madrid. That would enable us to get a fuller picture of exactly what happened to him.

How do you see the future of Catalonia from a political point of view?

I see, with great dismay, how disunited the Catalan political parties are. We have *Convergència i Unió*, a nationalist coalition that won the 2006 election but was not able to form a governing majority with other parties with Catalanist leanings. That enabled the Spanish Socialists, who obtained fewer votes, to continue to rule in Catalonia, as they had done since 2003. CiU had made deals with the Partido Popular (PP), such as the famous Majestic Agreement,[4] which is pretty hard to comprehend. But in the end one cannot help recognizing the very limited results these agreements led to. I think it is time to acknowledge that the situation is not getting better. Strategies aimed at progressively diluting Catalonia within Spain are becoming dangerously consolidated. However, all the Catalan parties seem to have their excuses for doing nothing about it. For instance, one of the main Catalanist parties designed a strategy which involved the creation of the three-party governing coalition[5] which was theoretically meant to attract to our cause everyone who lives and works in our country. But you end up realizing that it was a hoax. The other Catalan party, the CiU, reached an agreement with the PP and, again, you see that the results were disastrous, because the PP is fuelled by extreme Spanish nationalist pride. What I've been thinking for quite a while now is that there is room for a political option aimed at changing the structure of the Spanish State. And I think the best thing would be for Catalonia to have a state of its own. It's the only way I see of having any kind of influence internationally. A new party is needed because the structures of the existing parties are incapable of channelling the aspirations of the Catalan people. A new party will, hopefully, act as a catalyst for all these synergies and hopes. It may also encourage the other Catalan parties to stop battling on their own. If we don't join together to defend our rights, we won't get very far. I think what is required is for someone to lead them.

Do you see the 2010 Catalan Parliamentary elections as basic to your project?

Yes, I do. I really don't think we can wait any longer. It's a question of national dignity. Our country is dying and it's dying because they are killing it. It's that simple. The other day I was invited to celebrate the Chinese New Year, with the introduction of the Year of the Tiger, an animal which is the symbol of revolution. I think that's what we need to do: make a revolution! That is why I have created the party *Democràcia Catalana* which I hope will form part of a coalition capable of responding to all the unrest recently expressed in our country at the July 10th rally after the ruling of the Spanish Constitutional Court against our home rule. I think the only option left open to us is now is independence.[6]

Alfons López Tena
The jurist behind the independence movement

Alfons López Tena (Sagunt, 1957) is a prominent Valencian jurist who became a Catalan media figure when in 2001 he was appointed as a member of Spain's most important judicial body, the General Council of the Judicial Power. He held this post until 2008 as the representative of the Catalan coalition Convergència i Unió. Before then he had held the post of notary in Barcelona and other cities, and was a founding member of the Catalan Notaries' Forum, of which he became Vice President in 1999. He is also on the Executive Committee of the Comissió de la Veritat [Truth Commission] set up in 2007 to investigate Franco's crimes in post-civil war Valencia.

In 2007 he founded the influential Cercle d'Estudis Sobiranistes [Sovereignty Studies Circle] with the support of Scottish leader Alex Salmond. This organization aims to encourage a public debate on the advantages and viability of a Catalan State. He has written several books, the best known of which is Catalunya sota Espanya: L'opressió nacional en democràcia [Catalonia under Spain: National Oppression in a Democracy],[1] *in which he reflects on the need to sever Catalan subservience to the Spanish State. He uses his judicial, political, and economic experience to argue that Catalonia must follow the example of so many other European nations (Poland, Ireland, Norway, and others) in its aspiration to become a free state.*

Since late 2009, he has become a leading member of the National Coordinating Body for Independence Referendums (Coordinadora Nacional per la Consulta sobre la Independència), the movement that has organized plebiscites on independence in Catalan municipalities. He is also on the board of the prestigious cultural association Òmnium Cultural, which on July 10, 2010 organized the biggest march ever held in support of Catalan national rights in response to the June 30th Constitutional Court cut-back on Catalan autonomy. As the world's mass media reported, over one million demonstrators took part in what was to be one of the biggest demonstrations to take place in Europe this century.

What is your opinion of the Constitutional Court's June 2010 sentence on the Catalan Statute of Autonomy passed in 2006?

For Catalonia, this sentence marks the end of self-government and puts an end to any speculation regarding the possibility of our country progressing within the Spanish State. All that is offered to us is a form of subordinated administrative decentralization made available to us by way of the unilateral concession of the Spanish government and parliament. We are entirely in their hands. The Constitutional agreement of 1977, whereby we were to have home rule in exchange for institutional loyalty to Constitutional Spain, has been blown to pieces. At this point we have three options open to us, the first of which is pure resignation. So we'll discard that. Another is to try and change the Spanish Constitution, which needs the support of three fifths of the Spanish Parliament. So this too is entirely out of the question. And lastly, there is independence, if the majority of Catalans want it. And this option is within our reach. Indeed, the massive demonstration of July 10, 2010, has very much given a spur to this option.

You are the visible head of the movement to promote local referendums on independence, which have been held in over four hundred Catalan towns since September 2009. What have they achieved?

These referendums have largely done away with the defeatist syndrome that has for so long been dominant among Catalans. They have shown people that Catalan society is capable of organizing such initiatives under its own steam with the participation of tens of thousands of volunteers from different social and ideological backgrounds. Despite the lack of resources and the many obstacles in our path, these polls have been a success. They are being conducted under fully democratic conditions and have brought in almost 600,000 votes in favour or independence. It is a popular initiative aimed at taking our future into our own hands. In this sense we have outmanoeuvred the political parties and the rigid status quo they stand for. It is the peaceful strength of the people that has now come to the fore.

What position do you think Catalonia might justifiably aspire to in the future to ensure her betterment and identity?

The only possible way out is independence within the European Union. All other options, such as the ones tried out during the Transition period—with the new Constitution and the two Statutes of Autonomy (1980 and 2006) in force—have depended on agreements with the Spanish. Now it has become clear that they neither want to share power with us nor intend to relinquish the direct control they have over the economic resources of Catalonia. It's an arrangement that works magnificently for them—economically, culturally and politically—and so they have no intention of changing it. The new Statute, which has been completely debased, offers no workable opportunity for ensuring our future. If we accept the present situation with resignation, we will end up in the same bracket as other European stateless countries that have become marginal minorities stung by economic discrimination.

You have often spoken of a democratic deficit in the State...

Yes. My own hypothesis is a bit more sophisticated than the one generally held. I think that one of the reasons for this deficit is Spain's need to maintain a position of national domination over us. Karl Marx once said that it was impossible for the United Kingdom to dominate India while having a liberal constitution back home. Sooner or later, either the Empire or democracy collapses. Here it is exactly the same. According to the international Davos Forum, Spain ranks eightieth in the world's ranking of democracies. That places it beneath Botswana, Namibia, Uganda, Togo, Nepal, Malaysia and Egypt! The bottom line is that you cannot have an independent and impartial high court if there is a situation of national domination. You need the judicial system to be at the orders of political power because, if not, you have to apply laws that are formally democratic and which, on paper, offer guarantees for what is laid down in the Constitution. And Spain cannot afford to do that.

Can you give an example?

Sure. For example, the Constitutional Article that establishes that all Spanish languages other than Castilian will enjoy 'special respect and protection'. Only in a limited democracy can you let thirty years go past without doing one thing to aid those languages, either at home or abroad. They have simply imposed the State language on all and sundry. In a limited democracy such as ours, it is possible to go about boycotting those languages and simply ignore the international treaties that the State has signed. This is what happens all the time. The situation in Spain, without any real separation between the State powers, is closer to an elective dictatorship than it is to a real democracy. All right, you may say, formal liberties are apparently respected and there are free elections. But otherwise the government party is free of practically all forms of democratic control. Its power is almost unlimited.

Can you give a further example of what you mean?

I remember a special issue of *The Economist*, after the 2004 elections, which delved into this question. Bodies such as the large state-owned corporations, the Cervantes Institute or the Prado Museum have their management boards renewed after each election. This is done just to suit the governing party. So there is really no neutrality. Likewise, major business operations cannot take place without the permission of the Spanish government, which conducts them according to its own interests. This is the model that is applied in states in East Asia, Indonesia etc., where state intervention is rampant. In this sense I remember something Philip Man used to say: 'when investing in the world, you have to distinguish between countries where you have to ask what the law says and others where the question is who must I speak to.' In Spain the latter case holds firm. The problem for national minorities in a state such as Spain is that they are condemned to disappearance, because all the State's institutions are working together against them.

Why should it matter to a globalized world that Catalonia might disappear?

I think it's worth asking an average European or American what he or she would feel if his or her nation disappeared. Indeed, why should it matter to anyone if France or Britain disappear as they may well do one day? In 1940 France might well have become part of Germany. This question always seems to be made with respect to others, but never about one's own 'untouchable' nation. Then there is another question. History shows us that no country that has achieved statehood has ever spurned it later on. This always occurs in a situation of subordination, when there are first- and second-class citizens. Those who form part of the dominant nation, and those who do not. The latter are second class. It is only after a long period, when assimilation is complete, that 'equality' becomes complete. Significantly, only in three or four years in the whole 19th century were there Catalan prime ministers and ministers in Spain. In the last hundred years, there have been no Catalan prime ministers of Spain. Over the centuries, the presence of Catalans in key posts in the state has been way below her quota in terms of population and economy. Neither were there Indian ministers when India formed part of the British Empire! Again it's a question of first- and second-class citizens. No country wants to disappear. The process of assimilation means a lack of democracy and rights. It is therefore logical that the European Union, as a body based on democracy and rights, should repudiate the assimilation process taking place in Catalonia.

How does this assimilation process occur?

Although the Spanish king has publicly denied it, the Castilian or Spanish language has been imposed on us by Spanish regimes of every persuasion.[2] And now the systematic concealment of the very existence of the Catalan language and culture—along with those of Galicia and of the Basque Country—is a regular habit when projecting the image of Spain abroad. The Spanish State has dedicated zero euros to the promotion of Catalan culture abroad. On the rare occasion that Catalan authors have been invited to participate in activities organized by the Spanish *Instituto Cervantes* overseas, the Catalan government has had to foot their travel expenses. Spanish authors' transport and accommodation costs are fully covered. Apart from this, almost 100% percent of official web pages produced by Spanish ministries are available only in Spanish, the only exception being those which have versions in English. Yet Catalans pay their taxes like anyone else. Besides, the State systematically disregards the unity of the Catalan language with the idea of creating a separate language they call 'Valencian'. It is as if the British government were to edit texts in 'northern Welsh' and 'southern Welsh' to gratify some obscure maverick academy. Though illegal and contrary to the teachings of any university, and indeed Spanish law, this is common practice today. Their respect for our language and culture is null. A recent study on the language used by state and public enterprises in their publicity in Catalonia gives a quota of 94% in Spanish…

Do you think this is due to Spain's inability to get over her Francoist past?

Possibly. In any case, the example of the Spanish State is almost unique in 20th century Europe. Along with Serbia and Belarus—and in some senses Moldova—it is the only democratic country where there has been no clean break with the former dictatorial regime. All other European dictatorships—be they Communist or Fascist—have fallen before being replaced by democratic regimes. Those responsible for the crimes committed were made to pay, sometimes dearly. In the more lenient cases, in exchange for a blind eye being turned on some episodes, those who had collaborated with the dictatorship were often let off with a public moral reprimand. Spain is the only place where not even this has occurred. No politician, businessman, army officer or judge had to undergo any form of inquiry no matter how foul their record. No one reproached them in any way. So the continuity of the 'nomenklatura' was guaranteed, and in many senses remains intact today. A joke currently going around illustrates this to a tee.

Would it be too much to ask you to repeat it?

I'll have a go at an abridged version if you insist. It's called 'The day Franco rose from the dead'. It goes like this: 'On January 1, 2010, General Franco rises from his state tomb in the *Valle de los Caídos* crypt.[3] The first person he meets is the uniformed guard. "My good man. Stop gaping at me like a half-wit and inform me about who is running Spain today." "Well, your Excellency, the Vice Prime Minister is one Fernández de la Vega." "You're joking! What, old Wenceslao, the chap who did so well in my Labour Ministry that we granted him special industrial favours in Ávila?" "No, no Excellency. Actually it's his daughter María Teresa." "Well… well that sounds all right. Tell me more. Who would the President of the Cortes be now?" "It's one José Bono from Castilla-La Mancha." "Heavens! Not that model Falangist from La Mancha that I appointed mayor of his home town?" "No, your Excellency. Actually it's his socialist son José, who always says how proud he is of his Falangist father." "How splendid! We are doing well then. But tell me, who is the State Attorney now?" "It's one Conde-Pumpido." "Ah, that grand military judge who rid me of so many Republican rabble before the firing squads." "Well, not exactly *Generalísimo*. That was Lucio. This is his grandson Claudio. The one who advised the current president not to annul the death sentences you signed." "Bless him. And tell me, who runs the media now?" "Well there's one Cebrián at a newspaper called *El País* and…." "Well I never! He was head of the Falangist press and great at swinging things in my favour." "Well no, Excellency. Actually, that was his father. But you may well remember appointing his son head of the TVE news desk." "Ah yes… What excellent news then. Things couldn't be better it seems. I see Juan Carlos has done an excellent job keeping the show on the road! I think I'll just slip back into my tomb then."' As can be imagined, a much longer and probably wittier version is available for postprandial sessions… If required, the list of heirs is quite inexhaustible.

José Montilla
A President of Catalonia born in Cordoba

José Montilla was the President of the Catalan Government or Generalitat[1] from 2006 until losing power following the elections of November 28, 20101. He took office in November 2006 as the second Socialist to occupy the post since the institution came back into being in 1977 after a 38-year parenthesis imposed by the Franco dictatorship. Montilla is the first of the presidents of the modern Generalitat government to be of non-Catalan origin. In fact, he uses his name in its Spanish form 'José', and not its Catalan equivalent 'Josep'. He does so, he says, to be faithful to his roots. 'I'm Andalusian by birth,' he said in one interview when he became president, 'but I'm Catalan by conviction and choice.'

Montilla's family moved to Catalonia in 1971 when his home town, El Remolino (near Iznájar, Córdoba) was flooded over by one of Franco's latter-day hydroelectric schemes. In 1985 he became the mayor of Cornellà de Llobregat, a satellite town outside Barcelona where Spanish-born immigrants form a large majority. In addition to being appointed to posts high in the echelons of the Catalan Socialist Party—he was elected its First Secretary in June 2000—Montilla served as president of the Barcelona Provincial Council in 2003–4 and as Minister of Industry in the Spanish central government during Prime Minister Rodríguez Zapatero's first term of office (2004–6). In his investiture speech as President of the Generalitat in 2006, he confessed: 'I am discreet but transparent. I don't shout, but I know how to manage people. I don't gesticulate, but I will know how to govern. I do not laugh very much, but I'm happy to be able to serve my country.' Whatever the case may be, many Catalans appreciate the huge efforts made by Montilla to improve his spoken Catalan, a language he did not use when he was mayor of Cornellà in the '80s.

As Montilla himself admits, he is indeed a 'discreet' politician. To his opponents he often gives the impression of being almost absent. When he does become visible, it's generally in a very low-key manner. Some observers say he looks a bit like a ventriloquist with a gentle smile fixed on his face. For his followers, however, he is an efficient administrator who was able to iron over the squabbles that the cabinet of his predecessor as Generalitat President, Pasqual Maragall, had been renowned for. Others even consider that his presidency epitomized the predominance of the more pro-Spanish wing of the Catalan Socialist Party (PSC).

However, it would probably be an oversimplification to see Montilla as a mere yes-man to Madrid. In fact, his tendency to 'warn' of the serious consequences that would ensue from a cut-back to the Statute of Autonomy at the hands of the Spanish Constitutional Court often irritated Madrid in the period prior to the June 28th ruling. In his speeches in Madrid, he twice spoke of the 'growing disaffection' of many Catalans with Spain. To some this was the sign of a responsible president who challenged the position of his own party leaders in Madrid. To others it was the antics of an emissary seeking to put things right in the capital in order to save face and retain his post.

Sr. Montilla, what is the situation of Catalonia after the June 28, 2010 Constitutional Court ruling against the Catalan Statute?

The ruling has been received with indignation by a great majority of Catalan citizens. They are angry about the lack of respect that has been shown for the democratic process that we followed. They also perceive the harm the sentence causes to the political agreement we reached regarding our home rule. It cannot be overlooked that the Statute had been approved in the Catalan and Spanish Parliaments and ratified by the people of Catalonia. Some of the interpretations made by the Court are also offensive from the point of view of our national identity, our culture, and our language. It was in this state of mind that Catalan society responded with the massive rally of July 10th in Barcelona. What has been most evident is an increase in the disaffection that people feel with regard to a particular way of understanding Spain. Some time ago I myself issued warnings that this was the risk we were running. We now have a collective frame of mind which will leave a mark on people's future intentions. All this may well affect the course of Spanish and Catalan politics in the next few years.

Shortly after the ruling, you described it as a mistake...

Yes. I think it is a very irresponsible mistake. This sentence damages the political agreement that is enshrined in the Constitution and in the Statute of Autonomy. I think the Constitutional Court has come to be perceived as a most suspect institution both as regards its current composition and the insurmountable insistence it has shown for defining the form of the State, a prerogative which goes way beyond its powers. The Statute was a wonderful opportunity for tackling the age-old problem of Spain and achieving the democratic incorporation of Catalonia into the State. After the Court's ruling, this problem has now become more serious.

How must Catalonia confront this new situation?

It is the duty of Catalans to continue persevering. All democratic options are obviously legitimate. In my role as president, however, I think it is my duty to preserve the political agreement on which the Statute is based and to insist that it be fulfilled. We must explore the possibilities we have of achieving the powers and jurisdictions that the Statute originally included. We shall do so by using all the mechanisms we have at our disposal, without discarding any of them. We not only need to make the right political gestures but also take the right and legitimate political actions that are needed to bring together the different political parties and institutions. That is what I am determined to do.

Before the sentence, you went to Madrid on more than one occasion to warn of the possible growth of 'disaffection' between Catalans and the idea of Spain. Did they listen to you?

I decided to do this because a significant portion of the Spanish right-wing had been involved in a campaign that sought to condemn the legitimate aspirations of our country to self-government. Without any scruples, this campaign sought to conjure up a false image of our country, our institutions, and our people, based on slander. They made us out to be a privileged, mean people who only do what suits us best at the expense of the rest of Spain. They've done their utmost to conceal Catalonia's continuous economic contribution towards interregional solidarity, by ignoring the great contribution we have made with our taxes. They have also done their best to confuse people by muddling up concepts such as 'autonomy' and 'privilege', or 'difference' and 'equality'. Faced with this lie, I decided a warning had to be issued in a loyal but resolute fashion. I warned them about the negative effects all this could bring with it, and pointed to the damage that could be caused by the ongoing bloody-mindedness displayed by many Spanish politicians and media. I believe that regularly highlighting these things has had an impact on Spanish public opinion. People are beginning to realize that the growing unrest felt in Catalonia, as regards our country's relationship with Spain, could end up being more of a headache for Spain than for Catalonia.

During your presidency you negotiated a new financial agreement with Madrid. Yet several independent economic experts expressed their doubts about the possibilities it really offered of correcting the current fiscal imbalance between Catalonia and Spain…

The Statute of Autonomy laid down the basic outline of a model we had to develop to achieve the improvement of a financial system which was negative for the interests of Catalonia. That model is to form part of a new budgetary arrangement which has finally been agreed on after long and arduous negotiations. We now have a financial system that fulfils all the requirements of the Statute. Once it's fully operational, it will bring in an additional €3,600 million to Catalonia. Over and above that, the third additional provision of the new financial system states that the State will make a great effort to invest in Catalonia to compensate for the deficit we have accumulated in this field over the years. That provision is being carried out in a scrupulous manner and will result in investment amounting to €34,750 million before 2013.

With regard to the average for Spain as a whole, experts say that Catalonia has lost ground in terms of its productivity per capita in the last few years. Do you think that is a transitory phenomenon or is it the result of the lack of investment you have referred to?

We're moving forward in an increasingly complex economic and industrial context. We are interdependent within the Spanish, European and global economies. But I think that Catalonia, despite having entered a period of decline in the '90s, has been reacting adequately in the past five years, especially since 2004, when serious work was undertaken to strengthen the Catalan economy by way of the Agreement for Strategic Internationalization, Quality of Employment and Competitiveness. I think that the concerted effort that has been made during the last two legislatures to try and encourage the transformation of our productive model has been remarkable. This will be seen by all once we get over the period of global crisis we are currently affected by.

Political analysts have traditionally divided Catalonia into 'nationalists' and 'non-nationalists'. From outside Catalonia, in other parts of the Spanish State, you are sometimes accused of conniving with the nationalists without being one yourself. How do you see this?

Catalonia is made up of free citizens with different origins, languages, cultures, religions, and ideologies. My principal duty is to maintain and strengthen the social unity of the Catalan people and to encourage social cohesion at all levels. It is my aim to achieve the ideal of 'Catalonia, one nation'. You'll therefore appreciate that my objective is not based on ideological division. I see it as my duty to strive towards agreement and cooperation among my fellow nationals. Whether they understand that or not outside Catalonia is a different matter. I'm not a nationalist and that is why they accuse me of connivance from both sides. But I think there must be another way of seeing one's own nation and, indeed, the world.

You define yourself as a 'Catalanist' but not as a 'Nationalist'. What's the difference?

My political activity is guided by a broad conception of Catalanism which I understand to be the largest common denominator for the majority of Catalan citizens. With them I share the will to live together and the prospect of greater self-government. Having said that, within this broad scenario there are different views on how to develop our self-government. We mustn't forget that there are citizens of Catalonia who don't identify with Catalanism at all. From my point of view, I think we must choose if it is preferable for there to be division amongst Catalans regarding the different conceptions of self-government available or if it is better to maintain a basic unity in order to defend and build on the degree of self-government we already enjoy.

For years the international media did not take much of an interest in Catalan issues. But recently things seem to have changed. What do you make of this?[2]

I think Catalonia and Barcelona's current international profile is primarily based on the image gained during the 1992 Olympic Games. Never before had we been so much in the news. However, it's true that lately we have also been in the news rather a lot. But I wonder if that is a good or a bad thing. I think we need to develop an image of a positive kind and, quite frankly, I don't think it's very positive to appear in the world media as a result of issues, controversies, or conflicts such as the independence referendums. I think our presence at the Frankfurt Book Fair, the international renown of our chefs, artists, and musicians, the excellence of our scientists, and even the great achievements of FC Barcelona are far more positive things for us to be known for. The rest of the world is more interested in what we can contribute in terms of distinctive achievement and innovation than in 'the Catalan problem', which is something that doesn't really affect them. To aspire to stepping up the presence of Catalonia in the world media by way of the so-called 'internationalization' of our conflict—as some people term the phenomenon—seems a poor kind of ambition to me.

Do you think the Catalan language is treated fairly in the EU?

No, I do not. But some first positive steps have been taken to improve the situation and now we must keep on insisting. I feel particularly proud of the fact that, twenty-five years after joining the European Union, it has been the more progressive governments of Catalonia that have first achieved official acknowledgment for our language. Nevertheless, I do feel that the situation we've attained so far is not good enough and that the full acknowledgment of Catalan, both in Spain and in Europe, is an objective that we must keep working on.

Jordi Pujol
President of Catalonia, 1980–2003

'Catalonia is a nation which in synthesis is based on its medieval history and the economic revolution of the 18th and 19th centuries.' That is how former president Jordi Pujol i Soley describes his country. A moderate nationalist, Pujol was the surprise winner of the 1980 Catalan parliamentary elections (the first after Franco's death) when the Catalan socialists had seemed poised to win.

Jordi Pujol qualified as a doctor, though he never practiced medicine. From an early age, he saw Catalanist activism as a way of protesting against Franco. In 1960 he was arrested for having instigated a protest in Barcelona's Palau de la Música, where a patriotic song was sung in the presence of the Francoist authorities.[1] He was tortured and sent to prison in Zaragoza for nearly three years. The words 'Jordi Pujol', painted on walls, became a symbol of opposition to the regime. Aware of the difficulty Catalonia had traditionally had in creating viable banks,[2] Pujol founded Banca Catalana in order to ensure funding for Catalan industry. However, since it granted over-generous loans in the period prior to the crisis of the late 1970s, it too was taken into administration by the Bank of Spain following a fierce smear campaign in the Spanish press. In Catalonia that was seen as an attempt by Madrid to destroy Pujol's political prospects. Even the Communists gave support to Pujol on this account. In the end, no charges were brought against him, and he was able to continue his political career and lead the Catalan Government—for twenty-three years, no less! Amongst what are generally considered to be his major achievements are the creation of the new Catalan administration, the improvement of the country's economic situation, the establishment of Catalan as the major language of education and the development of the Catalan hospital and university networks, as well as the creation of the Catalan public radio and television system and the autonomous police force (the Mossos d'Esquadra).

Now retired, Jordi Pujol is still one of the country's leading figures. Although a favourite pastime amongst Catalans was to discuss whether, deep down, Pujol was really in favour of Catalan independence, it has only been recently that he has declared that he no longer has "any arguments against independence". In autumn 2009, when an independence referendum campaign started up in the towns and villages of Catalonia, he started to make statements to the effect that if things were handled properly, 'the pro-independence movement will become very strong'. Indeed, several members of his party and ex-ministers participated actively in the campaign, and are now openly advocating independence.[3]

Since 2002 you have repeatedly pointed out that the relationship between Spain and Catalonia has never been worse, and that the brand of compromise that led to the Transition has vanished…

A willingness to compromise existed in 1978–79. It made it possible to restore democracy and Catalan self-government after the dictatorship. But that spirit no longer exists. The relationship with Spain has become worse than ever. Even President Montilla speaks of 'disaffection' between Catalonia and Spain *(see page 48)*. He even issues warnings that speak of the 'increasing hostility' there is in Spain towards Catalonia. That comes after two or three years of euphoria in Catalonia arising from the controversy over the new Statute of Autonomy and the new finance agreement, when the negative effects of the three-party Government were being felt. Now I think it's Spain that will enter a period of crisis. In any case, some people in our country have been excessively arrogant. 'We're going to do this, we're going to do that,' they bragged. In Spain, too, they became very cocky and thought they were level-pegging with France and England. In their elation, they even saw themselves as superior to Italy. Now they've come round to seeing that they're leaders in just one area: the creation of unemployment.

Politically, who can be blamed for the hostility you mention?

The Partido Popular (PP) is the party that's most openly hostile to Catalonia. They are prey to a syndrome that has been termed 'Catalanophobia'. It brings them votes. However, there has also been opposition to Catalonia from the Socialists in areas such as the finance debate. In fact, amongst certain Spanish Socialists, there is also a good deal of hostility towards Catalonia. It's especially evident amongst intellectuals, and in articles even in liberal newspapers such as *El País*. Things could have been worse, because not reaching any form of agreement with Catalonia over the Statute would have been catastrophic for Prime Minister Rodríguez Zapatero, for whom Catalan votes are vital if he wants to stay in power.

Some years ago, Catalan parties—among them CDC—tended to see the EU as the political forum where Catalan problems could be solved by bypassing Madrid. Does that still stand?

That's an interesting question. Unfortunately there is a growing reaction in the EU against the powers of the autonomous communities and regions of Europe. We have come to a point in which it is the European Commission that is inciting member States to unify their internal arrangements. It even gets annoyed when Madrid says Barcelona must be consulted on a particular issue. This presents a magnificent pretext for Spanish politicians to insist that it is Brussels, and not Madrid, that imposes the need to unify the state. States are trying to recover some of the power they lost in the past. I think we should oppose that by building up our own strength and self-esteem. We must wait for more favourable times to make progress on the international front.

How does Catalonia stand in relation to other stateless countries in the EU?

For British public opinion, the Scottish question makes our case relevant. The question of how multinational states are to develop is of interest in the United Kingdom and comparisons with Catalonia are constantly being made. Maybe Britain and Spain can learn from each others' experiences with the multinational states they administer. They ought to become aware that if you draw a line across 18th-century Europe, from Dunkirk through Paris and on to Milan, including all south-western Europe, you will only find two countries which can boast of having undergone an Industrial Revolution: Catalonia and Lombardy, where the textile and leather trades were very important. The model for us was England. Our factories were replicas of English ones, powered by coal. Hydraulic power was important here, too, despite the relatively small size of our rivers. It was England that taught us how to power engines. It's a country with which we were allies in the War of Spanish Succession (1701–14), even though, in the end, Europe largely pulled out of the war. The Catalans were then left high and dry with no-one to help them

in their struggle against the joint armies of Louis XIV of France and Philip V of Spain. The amazing thing is that we still held out for over a year!

You presided over the Assembly of European Regions for a time. Are there any other cases like that of Catalonia in Europe?

Very few are as consistent as ours. As regards fully fledged nations, there is the Basque Country and the two nations of Belgium, the Walloons and the Flemish. There are also the Scots and the Welsh. Scotland, despite the Act of Union with England, preserved many features of its nationhood, with its civil law code, an education system and a culture of its own. Apart from that, there are regions that are much less powerful from a national point of view. What makes them a nation is having a national consciousness and a language of their own. They need special characteristics that distinguish them in a particular way and they generally have a rich historical heritage. Other regions may have had these features, too, and may have lost them. Regions such as those of Germany and France, for example, though strong in some respects, have in many ways lost their national status and just become regions.

In view of developments such as these, more and more senior members of your coalition (CiU) are now openly backing independence for Catalonia…

That's logical. What Agustí Bassols[4] now stands for is the 'disaffection' that is growing in Catalonia with regard to Spain. The appearance of a broad front of supporters of independence is a natural result of the present situation, in which the 2006 Statute of Autonomy has been seriously cut back by Madrid's Constitutional Court. There are lots more supporters of independence now than five, ten, or fifteen years ago. Many of them are pro-independence at heart, but there are a lot more, like Bassols, who have held important posts in my governments and have been loyal to my policy of not backing independence. What they are saying now is 'we've had enough!' It's the logical result of disaffection. I understand it. But just how workable an independence movement could be in Catalonia today is another matter. We'll see.

But is it good enough to tell people to just grin and bear it?

I often ask friends of mine who are in favour of independence: 'What now?' You see, to be successful in politics, there are three things you need to know about: History, Geography, and Demography. We must ask ourselves where we come from, who we are, and why things are the way they are. We live in one corner of the Mediterranean, and we are surrounded by very powerful neighbours: Spain (or Castile) and France. The Mediterranean is a turbulent sea. The Pope has always been opposed to us, for religious and geographical reasons, and has preferred to be friends with France and Spain. But we've also got some advantages. We have more contact with Europe, even though the part of Europe we share borders with is less developed than we are. Demography is also vital. Our population is very sparse. Countries disappear less as the result of wars than because of population substitution and assimilation. The Bretons are disappearing largely because France is gobbling them up! Scotland and Wales haven't disappeared, but successive military defeats at the hands of a powerful kingdom like England weakened them historically. Colonization, economic absorption, cultural substitution, and homogenization are processes that come in the wake of military conquest.

What do you mean by 'population substitution'?

Population substitution by way of immigration is a very effective way of making small nations disappear. It's what the Chinese are doing in Tibet and in other regions of China. Here we have had massive immigration from Spain, and now from Africa, Eastern Europe, and South America. Some people say it's easier to make a recent Sub-Saharan immigrant favourable to Catalan independence than it is a die-hard Spanish immigrant. If they are told how economic discrimination affects our country, that may help them to identify with us. Whatever the case, a lot of immigrants end up integrating. They become Catalans. President Montilla is a fine example.[5] As in the famous American Dream, immigrants can move up the social ladder in Catalonia. It's been happening for over fifty years. And, who knows? There may come a day when it will be easier for someone like Montilla to favour Catalan independence than for some compatriots sporting fine old Catalan surnames like Puigdemont or Vilaregut!

Why do some Catalans have little sympathy for Catalanism and aspire to be 'universal' or simply Spanish instead?

One of the great fads that some Catalans go for is the golden calf of so-called cosmopolitanism. They like to feel 'hip' and 'lefty'. When the Transition was in full swing, we were positively overrun with new-fangled social and political doctrines that ended up paralysing us. A lot of people fell over backwards to show their solidarity with the most obscure dead-end causes. The more far-fetched they were the better. However, if you don't stand up for your own cause, it's doubtful anyone else will. A Basque politician once said to me: 'You Catalans are splendid at demonstrating for highfalutin causes that don't really have anything to do with you. But you turn your noses up at anything Catalan that needs attention!' It's true. I suppose it's a question of priorities.

Why do you think this happens?

The period in which so many of our leading men and women were in exile was altogether negative for us. People thought that the fact Josep Tarradellas was our president in exile[6] was enough, and that maintaining that symbolic institution would pull us through when he returned. But it didn't. While he was in exile little was done of any real worth. Tarradellas thought the people would go and fetch him back from exile when Franco died. He was right. They did go and fetch him. But very little was achieved and the new situation was not taken advantage of. The Statute of Autonomy drawn up in 1979 was quite insufficient. It isn't enough to bring out the big drums and rant about unity. I think countries go forward when there is one important party that's dominant and shows the kind of leadership that other parties can follow. There is pitifully little to be gained from sitting around a table and debating every step that's to be taken in the process. The Basques were staunchly behind their institutions and that gave them a lot more power. And then they had ETA. Deep down, that's why they're so much more powerful than us.

What do you think of the June 2010 Constitutional Court ruling against the Statute of Autonomy?

The sentence has been doubly harmful. On the one hand it has had very negative political effects. It spells out severe restrictions on our financial capacity, our scope for home rule and the status of our language. But the persistence and lack of respect they have shown for us has also been most morally damaging. I don't think that these political and moral affronts can be easily repaired. It is therefore not surprising that the polls should show a steep rise in the support for independence.

How would you evaluate the effect of the July 10, 2010, rally in Barcelona?

Spain pretends not to have noticed our protest. And maybe it's true that in Madrid they take little notice of things like this. It must be a by-product of the 'despise what you don't know about' syndrome that has traditionally tainted so much of Spanish thought.[7] The Spanish World Cup victory in South Africa also did its bit to muffle the effect of the Barcelona rally. But for us Catalans the demonstration has marked a clear turning point. Things will never again be the same. Spain cannot continue to ignore us.

Joan Ramon Resina
The Catalan voice at Stanford

I met Professor Joan Ramon Resina in the hallway of the Catalan National Archives at Sant Cugat. Thirty years spent in the United States with ten in Californian academic circles have rubbed off on him in expressions and even his looks. He is now a professor in Stanford's Department of Iberian and Latin American Cultures, where he has set up a visiting Chair in Catalan Studies. His books and articles are awaited with expectation by some, and with awe by others. He is considered the hammer of the Barcelona-based Socialists.

His recent book Barcelona's Vocation of Modernity: Rise and Decline of an Urban Image *defines the idea tourists are given of Barcelona as a 'non-place', a site bereft of Catalan culture and historical identity. Resina sees it as little more than a destination for yuppy weekends. He stands out among those academics that fear for the future of the Catalan identity and are prepared to back political change.*

Resina has a doctorate in Comparative Literature from the University of California at Berkeley (1986) and another in English Philology from the University of Barcelona (1988). His specialist areas include modern culture, literature, and cinema, the modern European novel, historical memory, nationalism, and urban literature. He has held academic posts in North American universities almost permanently since 1986. His most recent books include Del hispanismo a los estudios ibéricos: una propuesta federativa para el ámbito cultural" (1990) *and* El Postnacionalisme en el mapa global [Postnationalism on a Global Map]. *Since 1980 he has published dozens of articles in the Barcelona newspapers* Avui, Ara, *and* La Vanguardia, *and is regarded as one of the leading exponents of the need to redefine Catalan nationalism in the age of globalization. In 2009 he founded the Catalan Observatory at Stanford, an institution which he now directs.*

What panorama faces Catalonia after the June 2010 Constitutional Court ruling against the Catalan Statute?

The sentence comes as no surprise to me. It certifies the decease of the so-called Constitutional Agreement of 1977 and effectively puts an end to the future possibility of developing Catalan home rule. To my mind, it even cuts back on the Statute of Autonomy Catalonia has had since 1979. The sentence is particularly aggressive in that it repeatedly refuses to acknowledge the national status of Catalonia and the consideration of Catalan as our own language, stripping it of the status it had of 'preferential' language. It is incredible that a court deprived of all legitimacy and in which Catalans have no proportional representation should have cut back on a Statute that was passed in the Spanish and Catalan parliaments and approved in a referendum in Catalonia. The people won't even be given the right to approve the changes. All in all it makes a mockery of democracy.

How does this affect a State that defines itself as *autonómico*?

Indeed, the panorama is quite bleak for the 'Autonomous State', which Spain theoretically defines itself as being. A clear attempt is being made to try and dissolve Catalonia in the magma of a provincial Spain. Catalonia cannot even decide on her own internal territorial divisions, and is condemned to an increasingly decadent economic, industrial, and institutional future, with a deficit in infrastructures that may prove crippling. The only alternative to this—as so many people are opening their eyes to daily—is to pull out of the Spanish State and create state structures of our own. Without this step we really won't be able to develop our potential and guarantee a better future for forthcoming generations.

What was the response to this sentence in Catalonia?

The rally held on July 10th in Barcelona, with over one million demonstrators,[1] is said to have been one of the largest held in Europe in recent years. Under normal circumstances, this would immediately have made politicians think. However, the Socialists soon claimed it had been an anti-PP (Partido Popular) rather than a pro-sovereignty rally. In this way they helped disguise Prime Minister Zapatero's broken 2003 promise to respect whatever Statute the Catalan Parliament drew up. It seems that the major political parties are incapable of connecting with people's feelings. Of course, in response, this all adds to the contempt people feel towards them. Nevertheless, the moderate Catalanists of CiU do seem to realize that the demonstration marks a turning point which places the demand for sovereignty in a central position in the political arena. But they have cold feet about leading it, and prefer to continue as undefined as ever. On the other hand, the Republicans (ERC) are trying to ride the wave, and claim that it is their strategy that has sparked off the pro-independence fever. They seem to forget they upset many ex-voters with their unfailing support for Montilla between 2006 and 2010.[2] Maybe a new political force is needed.

Why has this pro-sovereignty boom occurred now?

I see it as having multiple causes: the conservatism of Pujol's party (CiU), the cynicism of the Socialists, the appearance of new more open-minded generations of young Catalans who have not been exposed to age-old bias and fears like those who came before them. Then there is the growing acceptance of the independentist discourse by prestigious intellectuals and academics. But perhaps above all one must single out the enormous contribution Madrid has unwittingly made to the sentimental divorce many Catalans feel towards Spain. This must inevitably make its mark on the political scene.

What about the response to the July 10th demonstration by the international media?

Though the international press coverage for the rally was quite extensive and neutral, I was surprised to see some media interpreted the demonstration as if it had been a demand for greater autonomy. Thus a major German channel presented the pro-independence movement as one representing a minority. Oddly enough the only politician interviewed by this channel was conservative nationalist Artur Mas (CiU).[3] I

think this reflects the difficulties the European Union has in comprehending and assimilating the full weight of the Catalan cause at the present moment. In contrast with all this, the Spanish press reacted—predictably enough—with a wave of nationalist disgust and much gnashing of teeth. The fact that they estimated the number of demonstrators at the rally at 56,000 doesn't say much for their credibility! Their lack of respect for Catalonia once again won the day.

Is it hard to explain Catalonia and her culture in the US?

Yes. But things have improved in the thirty years I've lived there. Catalonia has evolved from being something quite remote and unknown to being a cause that rings a bell with more and more people. Whereas for many undergraduates it is still an unknown country, the same cannot be said among postgraduates, many of whom come into contact with it.

The world feels sympathy for stateless causes like Tibet but little or none for Catalonia. Why?

You're right. World attention and sympathy are more easily aroused in Third World countries with nasty dictatorships or with racial and religious fallout from colonialism. In contrast, Catalonia is perceived as a relatively well-off country. This undermines our credibility when speaking in terms of being 'oppressed'. Indeed, at times—amazingly enough—we are actually portrayed as a people that oppresses Spanish minorities! For many people we have moved on from a situation in which we suffered repression at the hands of a dictator to one in which we command little sympathy because we keep on making demands when we supposedly enjoy full democratic freedom. Some see us as the owners of an institutionally protected language that imposes itself on others. Then there is also the perception that we are 'rich'. Only a cultivated minority is in a position to see that our national rights are not respected.

Some of that hostility has emerged in the international press…

Indeed, it sometimes appears to be becoming shriller and more frequent. It looks to me suspiciously like an orchestrated campaign. Some *The Economist* headlines look like translations of Madrid press blasts against Catalonia. Of course it doesn't help that so few foreign journalists are actually based in Barcelona. Foreign correspondents tend to see Catalonia through the eyes of the Madrid-based media. When Catalonia was the guest of honour at the 2007 Frankfurt Book Fair, the event was successfully sabotaged by systematic attacks on the organizers and the Catalan government for supposedly excluding Catalan writers who didn't write in Catalan. This was an absurd argument clearly inspired by the Madrid press. Nearly all foreign journalists move about in Madrid's influential cultural and political circles. Do they ever read the Catalan press, I wonder? Do they understand Catalan? All of this makes it hard for them to understand our situation and easy for them to construe an idea of Catalans as obtuse and obstreperous. Incidentally, when Catalan writer Manuel Vázquez Montalbán was confronted with the accusation that Catalans were always complaining about things, he insisted that there was nothing worse than being paranoid when persecution really exists!

Do you think Catalonia has trouble making its views known?

Catalonia lacks institutions capable of arousing debate beyond the borders of the Spanish State. As Catalonia does not have a diplomatic corps, the best way to gain international presence is via the press. As regards the academic world, I have for years been calling for the introduction of linguistic immersion in English in Catalan schools. This is what they do in Scandinavian and in Holland where everyone ends up speaking English fluently. This gives them direct access to the international scene. Few Catalan academics or intellectuals are capable of addressing an American audience in English. Catalonia needs to make an effort to compete with other countries in promoting her knowledge producers. She must also encourage her academics to take up posts in elite universities worldwide.

You have defined Catalonia as a country that 'doesn't want to disappear'. Why is the anguish reflected in this expression so far removed from the view currently reflected in Catalan media and politics?

I think we need to take a close look at the position adopted by the political parties on this respect. In the 'golden' period of *Convergència i Unió*, I remember the question of the slump in the social use of Catalan being brought up at a meeting between American academics and the Catalan Minister of Culture. Before he agreed to reveal the relevant figures to those present, the Minister asked for media microphones to be switched off. So even then the government was aware of the divorce between official discourse and the stark truth. Indeed, in Pujol's last term of office he sometimes admitted that the language issue had been his biggest failure. The *Tripartit* government has also been unwilling to admit its failure in this area. The language crisis is very real although it has nothing to do with political attitudes. Indeed it would be unimaginable that Catalonia could be governed by anti-Catalan forces. On the other hand, living abroad as I do, whenever I come back I get the unpleasant sensation that the Catalan world—not just the language—is being slowly eroded away.

But in your writings you also talk about an increase in the number of people in favour of independence…

Yes, that's true. This is occurring because people perceive the politicians to be incapable of achieving the degree of home rule that was called for in the seventies. People increasingly see civic movements as the answer. Whereas ten or fifteen years ago plenty of people thought that to push for independence was irresponsible, even crazy, now the call for it is growing fast. I see it in my own father, who is 83. A few years ago the word independence scared him. But now he sees it as the answer. If people who've lived through the blackest periods of Francoism now see independence as the only option, it means that things are obviously changing. The extraordinary demonstration of July 10th, organized by Òmnium Cultural, shows that people are prepared to take the lead quite spontaneously when they feel the official institutions are not taking their aspirations seriously.

Why do you say that the Catalans are the 'Jews of Spain'?

They are in many ways treated as such. Spain was created in a process which involved the expulsion of discordant elements. In the beginning what mattered were religious and racial differences such as the lack of purity of people's blood. Spain defined itself as Christian. When it feels threatened, it tends to desperately search for those elements which made it feel strong in the past. The conquest of America is therefore often portrayed as an extrapolation of the victory over the Moors. The same happens with the question of Spanish unity. There's always a need to find the offending enemy within. The one who fails to fall into line. In the modern era—after 1640,[4] basically—I'm afraid this role has been increasingly assigned to Catalonia. From the mid-19th century onwards, the Catalans have tended to be portrayed as the Jews of Spain. I'm thinking of the cartoons of Francesc Cambó[5] in the Madrid press, the rhetoric of Pío Baroja, Valle-Inclán's *Luces de Bohemia*. Anti-Catalanism increased as anti-Semitism came to the fore again in early 20th-century Europe. Catalonia was once again depicted as the grave danger facing Spain. The degree of 'Catalanophobia' raised by the new Statute in 2005–6 did not appear out of the blue. This all goes back over a hundred years.

Hasn't immigration been used as a Trojan Horse to strengthen the pro-Spanish contingent in Catalonia?

Undoubtedly, though it's politically incorrect to say so. I think the majority of people in this country are of immigrant origin and non-Catalan surnames abound. My own grandmother arrived from Andalusia with her young children before the Civil War. My own daughters are only 25% Catalan in that sense. The problem has nothing to do with people's origins. It is really a question of the conditions under which people come to Catalonia. My greatest concern is that many of them have not been allowed to evolve.

Economy

Germà Bel
The concern over infrastructure

Germà Bel i Queralt is professor of Economics at Barcelona University, where he specializes in economic policy and the public sector. He was born in 1963, and brought up in Les Cases d'Alcanar, a town with seven hundred inhabitants which lies very near to the imprecise line—linguistically and culturally speaking—where Catalonia ends and Valencia begins. Bel likes to recall that he was 'brought up in a bar' that his parents ran. He read Economics at Barcelona University, has an MA from the University of Chicago and obtained his PhD back in Barcelona. From 2004 to 2006 he was an associate professor at Cornell and Harvard universities in the US.

His current research focuses on the economics and politics of infrastructure and transport. He is also interested in the reform of the public sector—especially the question of the privatization of state enterprises—the regulation and competitiveness of markets, and the reform of local services. His most recent books on these issues are: Economía y política de la privatización local [The Economics and Politics of Local Privatization]*(2006)—awarded prizes by the Catalan Economics Society (IEC) and the College of Economists of Catalonia,* Aeroports i poder [Airports and Power] *(co-authored with Xavier Fageda, 2007)[1] and* Espanya, capital París [Spain, with Paris as capital] *(2010).*

Bel has acted as economic consultant for the Barcelona Provincial Council [Diputació de Barcelona] as well as of the Ministry of Public Administration and the Ministry of Public Works and Transport in the Spanish central government. From 2000 to 2004 he was an MP in the Spanish Parliament for the Catalan Socialist Party (PSC). Currently, he is a consultant for the United Nations Development Programme and the Corporación Andina de Fomento [Andean Development Corporation]. He regularly writes articles in La Vanguardia *and participates in* Cadena Ser *radio debates.*

Are Catalans justified in airing their grievances about the state of infrastructures in their country?

I think the Catalan position—I don't like the term 'grievances'—really has more to do with the management of the major infrastructure elements than with the infrastructures themselves. For example, a new terminal building was recently opened at Barcelona Airport.[2] But will it really solve any of our transport problems? All right, in the future the terminal will give us more capacity. But Barcelona airport's main problems have more to do with control than with cement. Likewise, when the TGV[3] train line to France is completed, we'll continue to be badly connected to Europe because no plans have been foreseen to improve rail freight transport in our country.[4] True enough, there are similar problems in other European countries. But the paranoia that the issue raises here is unparalleled! This is so because there is no other country in which the central government exercises such tight control over transport. In other countries, even large airports are privately controlled. Here everything depends on the Spanish air transport authority, AENA, which in turn depends entirely on the Madrid authorities.

So the existence of AENA is negative for Catalonia?

Not only for Catalonia, but for Spain in general. Madrid Airport is probably the only one that is not negatively affected by AENA. However, were AENA to disappear, Madrid might well benefit too! AENA is determined to run all Spanish air travel as if there were just one airport: Madrid. They actually admit to this in their own literature. Their whole policy is designed around that one airport. Some smaller airports would greatly benefit from the suppression of AENA and its control of the Spanish air transport zone. It is actually much more realistic and beneficial not to think about 'zones', as such, but about the interests of the airports. These should be seen as individual concerns, with their own priorities. And run accordingly. This is really necessary in the case of Catalonia because Barcelona has the potential of becoming a major hub, an option that other airports have not got to the same degree. But they too would also improve, because the AENA model is hampering their prospects as well.

What about the policies of the airlines themselves?

In 2006 Iberia reinforced a tendency it had initiated earlier, which involved the suppression of all connecting flights originating at Barcelona except for those supplying air traffic for Madrid. At present, Iberia limits its offer, in practical terms, to Barcelona–Madrid flights. Iberia knows that if it centralizes all its flights in Madrid it will increase its profits. Previously, Iberia had flights to New York from both Madrid and Barcelona. But the Barcelona route was shut down. They said it was losing money, which was a lie. It was just that they increased profits by concentrating flights in Madrid. The profitability of the Barcelona–New York line is proved by the fact that three other companies now do the run very successfully. In fact, for Delta Airlines, it is now their third most profitable route in the world! For Iberia, however, it is more profitable just to fly from Madrid.

So why did they create the T1 terminal in Barcelona airport?

That's a good question indeed. What is happening now at this new terminal is that the fastest access route to any departure gate is provided for Barcelona–Madrid flights. The decision to design things that way was taken in 2007. To my immense surprise that decision was loudly applauded by the political and economic authorities of Catalonia. At that time we were told the lie that the route would be open to any airline that so wished. But the truth is that there are administrative restrictions which ensure that it is only Iberia that can use that corridor, enjoying all the logistical advantages imaginable to enable it to do so. Why's that? To enhance Madrid Airport!

So Iberia wins out with all this…

Yes. In the age of the state monopolies, Iberia played the role of commercial delegate at all Spanish airports. Now Iberia is private. Surprisingly enough, though, its role has not changed. AENA continues to favour Iberia, because the idea is pushed that 'Iberia

connects Spain to the world'. It's a highly nationalistic view, and clearly one that is aimed at giving Barcelona Airport a subsidiary role. Hence Iberia's absolutely marginal presence here. It simply transports passengers to Madrid! If Iberia disappeared from Barcelona airport, we would hardly notice the difference. As regards the January 2009 purchase of Spanair by a group of Catalan investors, it is still too soon to know what the outcome will be.[5] What is certain is that the group thought this could be a last chance for Catalonia to acquire a large conventional airline at a time when the air travel market is contracting.

What caused the famous 'infrastructures collapse' in Catalonia in 2007?[6] Does that sort of thing happen elsewhere?

What happened in 2007 was that the entire *Rodalies* railway system backed up. It had been renovated in the early 1990s. Since then no significant investment had been made, and it was suffering from increasingly heavy service strain. In addition, the Spanish railway company, RENFE, had become obsessed with building the fast train system (AVE) according to a highly centralized plan, as announced by Prime Minister Aznar in his April 2000 inauguration speech. The Catalan Government took the bait of this challenge, thinking it would enable Catalans to whizz to Helsinki in no time flat. Of course, for years this programme completely sapped the budget allowances available for other means of transport, including the *Rodalies* network and freight rail transport. In Madrid, on the other hand—where the AVE is very cheap—no restrictions were ever put on investments in the local train network. When I was an MP and asked for more investment in the Catalan local rail network, we always got the same answer: 'With all that we are investing in the AVE, there's nothing left for normal trains.' So throughout 2006 nothing was invested in Rodalies. The collapse the experts had forecast back in 2003 eventually happened in 2007. When the AVE reached Barcelona, the Rodalies network collapsed. It was hardly surprising, because thirteen years had gone past without one euro in upkeep investment! The governments of Spain and Catalonia had got their priorities wrong. They paid too much attention to 'glamour' infrastructures and none to day-to-day needs. In the end, the system crashed.

In Catalonia, the question of the motorways is controversial, because tolls have to be paid on most of them whereas they are free in most of Spain. Is that correct?

Yes. But I think it's worth considering the genesis of the Spanish highway network to understand how we have come to that point. The first motorways, in the 1960s, were all toll roads built by private companies. They were constructed in areas where they would be most profitable, especially in zones with plenty of goods traffic and tourism: principally the Mediterranean corridor and the Ebre Valley. The problem is that the formula for making motorways was based on a toll system. It was not a case of the Spanish Government deciding that in Catalonia people would have to pay, but not in Spain, as some Catalans say. In the '80s, when other main highways were built, the formula was different. So now we have a dual system in which some areas—including Catalonia—have toll motorways, and others have free highways *(autovies)* which are paid for out of the State budget. Of course, in areas like Catalonia, where you have to pay tolls, that affects the cost of living as well as of production and distribution. The problem that ought to be tackled is how to homogenize and rationalize the system so that it isn't always the same regions that have to pay.

The State could either introduce or eliminate tolls on all roads. A third option would be a formula applied in the USA, where the management of the highways is left to the states involved but it is the Federal Administration that owns them. If that formula were applied, the regions could decide whether to charge a toll or choose some other way of financing them. That would prevent the situation we have now in which some areas such as Catalonia not only have to pay tolls on almost all their motorways but also have to contribute to financing free highways in the rest of the state with their taxes!

So Catalans are right to complain in this case...

Yes. I think Catalans are quite entitled to complain and demand changes. The economic harm done in terms of higher transport costs is unquestionable. But I think it is wrong to keep putting out the notion that the Spanish government resolved to make Catalans pay for their highways while making others exempt. It is obvious that changes must be introduced to make things less unfair for the areas that have to pay. What has failed up to now, on the Catalan side, is the capacity to make a correct diagnosis of the situation and adapt policy-making and demands to it.

And what is the situation now as regards rail travel?

In fact something similar is happening to us on that score too. We are concentrating all our attention on the TGV (AVE) links to France and Valencia, and have completely ignored the question of the freight line up the Mediterranean coast. The State has approved the plan for an Algeciras–Madrid–Zaragoza freight line, which will shift traffic away from our country in favour of the Central Pyrenean option. That's serious for two reasons. On the one hand, the Mediterranean corridor's long-standing deficit in terms of modernization will be increased. And, on the other hand, our demand for the TGV line to France offers us no guarantee that we will be able to travel to stations beyond Perpignan or Montpellier for a good many years. So, for the moment, it is not going to bring Barcelona any nearer to Paris. We seem to have a serious problem defining our priorities in Catalonia. Meanwhile the State is planning major rail infrastructures that will very much mark the future and threaten to leave us out on a limb. We run the risk of becoming absolutely marginal with regard to the principal rail transport infrastructures in Spain. And there's no changing that now, because all the major decisions have already been taken.

What is the State's philosophy behind this behaviour?

Madrid has for centuries been the political capital of the State. During the 1990s it also became the economic capital of Spain. They wanted to follow the French model, and they strived to turn Madrid into a sort of Paris. What they haven't managed to do, so far, is turn Spain into France!

Does that mean that the Catalan economy—which traditionally led Spain—will have finally been sapped during Spain's longest period of democracy?

Catalonia's economy is far from being the most buoyant in Spain, as it used to be. In terms of the relative production of wealth, the economies of the Basque Country, Navarre, and Madrid are well ahead, and those of Rioja and the Balearic Islands are quite comparable to ours now. Catalonia is relatively wealthy when compared to the Spanish average. But other regions have improved their figures much more than we have. Our standard of living isn't much above average.

What are the economic consequences of all this?

As regards the fiscal balance in Spain, and bearing in mind that the Basques and Navarrese pay nothing,[7] the truth is that the 'contributors' of Spain—i.e. those who pay—are basically the Catalan and the Balearic regions, and to a lesser extent Valencia. Contrary to what fudged figures suggest, Madrid has absolutely no fiscal deficit with regard to the State. Madrid receives a great deal of investment in the form of services and salaries which figure as investments made in Spain in general and not ones made in Madrid. However the sole beneficiary of this investment, in practical terms, is clearly Madrid. For example, my mother, who lives in Les Cases d'Alcanar near Tarragona, has to pay taxes which go towards funding the astronomically expensive enlargement being made at Madrid's Prado Museum. But she has never even been to Madrid, nor intends to go!

Joaquim Boixareu
International business, Catalan roots

Joaquim Boixareu is the Managing Director of Irestal, a metallurgical company that produces and distributes stainless steel products. The company's headquarters are just outside Barcelona, and it has branches in Spain, Britain, France, Portugal, Russia, the Czech Republic, Slovakia, Poland, and Ukraine. This leading Catalan entrepreneur very much sees the need to participate in business associations[1] to encourage Catalan enterprises and to connect them with society. He is an enthusiastic fan of business internationalization, a question that he sees as a prime concern for Catalan enterprises at this time. He also heartily recommends an international education for those engaging in business, and encourages students to spend part of their university careers abroad. To practice what he preaches, Boixareu speaks six languages fluently. As a past student of Barcelona's prestigious ESADE business school, he says: 'I was lucky to spend my last term at the HEC in Paris. I also studied some time at New York University. I believe that having had the opportunity to live in these two great world capitals at that age was a priceless experience.'

Boixareu has never concealed his feelings for Catalonia. Although based in Barcelona, he is proud of the Pyrenean roots of his father's side of the family. He has even been able to trace it back five hundred years! He remembers with emotion that his father was a nationalist and a member of the Catalanist party Nosaltres Sols [We Alone].[2] *'He had many difficulties and suffered persecution during and before the Franco dictatorship. So when things got really tough, he decided play it safe and set up a business.'*

Boixareu is aware that his mother's schooling at the prestigious Institut-Escola [School Institute]—a coeducational and secular school founded by the Catalan Government in 1932—marked his own view of the world. He points out that both his parents were Catalanists 'and fought for the country's freedom'. When asked about the controversial independence referendums held in 2009–2010, he says that he is 'all for freedom, both individually and as a country', and insists that they are fully democratic despite their unofficial nature. On the other hand, he sees a democratic deficit on the part of the Spanish State, and points out that there is 'a worrying lack of respect for the ideas of others' in the State. 'They tell us that either we are with them or against them. So they don't really offer us any kind of option. They don't accept us as we are.'

This prestigious industrialist sees a contrast between the Catalan and the Spanish traditions, associating the former with a 'a greater respect for democracy and compromise' and with 'a very active civil society'. To him it is obvious that Catalonia is a nation, 'not because the law may declare it so, but because we are a cultural, historical, economic and linguistic reality which goes back a thousand years'.

What do you think of the political developments that there have been in Catalonia recently?

I think there is a need for society to see which way our country is headed. For example, I think people are becoming increasingly aware of the very real lack of infrastructures we have in contrast with the economic and industrial position we otherwise enjoy. The most important thing is that we are not taking full advantage of our potential as a country, because we have restrictions. Barcelona airport is a good example of this. It is obvious that Catalonia needs to manage its own airports in order to be able to compete globally. Other issues that worry people in this context are education, research, and our shortcomings regarding the knowledge of languages. Many businessmen raise the question: if we are not able to compete with things as they are, what will happen in the future?

But isn't Catalonia seen as a privileged region in many parts of Spain?

I honestly do not think it is worth responding to clichés that are spread by the Madrid press. What we must do is consider our own country in the wider context of the global world. In the international context, we cannot forget that Catalonia has no natural wealth of her own: no oil, gas, or minerals. The only really sound resource we have are our people. There are top Catalan businessmen doing amazing things on all fronts. The funny thing is that all too often, they remain quite anonymous. Personally I see it as a shortcoming because it may prevent our youth from admiring the 'Bill Gates' we have among us! We also have world class sportsmen in many sports such as football, basketball, or motor sports. We have top class doctors, many of whom are acknowledged worldwide. We have high-powered research centres and outstanding scientists as well as first-class business schools. We even have a chef—Ferran Adrià—who has for some years been considered the best in the world. What I say is that, whatever our other shortcomings might be, it cannot be a complete coincidence that we have so many first-class performers in so many different fields. I would say this is the result of a certain tradition, and a particular environment which is conducive to excellence and high-quality work. This is the most important asset our small country has. Needless to say, there is still plenty more we could do to improve things. But the fiscal deficit we suffer at the hands of the State often makes that difficult!

Going back to your earlier point, why do you see it as important for Barcelona airport to be managed locally?

Airports are not only defined in terms of the passengers or merchandise they handle. They have a more strategic purpose which is to connect cities and countries with the world. This is what our country lacks at the moment. If Barcelona airport is to continue as a mere satellite of the one in Madrid, it's going to be a severe setback. It prevents us from competing. We do not want it to be a low-cost airport either because, although this may have a market, it does not serve the principal role the airport must have as an air transport hub. It must link up our country with the rest of the world. To do so, it requires three things: an important airline using Barcelona as its headquarters; unrestricted connections with the major international routes; and the management of the airport itself. And Madrid obstructs all this. The fact that we now have a new T1 terminal building is not enough. Nor is it enough that Spanair airline is now based in Barcelona.

Would you say there has been a conscious effort by the Madrid Government to restrict Catalan competitiveness by limiting infrastructures such as these?

Conscious effort or not, the problem lies in the centralist model being applied. This is a very serious problem as regards the railway network. The Mediterranean corridor (Barcelona–Valencia–Perpignan)—traditionally essential not only for Catalan and Valencian interests but also for the Spanish economy itself—is no priority for Madrid. Spain continues to be a 'railway island'[3] and there inexplicably seems to be no will to link up with Europe. As regards the airports, including Catalan ones, the fact that they are managed by a Madrid-controlled agency (AENA) means that the mentality with which they are run is highly centralist. At present, all airports in Spain act as mere appendices to that in Madrid. This is most

inefficient and totally illogical. In Germany, a country far richer and more developed than Spain, the main airline Lufthansa has two hubs, one in Frankfurt and the other in Munich, although the distance between the two is almost half of that between Barcelona and Madrid. The Germans and Americans are clever and true federalists. So they have seen the advantages of having more than one hub, as happens in most countries in which airports are not directly or indirectly run by the State administration. Munich airport has 35 fully-employed people working in the marketing department to promote Munich airport throughout the world. In contrast, Barcelona airport has one.

You mentioned the fiscal deficit that affects the Catalan economy. How does this compare with the situation in other regions of the world?

The fact that Catalonia has to pay 10% of its GNP in taxes to the rest of the State—taxes which do not return in investment—is a form of drainage that not even the richest economies in the world tolerate. We are not such a rich country! In the legislations of many countries there are generally reasonable limits for interregional compensation quotas. In Germany, for example, the Constitutional Court has decreed that 4% of a Land's GDP is the maximum it can be expected to contribute. Here that limit rises to 12%, three times more. Neither Baden-Württemberg nor North-Rhine-Westphalia could face such outrageous creaming off of their income. So this is an enormous problem for the Catalan economy. It means that our companies and industries do not receive the support they should be getting to help them develop their activities in international markets, in research, in development and in technology. All this severely affects our competitiveness.

How is this phenomenon perceived from Spain?

Objective data on this issue is sadly lacking in the Spanish media. The contribution made by Catalonia to the Spanish economy is imperceptible to most Spaniards. Indeed, it is concealed from them. Both the Pujol (1980–2003) and Maragall (2003–2006) governments of the Generalitat tried hard to educate opinion on this question, but to little effect. I think it is a bit like what happened after World War II: however much the Germans insisted they were no longer the enemy any more, no Frenchman was impressed. It was not until French leaders took it upon themselves to convince their compatriots that the situation changed. This is what Spanish leaders should have been doing with regard to Catalonia. But they seem to have no interest in doing so.

There have even been boycott campaigns against Catalan products in Spain.

That's right. This was primarily due to the debate over the new Statute of Autonomy. In principle I think all boycott campaigns are negative. But ironically enough, I think that by boycotting Catalan products, those seeking to harm us were in fact harming themselves, because the tax money those products generated was not coming in to them. On the other hand, Spanish companies also sell a lot of their products in Catalonia. So I think it is absurd that there should be a boycott in either sense. It's cutting off your nose to spite your face!

How do you think the economy would be affected if Catalonia became independent?

To be honest, I think there would be advantages and disadvantages. Although this issue has begun to be debated, I don't think there is a clear idea as to how things would turn out in the end. One of the obvious advantages would be the reduction or elimination of the fiscal deficit we suffer from. On the other hand, the possible loss of part of the Spanish market would be a disadvantage, albeit temporarily so. The Spanish market continues to be important for the Catalan economy, although not nearly as important as it used to be thanks to today's globalized economy. So things would have to be carefully weighed up one way or the other.

The Basques have a special economic status with their own taxation system…

Yes. It's a huge advantage for them. The Catalans made the fatal error—thirty years ago, when democracy began—of not opting for the economic quota system the Basques have. This would allow us to manage our own taxes and resources today and pay an agreed amount to Madrid on a yearly basis. This system would have allowed us to adapt our economic structure to our own economic, industrial, and sociological structure, which in many respects is different to that in much of Spain. Catalonia has been an industrialized nation since the 18th century. And Spain has not. This means that our priorities are often different. It often calls for divergent economic and industrial policies. Catalonia should be given the option of applying her own fiscal and economic policies.

Have Catalan business sectors made demands in this direction?

Well I think there have been significant developments on this front. In March 2007, when the effects to the economy by the shortcomings in infrastructures were becoming most visible,[4] a memorable event took place. The Catalan business elite came together for a meeting at the IESE Business School. They demanded Catalan control over Barcelona airport. Suddenly, it was as if a taboo had been broken. Catalan businessmen and women suddenly began to air their views about the appalling condition of State-run infrastructure in Catalonia. A meeting as determined as this had not happened for over a hundred years. In general I would say there is an increased awareness amongst Catalan business sectors regarding the need to work together and exert pressure to protect our interests.

Are Catalan universities prepared for globalization and current business trends?

I think Catalan universities ought to encourage international experience among their students, making them 'citizens of the world'. This would have an immense value for the country, because it would make students aware that the world is far smaller than they think but a lot larger than the Iberian Peninsula! The whole of the education process is fundamental for the future of the country. Internationalization is very important at all levels of education. It is for academics and researchers too. Being exposed to international competition makes you learn how to deal with it. We must be prepared to fare alongside the best in the world and take our place where we belong. This will make us more modest and humble, which is also a good thing. Another very important factor is the way our universities are governed. We have a lot of ground to make up for with regard to Finnish, Dutch, or Swiss universities. Even Portugal is ahead of us now. We still have an important deficit there.

How do you see the future?

Despite all the external obstacles, I think that the future of Catalonia really depends on the Catalans themselves. There are so many things that we can do because they depend on us. For example, we can improve the Catalan public administration. Why isn't it more efficient? For over 200 years, Catalan public administration has adopted many of the worst defects in the Spanish system. This must change. I also think we need to be very much more fluent in English. This depends on us and no one else! And lastly, I think we also need to have more truly internationalized companies. This too depends on us. So we have lots of work to get on with, don't we?

Josep Mateu
Managing an automobile club with one million members

Josep Mateu is the Director General of the RACC (Royal Automobile Club of Catalonia). It is a hugely successful enterprise with over one million members and two thousand employees. Car insurance, travel, and motor sports are three of the club's main areas of operation. RACC also takes part in organizing Formula 1 and Motorbike Gran Prix races, as well as major international car rallies. Apart from managing the RACC, Josep Mateu is also President of FemCAT (Fundació Privada d'Empresaris, or Private Business People's Foundation). This foundation was created in 2004 to promote initiatives that would contribute to the future progress of Catalan industry and society. One of the major objectives of this organization is to make Catalonia an economically competitive country at an international level. In the words of Mateu, we spend our time 'thinking about the country we are going to hand down to our future generations'.

In March 2007, FemCAT organized a high-powered international business forum called Sortim al món [Let's go out into the world]. *It was attended by the former US Secretary of State Colin Powell, and Steve Forbes, of the Forbes Group. FemCAT also signed an agreement to cooperate with the Catalan Parliament with a view to bringing the business and parliamentary worlds closer together. In June 2009 Josep Mateu told a VilaWeb journalist that what FemCAT wanted politicians to do was to 'concentrate more on strategy and less on short-term tactics'. When asked what country he envisaged as a model for Catalonia, Josep Mateu opted for Finland, a country which he sees as 'built on the principle of cooperation between the private, public, and individual spheres'.*

As regards his ideal city, he singles out Boston, a city which he sees as the result of a common project that has 'successfully blended social cohesion and inspiration in a wide range of initiatives'. In 2009 members of FemCAT bought Spanair airlines, an intelligent, private initiative aimed at providing Catalonia with a leading airline of its own. Mateu defines himself as a 'patriot', and defines the current semi-federal structure of the State as an obstacle for Catalonia. As a recipe for the future, he sees a very real need for Catalonia to recover powers and areas of jurisdiction that will enable the country to manage her own economy and infrastructure unhampered.

How has the Catalan economy evolved in the last few years?

The situation in our country has its own specific ingredients, over and above the general situation of economic and political crisis the world is faced with today and all the effects this has on social values. Not only are we no longer receiving European funds, but the political model of the State is also undergoing a severe crisis. It is a complex situation that other European states are generally not faced with because few question the state in those countries. In Catalonia the state is questioned.

Why is it questioned?

Well, to start with, the deficit in infrastructures we suffer from is hampering our capacity to compete internationally. The Catalan economy has weakened because of this. Apart from this, our society also seems less inclined to sacrifice and hard work than it used to be, a factor that in the last thirty years has coincided with the birth of a public administration system of our own. We have a powerful and innovative business sector. But it is by no means sufficiently well known abroad. What we need are business leaders who can help us overcome the idea that our limitations have no solution. We have to define a common project, and for this we need a determined political leadership that will ensure that we all advance in a coordinated fashion. Catalonia is too small a country to waste energies on domestic squabbling! We must all do our bit and make sure the real problems are faced.

You mention the question of infrastructures. What is the problem here?

In Spain the State administration is obsessed with a radial transport model based on Madrid. Limiting its scope to the Iberian Peninsula shows short-sightedness and severely affects our international connectivity. What we want is not only to have better infrastructures for our economy but the capacity to run them. Another problem stems from the fact that internal inequalities mean that the richer regions have to subsidize less developed ones. On paper that may seem reasonable. But there is no plan whatever to ensure that the fiscal effort we make is compensated for. Policies such as these are what most hamper Catalan potential for competing with the richer areas in Europe. The model is based on providing poorer regions with fish instead of teaching them how to catch them. One negative outcome of this is that the whole Mediterranean belt, from Girona to Málaga, lacks infrastructures and connections with Europe. This situation has the effect of crippling the richer and more dynamic regions while funding poorer regions with subsidies that altogether fail to contribute to their development.

The Spanish Constitutional Court has ruled out the possibility of effective powers in the area of fiscal policy…

Indeed. The current situation is seen by many as unjust and even absurd. The truth is that the Spanish State actually loses out by not granting us these powers and by not investing sufficiently in our country. This causes a chain reaction: while we become less competitive, the State as a whole becomes poorer. However, to be honest, at present there is no real guarantee that we can do things much better on our own. Our present model also has its limitations. Catalonia is paying a hefty price for not having secured an economic agreement like the Basques did during the Transition period. If we had that agreement, which is based on yearly quotas paid to Madrid in return for services, we would have been able to obtain the infrastructures we needed.

Some say the Spanish market is not as important as it used to be for Catalan business.

In the present situation one cannot discard any market however internationalized things may have become. Parallel to this, we also have to face up to phenomena such as the campaigns calling for the boycott of Catalan products in Spain, some of which are openly patronized by Madrid media. Miserable initiatives such as this result from attempts to manipulate the territorial conflict in Spain for electoral purposes. Whatever the case, Catalan and Spanish markets are not large enough nowadays. So it is essential to turn to international ones too. Indeed, large Catalan companies now find their markets on all three fronts.

The Spanish market is necessary but, in general, it is no longer essential. The Catalan economy accounts for one-third of the international exports produced by Spain.

What do you think of the fact that some Catalan businessmen are beginning to show interest in obtaining political sovereignty for their country?

Businessmen tend to analyse questions from a professional point of view. So they may well be increasingly inclined to regard the infrastructures deficit and other developments in the political world as factors that cause our country to be less competitive. This may in turn lead them to look for changes. Business is getting more and more global, so the need to adapt to a world marked by greater competitiveness is increasingly becoming a priority. This may one day lead to a situation in which practical businessmen who today want little more than to be more competitive will see fit to muck in with those who are emotionally inclined to favour sovereignty for their country.

As a businessman, what do you think of the unofficial referendums on independence that are being held in Catalan towns?

They are the result of the shortcomings of the state model that is currently in existence. In this sense, I think Catalans have every right to express their opinions and their feelings about the future. These referendums arise from the fact that many Catalans rightly feel that they are not understood in Spain. And the absurd thing is that—in the long run—I think this lack of understanding is really going to be much more damaging for Spain than it is for us. The referendums form part of the ongoing debate about our identity and national symbols. These elements are important for us as Catalans as they are for people everywhere, including Spain. Nevertheless, the need for a debate on the defence of our identity and culture must not make us overlook how important it is to become proficient in English, when it is quite feasible to master both languages to perfection. I think English is very important for our future.

What do you mean when you say Catalans are 'not understood'?

Let me try and give you an example. Several years ago the Spanish government did away with indicators of the home province on car number plates. While in some European countries each region or nationality bears its own official identifier on number plates—indeed in some, these have been introduced only recently—in Spain these were altogether eliminated at a very delicate moment when other clear threats to our identity were also being made. This may seem a triviality to some. But it upset many Catalans who felt that their symbols were not being respected, as is so often the case. The whole question regarding this lack of respect may well have to do with the fact that we have not engaged with enough decision in the game that is being played out in front of us. There must be a rational project to be working for, as well as enthusiasm and emotion. And symbols form part of that emotion.

Xavier Sala-i-Martin
Professor of Economics at Columbia University

For many, Xavier Sala-i-Martin (Cabrera de Mar, 1963) is 'the man in the eccentric-coloured jackets'. At least, that is the image that most Catalans have of him. Many do not even know that this flamboyant TV personality is in fact a leading economics professor at Columbia University in New York. Forced to place him on a professional map, many would probably situate him closer to the world of professional football than that of academics and the economy. Indeed, his green, pink, and yellow tailor-made suits and jackets have for years earned him the unofficial title of Catalonia's most loudly-dressed man at FC Barcelona matches (he was president of the club's advisory Economic Commission in 2006–2010, during the presidency of Joan Laporta) and on TV talk shows. His choice of jackets wavers little for the highbrow international economics venues he regularly attends. The press loves them, and generally places him at the centre of most group shots he's involved in. In a visit for the 'Malaria No More' solidarity campaign to the New York Stock Exchange on August 5, 2008, he and club president Joan Laporta opened the session of the day by jointly pressing the 'Opening Bell'. Sala-i-Martin's orange jacket was the star of the day's event, of which—jacket or no jacket—the professor is particularly proud!

Sala-i-Martin is one of a select group of Catalan intellectuals that make no secret of their expansive devotion for Football Club Barcelona, which they see as 'more than a club', the team's motto. While other staunch FCB-supporting academics open their web home pages with scholarly quotes and notes about meeting times, Sala-i-Martin's launches out with a portrait of himself in a turquoise jacket holding up the UEFA Champions League trophy. And that's not all. It goes on to show the masterly video that Barça coach Pep Guardiola showed to his players five minutes before playing the vital final against Manchester United in Rome in May 2009. From there he jumps, almost reluctantly one might think, to 'Academic Stuff' and a graph on the evolution of the world distribution of income. This is a favourite subject of his, and one in which he has challenged conventional thinking on the matter. Despite this penchant for sport and Barça, it would therefore be a mistake to think we are faced with a banal, clothes-obsessed eccentric. Far from it.

Professor Xavier Sala-i-Martin is consistently ranked among the most widely-quoted economists in the world. In 2004 he won the King Juan Carlos I Prize for Economics, awarded to the person the Bank of Spain considers the best economist in Spain and Latin America.[1] In 2006 he also won the Lenfest Prize, awarded to the best teacher at Columbia University. His study areas include economic growth, development in Africa, monetary economics, social security, health, and economic issues. He is a champion of liberal thinking, on which subject he wrote a book titled Liberal economics for non-economists and non-liberals. *Another of his best-known books is* Economic Growth, *written with Robert J. Barro. Xavier Sala-i-Martin writes regularly for* La Vanguardia, *often expressing views that are as critical of the policies of the Spanish government as they are favourable to Catalan independence.*

Apart from the present crisis, Catalonia has had to face the last 15 years with a fiscal deficit equivalent to 10% of its GDP. Is that right?

The fiscal deficit of Catalonia with regard to Spain is large if compared with other European 'regions' of a similar size. Indeed, forming part of the Spanish fiscal system actually means that the resources generated by Catalan enterprises and citizens are generally invested elsewhere. This means that it has effectively become pointless to pay taxes here. People do not mind paying handsomely if they get good public services in return, as in Sweden. They are also happy to pay little and get poor public services, because this enables them to have plenty of private resources to spend on what they want, as happens in the USA. The worst situation is one in which high taxes are paid, as in Sweden, but in exchange one gets deplorable public services and investment, as in the States. In this regard, the fiscal situation of areas such as Catalonia or the Balearic Islands is among the worst. In any case, although the fiscal deficit is a major problem for Catalonia, it is not the most serious. The most serious problem is that, through belonging to Spain, Catalonia has to maintain a very obnoxious institutional system. By this I mean the system of regulation, the educational system, the system of finance, the taxation system, and all the bureaucracy.

It is generally thought that the present crisis has generated a slump in demand and that this has led to the high unemployment figures we have. In the case of Catalonia, does one have to add to this the effects caused by the fiscal deficit?

I know that I am in a minority position among economists here. But I do not think that the crisis is a question of demand, but rather of supply. In this sense the problem is that the productivity of the Catalan worker is very low. In my opinion this is caused not by the deficit you mention but by the excess of norms and regulations that exists. In addition, our students are poorly prepared. I also believe that the Spanish welfare system snatches all forms of initiative away from young entrepreneurs. I think we must also talk about the lack of financing that there is for our businesses, because banks are obsessed with financing construction projects and mortgages.

Should the collapse of our infrastructures and the progressive indebtedness of the Generalitat be put down to the fiscal deficit?

Partly yes. But I think the poor policies carried out by the Catalan Government should also be taken into consideration. It has failed to establish priorities for expenditure.

What is your position regarding the future of the Catalan car industry and the SEAT factory?

SEAT will only be able to compete when its workers have either a higher productivity rate or lower salaries. Since lower salaries are not acceptable, nor advisable, the only option for survival today is increased productivity. But of course this means new educational reforms, new regulations, more flexible and modern public institutions, lower taxes, a financial system that funds innovative companies (and thus one which involves an important degree of risk), etc. We must completely overhaul the production system. This will be difficult to achieve with the restrictions and norms Spain imposes throughout the State.

So forming part of Spain, at the present moment, is a problem for the Catalan economy...

It is from the point of view that the Spanish government applies uniform policies in all its 'regions'. It does so in the field of education, universities, economic regulation, the public sector, the financial system, and energy, to mention but a few. All this makes our productivity rate daily come closer to those of the least productive areas of the State, such as Andalusia, Extremadura, or Galicia.

Does the present situation push Catalonia into having to decide between poverty and independence?

The truth is that the current situation prevents Catalan citizens and enterprises from developing their potential. I believe that the least one can expect from one's state is the chance to develop and grow according to one's possibilities. When a state castrates these

options, it limits one's potential and condemns one to being less than one could be. I think it is time to consider if it is really in our interest to continue forming part of this state. This is what Thomas Jefferson said in the Declaration of Independence of the United States. But while I have said that, I must point out that independence is not a real guarantee that things are going to be done any better. A Catalan State governed by politicians such as the ones we have had in recent governments would not be much of an improvement. It's not a question of whether the money is ill-spent in Spain and not in the Catalan Pyrenees. What is vital is that this money is not ill spent. If instead of Spanish rules and regulations that prevent private initiative we have Catalan ones, we will still be in a mess. And one does not have to be a NASA boffin to see that the obsession with environmental sustainability shown by the people who have governed Catalonia in the last few years indicates that, in a Catalan state governed by their like, things would not be much better than they are now.

Do you think that independence might in some respect help the country overcome the international crisis?

Not really. I think it's obvious that many independent countries have suffered the crisis. Indeed, almost all countries that did were independent. So independence does not enable one to dodge it. What independence does allow one to do is to not depend on a government of incompetents who don't have a clue about how recession should be handled, as has been the case with the Spanish government. The snag is that, as I've already said, being independent is no guarantee that a future Catalan government will be any better at guiding us through forthcoming crises. In fact I'd say that the government that led Spain through the latest recession is no worse than the one that led Catalonia in that same period.

Elisenda Paluzie
A university dean for independence

If you saw Elisenda Paluzie in the corridors of Barcelona's Central University, you might well mistake her for a student going off to a lecture. Again, if you didn't know how young some of the academics in the highest echelons of university governance are these days, you might be even more surprised to know that she is Dean of the School of Economics and Business. Like Germà Bel, Salvador Cardús, Carles Boix, and Joan Ramon Resina (all of whom are also interviewed in this book), Elisenda Paluzie belongs to a generation of academics with a clear commitment to political and social affairs.

While this inclination led Bel to take up a seat in the Madrid parliament for the Socialist Party, Paluzie is a member of Esquerra Republicana de Catalunya (the Republican Left of Catalonia, ERC), a pro-independence party with over twenty MPs in the Catalan Parliament. Paluzie forms part of a wing of the party that regrets that the leadership shelved part of its more nationalistic agenda to join a three-party coalition government of the Generalitat from 2003 to 2010—known as the Tripartit—together with the Catalan Socialists (PSC-PSOE) and the Eco-socialists of Iniciativa per Catalunya-Verds (Initiative for Catalonia-Greens, or ICV). The first of the two Tripartit governments was presided over by Pasqual Maragall, and the second, from 2006, by José Montilla.[1]

In the latter part of the Montilla legislature—largely marked by the political and juridical challenge to the 2006 Statute of Autonomy by the Spanish Constitutional Court—Paluzie and others began to consider that ERC's presence in the coalition was becoming too much of an embarrassment. During that same period (2009–2010), she took an active part in the movement[2] that organized the independence referendums, to which her prestige as professor of Economics of Barcelona University lent great weight.

How does the June 28th Constitutional Court ruling affect the future funding of Catalan self-government, in comparison with the original formula laid down in the Statute of Autonomy?

Before the ruling, the Spanish Parliament had already cut back on the formula during the parliamentary debate. The original Statute had proposed a model similar to the Basque quota system, in which the Generalitat was to be entrusted with the levying of taxes. The idea was that there was to be a yearly joint decision (between the Generalitat and the State) to decide on the Catalan contribution. The Generalitat's power to negotiate would thus have improved significantly. But all that was done away with. Changes introduced by the Socialists along with an agreement they reached with CiU[3] meant going back to square one. At that time economic experts had issued a warning about what it would mean if Catalonia failed to have the opportunity to reach bilateral agreements with the State. Now the ruling confirmed that. The creation of a bilateral Commission between Catalonia and the State was thus suppressed in favour of the traditional multilateral model, in which all the autonomous communities—barring the Basque Country and Navarre—would continue to bicker over funding. The decision regarding Catalonia's 'solidarity' contribution to the rest of the State would continue to be taken multilaterally, under the surveillance of the all-powerful State. As before, Catalonia would continue to have little or no say in the matter.

Article 206 of the Statute is one of the most affected...

Yes. This article refers to the way in which the State is to apply levelling and solidarity mechanisms between the contributions of the different autonomous communities. Article 206.3 had established a partial levelling principle whereby only the provision of essential social services was to be made equal, as occurs in most other democracies. Measures were thus to be introduced to make Catalonia receive a fairer share of the pie to compensate for the greater fiscal contribution she makes. However, prior to a decision being reached on the Statute, a new law was brought in for the funding of the autonomous communities (the Ley Orgánica de Financiación de Comunidades Autónomas or LOFCA) that did away with that principle. This leads us to a situation in which, despite being the third community in terms of per capita tax contribution, we have dropped to the tenth or eleventh position in terms of per capita funding for self-government. In addition, the Statute's third additional disposition has also been invalidated. It had been intended to introduce a binding commitment regarding State investment in Catalonia. This was interpreted by the Court to be no more than a mere political commitment devoid of any statutory obligations for budget legislators. All in all, it shows the complete lack of respect there is for the Statutes of Autonomy in the Spanish juridical makeup.

Before the ruling, how had the 2008 agreement for the funding of the autonomous communities affected Catalonia?

In fact things are going to change very little. Although the autonomous communities' part in the tax share-out was indeed to be increased, to 50% in the case of Income Tax, 50% of VAT and 58% of special taxes, the truth is that there are also to be important fund-levelling mechanisms that significantly reduce those funds. Besides, things are now going to be much more complicated to interpret and control than before. They say all this is an improvement. But what does it all mean in terms of the reduction of the fiscal deficit of Catalonia? Independent experts have recently estimated that it amounted to 9.8% of Catalan GNP. If we extrapolate this for 2009, it means over €20 billion in deficit for the year. That is an 8.8% deficit, just one point less than it was in 2005. It is such a pitiful reduction that it does almost nothing to solve the problem of our fiscal deficit. So, in effect, the whole exercise to improve the Statute for the sake of better finance—a process lasting four long years (2005–2010)—has proved to be a complete wash-out. Politically, we have been led down the garden path and made to waste four precious years in absurd parliamentary initiatives that have boiled down to almost nothing.

Do the last few years' figures indicate that Catalonia is losing its leading position in the Spanish economy?

Compared with the situation thirty years ago, Catalonia is quite clearly losing ground. We live in a highly competitive world in which countries that fail to have first-rate infrastructure and services are soon overtaken by those that do. The fact is that Catalonia has a poor and expensive electricity grid, expensive roadways, and an airport network that it has no control over. In addition it also has a very deficient freight railway system. The Barcelona-Valencia rail corridor is fundamental for exports, and has for years been a primary artery of the Spanish economy and Mediterranean tourism. But you'd never think so… The truth is that transport along this railway line is severely hampered by the fact that it is outdated and largely single-track. The motorway is also hideously expensive. What keeps our country above the waterline, for now, is its industrial tradition. Unfortunately, though, we are no longer fully competitive in many fields we used to excel in. What's more, the Spanish interregional compensation system, which awards economic funds to the poorer regions on an income-based system of transfers, actually pours funds into some regions that are in fact richer than the average! As a result, Catalonia is doubly affected. Not only does our country pay out a lot more in taxes than it should, it also gets a lot less back in investment. Although about 18% of the population of Spain lives in Catalonia, investment in Catalonia currently amounts to just 15.2%. As recently as 2000 it was as low as 13%! We are now the third most productive region in terms of effective per capita productivity, but we come eleventh out of fifteen after the interregional compensation process has been applied. One factor in this compensation process that could have benefited Catalonia was the competitiveness criterion. But it's now estimated that this will only bring in an additional one million euros. This is hardly going to help reduce the current yearly fiscal deficit we accumulate of around 20 billion euros, the equivalent of approximately 10% of our GDP!

How does this compare with the situation of other countries in Europe?

I believe it's a situation no European region other than the Balearic islands has to face, no matter how rich. German law prevents even the richest *länder* from contributing anything over 5% of their GDP to regional compensation funds. The bottom line is that, for large sectors of the population, life in Catalonia has become increasingly hard. It must be remembered that prices—particularly for real estate—are well above those in other parts of the State. The crisis has also hit our country particularly hard, and we lack the tools with which to counter its effects. For example, Catalan unemployment figures are now double those of the Basque Country, the other traditionally industrial area of Spain. Given the interruption in the devolution process occurring since the nineties, many businessmen see the need for drastic changes if we are to stay competitive.

Does that mean they are looking for political change?

They're certainly aware that, if the present tendencies prevail—and it very much looks as if they will—the Catalan economy will soon be facing increasingly tough conditions. Since 2007, key business lobbies in our country have begun to express their concern regarding Catalonia's lack of powers and resources in vital areas. This happens, for example, in the field of transport. The fact that the centralized airport system favours Madrid as its sole airport hub means that Barcelona Airport has become impracticable as a base for a whole series of multinational companies that might otherwise use it. All right, they recently opened the big new T1 terminal building at Barcelona airport. But the Catalan government has little say in running it and has few options for attracting international flights there. Indeed, the Spanish airport system is the most State-controlled and centralized one in Europe.

How does this affect business people?

Business people are pragmatic, and these shortcomings are beginning to affect their way of thinking. Some may think independence for Catalonia is too dramatic a step. But others are coming round to seeing it as the only way out. Whatever the case, I'm sure that the day after independence is declared, lots of those who are still undecided today will adapt to the new situation. At least, that's what happens when there are changes of government in normal countries. The same must be true when a new State is formed. In the break-up of the Austro-Hungarian Empire, after the First World War, businessmen in what is today the Czech Republic couldn't get their minds around the idea of a doing business in a new State. But when they saw that sales and exports were picking up under the new set-up, they were the first to adapt. Indeed, the country soon underwent an economic boom.

But wouldn't independence affect exports to Spain?

That's what some people harp on about. However, globalization is causing rapid changes to the market for Catalan firms. In just ten years—between 1995 and 2005—the percentage of Catalan sales to Spanish firms dropped by 7%, while the percentage of exports to other countries grew by more than 8%. At present only about one third of Catalan exports go to Spain. In the fifties, the figure was twice that figure. If we go back further, in the 19th century, almost all Catalan sales depended on Spanish buyers in the peninsula or in the Spanish colonies. The colonies no longer exist, and the Spanish market has also become quite globalized. So the issue is no longer such a decisive one. In the future, it will be even less so. Anyway, there is no reason why Catalonia and Spain shouldn't be good neighbours one day!

In Spain they say Catalonia is selfish and rich…

That's what they say every time there's any kind of economic controversy. It's a cliché that's been greatly overused in the last hundred years of Spanish history. It's time they took a look at the figures and looked for fresh arguments.

What is the state of the banking institutions of Catalonia? Doesn't a 2010 law jeopardize Catalan government control over the savings banks?

Catalonia has a great tradition as regards savings banks. But we cannot say the same for normal banks. Banc Sabadell-Atlántico is the only powerful Catalan bank to have survived. During the Franco regime, Jordi Pujol *(see page 54)* founded Banca Catalana with a view to offering the country the services of a first-rate bank. But Banca Catalana was unable to make it through the financial crisis of the eighties after investing heavily in comparatively unstable industrial projects. While the Spanish government of the time bailed out several major Spanish banks, Banca Catalana was allowed to go under. One may ask why? The Madrid-based Socialist newspaper *El País* certainly did its best to make that happen. Pujol's bank wasn't forgiven a single peseta of the losses it suffered, through the well-meaning and widespread substandard practices of the time. Other Spanish banks that did the same thing got off scot-free! In contrast, and despite the crisis, the savings banks in Catalonia are doing relatively well. But changes in policy are seen by many as a threat to the territorial basis on which they operate, contriving to favour mergers with savings banks in other regions and in this way watering down their Catalan allegiance. Indeed, this is what has happened with Caixa Laietana, which has been taken over by Caja Madrid.[4] In Valencia this step has been much worse for local savings banks. It's just another example of the lack of control our country has over its economy.

Memory

Dr. Moisès Broggi
The International Brigade surgeon

Dr. Moisès Broggi's home is a small haven of peace in a hectic district uphill from the centre of Barcelona. A small gate on a side-alley off a major avenue leads to narrow steps that transport one into a quiet garden home, where the 102-year-old doctor lives with his charming wife, Angelina. Small in stature, but universally admired in Catalonia, he is one of the last living vestiges of Catalan Republican dignity. Indeed, in 2009, he was shortlisted for the prestigious 'Catalan of the Year' prize granted yearly, on the basis of a popular vote, by the newspaper El Periódico—though FC Barcelona's triumphant coach, Pep Guardiola, eventually carried off the award. For the press and institutions, Dr. Broggi is a key figure to turn to when debates and tributes are being planned. In that same year, 2009, he was also awarded the Catalan Government's highest distinction.

Dr. Broggi was born in Barcelona in 1908. He studied medicine at Barcelona University, where he graduated in 1931, the same year that the ill-fated Spanish Republic was proclaimed. He specialized in a field that was going to prove vital in the tragic years ahead: surgery. When the Civil War broke out he had no doubts about taking sides for the Republic, which had enabled Catalonia to recover part of her political autonomy in 1932. Dr. Broggi joined up with the International Brigade's medical team. He was very active in the creation of mobile operating theatres placed near the trenches. At the end of the war he initially took up posts at the Vallcarca and Hospital Clínic hospitals in Barcelona, but his political record soon caught up with him and he was suspended. He was submitted to the usual reprisals to which most Republican medical staff were exposed. He was nevertheless able to continue practicing in different clinics, at a time when doctors were very much in demand.

After Franco had died, in 1980, Dr. Broggi was elected president of both the Royal Academy of Medicine in Barcelona and the Commission on Medical Ethics of the College of Medicine. He was also a founding member of International Physicians for the Prevention of Nuclear War, a prestigious association that won the Nobel Prize in 1985. Similarly, several universities have conferred upon him Honoris Causa degrees. In 2010, the new public hospital at Sant Joan Despí—just outside Barcelona—was named Hospital Moisès Broggi, an honour that greatly satisfied this venerable veteran of Catalan surgery.

Do you think the sacrifice of the International Brigades in the Civil War has been sufficiently acknowledged by present-day society?

I'm convinced that their contribution has not been commemorated enough. Their sacrifice was truly remarkable. All those people who came here to put their lives in peril for an ideal! At the Battle of the Ebre, in late 1938, there were still International Brigade volunteers present. It was extraordinarily memorable and praiseworthy. Not enough has been done to honour them. This could be put down to the way in which the political transition after Franco was handled. After Franco's death, things didn't change as they should have done. In many senses Francoism continued to exist, and in many ways it still does today! There are elements that subsist in the legislation that prove that the Franco regime is still alive and kicking. I think this has a great influence on things even today, despite the democratic gloss.

What kind of influence does it have?

I think there are admirers of Franco who still pull the strings. This effectively prevents Spain enjoying a fuller degree of democracy. There were a lot of people who, as we say in Catalan, 'swam between two waters', and who still hold office and wield power today. Look at Rodolfo Martín Villa presiding over Sogecable. Or the late Juan Antonio Samaranch's post as Honorary President of the International Olympic Committee.[1] Deep down, it's a disgrace to all democrats, and won't look at all good in history books. I reckon a large part of Spain's right wing is still Francoist. Their favourite motto is: 'We were better off under Franco'.

But lots of members of the Partido Popular say they have nothing to do with Francoism...

Of course they do. They deny it because they're ashamed to admit it. But, deep down, I'm convinced they do. They don't want to own up because, as is well known, the crimes committed during the Franco regime have begun to be publicized worldwide. As time goes on, more and more is known about the terrible crimes Franco committed. Although their perpetrators remain unpunished, the regime was morally reprimanded at the European Parliament and by the United Nations' Human Rights Council in 2008. All this makes things increasingly embarrassing for die-hards. This is why every attempt has been made to sweep all these crimes under the carpet.

What is your opinion of Allied non-interventionism during the Civil War?

That was a disaster for us. The rebellion of the generals in 1936 brought havoc on our country, and left us without law and order. At the outbreak of the war, extremists won the day on both sides. And it was then, thanks to Franco's coup, that the more radical factions—the FAI[2] in Republican areas and the Falangists in Franco-controlled zones—took over completely. That was disastrous for us because Franco continued to enjoy the support of Hitler and Mussolini, whereas the negative image created by the FAI led the democratic nations to abandon us, hoodwinked as they were by the propaganda put around by the conservative and Catholic press in Europe.

Do you think the Republican and Catalan governments could have done more to stop the crimes in the Republican rearguard?

No, I really do not. Our government just didn't have the resources to face up to the situation. It had very few military assets, and it was at the mercy of the anarchists who had hoarded large quantities of arms during an uprising prior to the Civil War, in October 1934. The economic situation was also desperate. Unemployment was enormous because work on building the underground railway in Barcelona had come to an end. Lots of people had been made redundant. There were a lot of people on the streets, some of whom were armed and more than willing to kick up trouble. There was no stopping them when the coup unleashed violence in its worst form.

In 2008, the Consuls-General of France and Germany publicly apologized for their countries' part in handing over President Companys[3] to Franco...

Yes. But for some strange reason, the ceremony conducted at the Generalitat Palace did not get the coverage it deserved. I know, for example, that the Consuls-General were unwilling to let their speeches

be published. It was as if they had subsequently been put under pressure to hold back. And that would surely be because the diplomatic corps, despite accepting the invitation to participate in such a noble act, knew that influential members of the local establishment are associated—either by family or ideological connections—with the Fascists who had Companys shot. They weren't happy at all about that ceremony. I'd say they had strings pulled to have the tribute muffled.

What about the position of Madrid with respect to Companys?

They have never apologized for what the State did. They have not even annulled the sentence with which Franco sentenced him to death! Now I believe they have issued the family some kind of 'good conduct diploma', that they were made to apply for at the Ministry of Justice. It's humiliating, and quite unlike anything that has happened in other countries that have overcome dictatorships and civil wars.

Did you ever meet President Companys yourself?

Yes, I did. And I pride myself on being able to say that I enjoyed a personal friendship with him. I remember we had a meal together with him in the company of other doctors. He was a most inspiring and dignified leader. It's curious, because my mother had a small shop with an assistant who was an orphan. Her name was Carme Ballester. My mother had taken her on and treated her like a daughter. And it was that girl who, when she grew up, became Lluís Companys' second wife! So I've got plenty of memories of him, all of them positive. Such was the relationship president Companys had with our family that he entrusted a very delicate matter to my father during the war.

Do you think that the Catalan issue was one of the reasons Franco declared war?

Yes, I think it was very important. The Republic had accepted an incipient form of devolution for Catalonia with the 1932 Statute of Autonomy. Subsequently there were achievements as significant as the creation of the Autonomous University of Barcelona. These greatly upset the Spanish right and the military. But the spark that really set the Civil War alight, in my opinion, was the fact that in 1936 the Republic was considering the economic question and the need to finance Catalan self-government. That is very often overlooked. But I do think anti-Catalan feeling was a key issue in the outbreak of the war. It's very similar, in that sense, to the current situation, in which the financial issue is what most seems to infuriate Madrid.

Senator Francesc Ferrer coined the term 'Catalanophobia' to refer to the dislike many Spaniards have for things Catalan. Do you consider the term appropriate?

As I see it, there is outright antagonism between Catalonia and Spain. That's nothing new. It has age-old roots. It's a gut feeling both for them and for us. The reason is that we are completely different. We belong to two different nations. They are Spanish and we are Catalan. The problem is we are completely and utterly subjugated to them. They take advantage of the power they exert over us. Little by little they are throttling our economy, and taking advantage of us without showing us the slightest respect or indeed gratitude for the economic solidarity we show. They need us for the tax levies they get out of us. But at the same time they mistreat us. The big change occurring now is that Catalonia no longer needs Spain.

In most democratic countries the administration goes to great lengths to curtail inter-ethnic strife and prevent tension between communities. Is this so between Spain and Catalonia?

For reasons that escape me, the Madrid government seems to have no interest whatever in improving the relationship between Catalans and Spaniards. They could do so by encouraging mutual understanding, and the right of each community to choose the political future that best suits it. They could strive to get these choices respected. Even the king could do something about this. But his incapacity or reluctance to do so is more than our patience can put up with any more. I think the king is anything but impartial. He has no interest in Catalonia and how Catalans feel. He has just been to Santiago de Compostela to pray for national unity before the tomb of Saint James. And that's no joke! The truth is that we have reached a point at which the only option left is separation.

At present there is political unrest in Catalonia. Why is that so, in your opinion?

I believe it is because people have been able to overcome the fear that memories of the Civil War inspired in them. People do not remember it so much now. Fear has largely been overcome, even though there are lots of people who are still unwilling to talk about the past. War is a very serious matter. Many people cannot forget that the others, the right wing, have always had the army behind them. And the army is constitutionally primed to act against us if necessary. In that sense, the situation is not so very different from that of Yugoslavia in the nineties.

Can the situation in Catalonia be compared with those in other countries?

The situation we are going through cannot be seen as something entirely remote for a lot of people in Europe. Before the 1914-18 war, situations like ours today were widespread. There were the Ottoman and the Austro-Hungarian Empires, whose disappearance after the war enabled the emergence of a whole range of nations, some of which had lacked freedom for centuries. Greece and the Balkan countries had been dominated and exploited by the Turks. Sweden and Norway separated peacefully in 1905. Likewise, the British granted independence to many nations after World War II, largely without bloodshed. Now Catalonia needs that same kind of treatment. Like Scotland, Catalonia is awaiting an opportunity to be free. I really cannot think why it is seen as so impossible for Catalonia to separate from Spain! Now is the moment to lay our cards on the table and make our demands as clear as possible. We want to be free. It's that simple.

Do you think the international community will understand that?

The main problem is that no-one seems to know about us. Nobody knows about our problems. People think we're just Spaniards with a stupid tendency to complain about things all the time. I think it would be a very good idea if we tried to carry on with the excellent work done by people like Pau Casals, Josep Maria Batista i Roca and Josep Trueta.[4] They were able to put across our case most effectively. I also think tourism should be exploited more in this sense. People ought to be told who Gaudí really was. Aren't his buildings the most visited monuments in Barcelona? When you visit Italy, they tell you all about Michelangelo and his ideological position. Here it seems to be a taboo to let anyone know that Gaudí was in favour of Catalan independence or that he was arrested for speaking in Catalan. Maybe if these things were explained, people would have more of an insight into what is going on here.

Josep Cruanyes
Getting Franco's death penalties annulled

Josep Cruanyes was born in El Masnou, just north of Barcelona, in 1952. As a lawyer and historian, he has the perfect profile to play a major role in the Historical Memory movement that has been so active in Catalonia in the last few years. The question to be answered for many is how the Franco regime and its victims should be treated today, so many years later. Cruanyes is one of a wide range of public figures to have spoken up against the ongoing impunity of the State. He points to the fact that—in contrast with what happened in Germany, Italy, or Argentina after their military dictatorships came to an end—pitifully little was done in Spain to steer things back onto a truly reconciliatory and democratic course.

For years Cruanyes has acted as the lawyer representing families that want to achieve the official annulment of sentences applied against their Republican and anti-Francoist forebears. One of the families he assists is that of Republican Justice Minister Joan Peiró. He was executed in 1940 after a mock trial. Another is that of young anarchist activist Salvador Puig-Antich, who was garrotted—the cruellest form of execution—as late as 1974. In both cases, Spain's Supreme Court rejected demands for the sentences to be annulled.[1]

Cruanyes is the spokesman of the Dignity Commission [Comissió de la Dignitat], an association set up in 2002 to put pressure on the State to return hundreds of thousands of Catalan documents known as the 'Salamanca Papers' that were confiscated by Franco in the last stages of the Civil War in 1938–39. Many of the documents are still stored in an old police depot in Salamanca, which today has been converted into a historical archive and Civil War study centre. The objective of the Comissió de la Dignitat is to get these documents returned to their rightful owners: the Generalitat, municipal councils, private bodies, political parties, trade unions, private individuals, and so on around Catalonia and has the support of an impressive list of international personalities headed by ex-heads of State such as Francesco Cossiga and Mario Soares, followed by professors Noam Chomsky, James Petras, Paul Preston, and Howard Zinn, musician Peter Gabriel and Nobel-Prize winners Rigoberta Menchú and Adolfo Pérez Esquivel, among many others. The petition was also backed by over a thousand university professors from over 220 universities on the five continents.

In 2007 a law on 'Historical Memory' was passed by the Spanish Parliament which some saw as a step forward in condemning the Franco regime. Would you agree?

I honestly see the law as a swindle. To my mind, it altogether fails to challenge the major taboos that were set up by the Francoists during the Transition period after 1975. Ominously it starts out by not recognizing the legitimacy of the Republican legal system prior to Franco. Nor does it allow individuals to be put on trial for crimes and breaches of human rights committed by the Francoists during and after the Civil War, and—indeed—right up to 1978. Unlike what happened in post-1945 Germany or post-Videla Argentina, the law has not even opened the door to such elementary acts of justice as declaring the political trials conducted by the regime legally invalid. The only thing the new law introduces is a timid form of moral acknowledgement for the victims of Franco. I see that as a poor result for a law passed thirty-six years after the death of Franco! If they cannot do any better than that it's a sign that something is still very wrong with Spanish democracy.

What about the question of indemnities for the victims?

That has not been solved either, as had been hoped. In fact, the law introduces a new form of discrimination by distinguishing between victims according to the different periods in which they were subjected to repression. It is also unacceptable in the extent that it evades real government engagement in the question of the mass graves and the missing. The Government will not take any responsibility for mapping these graves, or investigating their contents. In what democratic country could one imagine that such a dramatic matter would be left in the hands of possible relatives? They are not even going to provide these relatives with legal and forensic support to oversee the clarification of the circumstances in which these killings occurred. This law effectively allows the State to wash its hands of the whole affair. In addition, the archives containing documents that record the workings of Francoist repression are not to be opened. It is shameful that a Socialist government should have allowed this to happen. We must inevitably conclude that the Franco regime continues to be quite untouchable.

In 2007 you said that the Oscar-winning film *The Lives of Others*[2] could not have been set in present-day Spain...

Yes, I did. That magnificent film is set in East Germany, before and after the fall of the Berlin Wall in 1989. It ends with the main character going to the Stasi archives to find out who had spied on him during the socialist regime. Needless to say, it was perfectly possible to do that after the reunification of Germany because victims were guaranteed their right to know the truth. The equivalent to this in Spain is out of the question. Here Franco-era police files are inaccessible. To try and justify that, the Government has wielded the absurd argument that it must 'protect the honour of the police'. In Germany, personal honour and other such basic rights are respected too, naturally. But the right of victims to know the truth about the repression they suffered has absolute priority. The UN convention on civil and political rights fully supports that. How else can a true democracy be built?

You have been very critical about the way the State purports to have 'rehabilitated' Lluís Companys.[3] Why?

Given the formula they propose, you cannot really talk about any recognizable form of rehabilitation for Companys. The State views the 1940 execution of Companys as if it were a minor matter. But for Catalans it's important. Companys was our democratically elected President. In 1940, he was deported from France to Spain with the intervention of the German military police, in collaboration with Spanish agents, and thus in contravention of the extradition treaty between France and Germany in force since 1877. Indeed, all the deportations of Republicans were crimes. But especially so that of a president of a country who was himself a political refugee. The Spanish State was as guilty here as the Germans were. Yet only the latter seem to have uttered any form of apology. In 2004 Spanish Deputy Prime Minister María Teresa

Fernández de la Vega, standing on the very spot where Companys had been shot sixty-four years before, solemnly promised that a law would be passed to annul the sentence against Companys and other Republican victims. But to this day, no such law has been passed. Not one sentence has been annulled.

What has the reaction been to this in Catalonia?

Spurred on by a resolution of the Catalan Parliament, the Generalitat requested that the Catalan Attorney General should take the necessary steps to annul the sentence. In Madrid they responded by arguing that an annulment had already been implemented by means of the Law on Historical Memory. It is unacceptable for them to try to sell such a thing, when such an option had been categorically ruled out during the parliamentary debate! Another thing I find incredible is that the Catalan Government itself should have bought the excuse offered by Madrid. President Montilla went to the extent of proclaiming that the Attorney's words had marked 'a great day for Catalonia'. It shows that our Government is willing to grab at anything to rid itself of this awkward issue, quite ignoring all its deeper and more serious implications. Any lawyer knows that a sentence can only be declared null and void when a judge passes a sentence to that effect.

You have often criticized the fact that people who held public posts in the Franco regime continued in power after democracy arrived in the late seventies. Wasn't it an achievement to incorporate them into democracy?

I do not deny the wisdom involved in integrating Francoists into democratic practice. What cannot be accepted, however, is the attempt to hold them up as models for the democratic era! Let's face it, they would have been treated as criminals in most other democratic countries. One thing is the reconciliation rightly praised by John Carlin in South Africa. But it was quite another thing to empower the old Francoists to create a democracy to suit their own interests. Martín Villa[4] ordered the destruction of thousands of files recording the political repression conducted by the Falangist Movement in Barcelona. Could a person known to have destroyed Stasi or Gestapo files have become a minister in democratic Germany in 1945? Could he be presiding over the country's leading 'progressive' media group? Manuel Fraga[5] was a member of Franco cabinets that condemned people to death on political grounds well into the 1970s. Not only did he for years preside over the democratic government of Galicia, but he is also the current honorary president of the Partido Popular! Then again IOC president Juan Antonio Samaranch had gone around in a blue Falangist shirt and saluted Fascist-style well into the seventies.[6] All right, we reincorporated him into democracy. But isn't a society that sets up characters like this as its leaders creating a frightful model for its younger generations? None of these characters have so much as hinted that the Franco regime might have been wrong in any way. I think we are paying the consequences today.

What do you think about the dismissal of Judge Baltasar Garzón[7] from the Spanish *Audiencia Nacional* (High Court) in Spring 2010?

Whatever one may think about Garzón on other accounts,[8] the fact is that he stood up for the application of the principles of universal justice in cases involving the abuse of human rights and crimes against humanity. In autumn 2008 he bravely ordered enquiries to be made about people who had gone missing during and after the Civil War. He wanted to investigate the mass graves that were known to exist in many parts of the Spanish State. Over sixty years later, it was high time something was done about identifying the dead, discovering why they had been killed and who had been responsible. When he asked for the people to report cases, he was flooded with petitions regarding 140,000 missing. What was most shocking about Garzón's dismissal is that one of the parties calling for it was the fascist *Falange Española*, many of whose members had been directly involved in those killings! The reason given for suspending Garzón was that the Amnesty Law of 1977 forbade the investigation of crimes committed under Franco. It was also alleged that the Historical Memory Law of 2007 had made the opening of mass graves a purely administrative matter. This just goes to show that the

Spanish Government had really meant that law to be a 'Full Stop' measure, clearly ignoring the fact that Spain had signed the International Civil and Political Rights Agreement of 1966 which lays down that there is no time limit for the prosecution of crimes against humanity.

Would you say there is still fear in Spain and Catalonia?

I think this is quite obvious from the meagre confidence people show in the Spanish democratic system. In a lecture I recently gave in Roses[9]—on Francoist repression—I talked about the need to make the old police files accessible to the general public. At question time, a gentleman in the audience, who had been a trade union leader during the Franco era, asked me in a manner of considerable distress why the files were still being preserved. I told him they were a historical artefact, and proof of the dictatorship's criminal actions. He was clearly afraid that they were being kept in case the dictatorship returned. For a lot of people this is the only possible explanation for archives that they know exist, but which are doggedly withheld from public inspection. Where else does this occur in the democratic world?

Do you think the World War II Western allies (the UK, USA and France) are in any way indebted to Catalonia and the Spanish Republic for their callous attitude in the 1930s and 40s?

Yes, in many ways I sincerely do feel this. To protect themselves against the Nazis, they hypocritically abandoned the Republic to its fate when everyone knew the Germans and the Italians were giving large scale military aid to Franco. We cannot forget that their formal opposition to Franco—who was, remember, the last Fascist leader in Europe—petered out very fast. I don't think the excuse of the Cold War justifies their attitude. They clearly couldn't care less that democrats were being persecuted by a dictator. Not as long as the Americans could have their military bases here. Not while France and Great Britain could send their tourists here. Their so-called 'defence of democratic principles' was sheer hypocrisy. What really mattered were the economic interests involved.

Indeed, I feel sure that Spain's democratic deficit today can partly be put down to these countries' long and active support for Franco. And I think one way these and other countries could put the record straight would be to admit their fault.

As a historian, do you think the Catalans have historical rights? Do you consider it right to think of 1714[10] as a turning point in history?

Nations are built over the course of time. And Catalonia has figured—since 1421—as one of the first states to have a parliament in which the king was obliged to submit to parliamentary law. This forms part of our culture and our democratic heritage today. Unfortunately in 1714 Catalonia was abandoned by her allies—Austria and Great Britain—who did not keep their promise to protect Catalan liberties. For Catalonia, 1714 is indeed a point of reference, because it was then that we lost our State with all its attributes of power. In 1931, two hundred and seventeen years later, Catalonia began to recover part of her right to self government when our old government—the Generalitat—was restored. But that only lasted until 1939. In 1977, after Franco died, the Generalitat was again restored to enable the Catalan people to govern themselves again. Significantly, that occurred before the 1978 Spanish Constitution had been passed. That is why the Catalan people's right to self-government cannot now be hedged in by the neo-Jacobin Constitution of 1978. One cannot forget—as Madrid constantly tries to make us do—that Catalonia was a nation long before Spain ever had a Constitution. Long before Spain even existed.

Hilari Raguer
The monk-historian from Montserrat

Father Hilari Raguer lives at Montserrat, which is the spiritual heart of Catalonia. Famous worldwide, the monastery perches like a mountain chough on the amazing 1,200-metre-high cylindrical conglomerate of stone cones that rises above the central Catalan plain. The word Montserrat means 'saw-cut mountain'. The peaks of Montserrat are visible from almost anywhere in northern Catalonia. On clear days, the mountain can even be seen from Mallorca, hundreds of kilometres away over the sea to the east. The Madonna who reigns here—and whom Catalans refer to as la Moreneta[1]—is one of Europe's famous 'black virgins', a small figure in dark wood believed to date from the 12th century. In contrast with the stuffy, pious conservatism of many Spanish monasteries, this shrine—which Napoleon blew to bits, and Himmler visited in 1940 in search of the Holy Grail—became the sanctuary of Catalan nationalists and anti-Franco activists during the dictatorship. Montserrat's Abbot Aureli Escarré was forced into exile in 1963 for criticizing Franco. Much-loved Abbot Cassià Just (in office 1966–89), known somewhat exaggeratedly as the 'red abbot', ran considerable risks when he harboured opponents of the regime, and hosted their clandestine meetings. On one notable occasion, on December 13, 1970, three hundred Catalan intellectuals locked themselves up in the monastery to protest against the trial of Basque separatist militants. Romantics say there is something symbolic in the fact that the highest peak above the monastery looks as if it is topped by a Phrygian cap, a symbol of republican freedom since Roman times.[2]

Hilari Raguer[3] is a very much respected historian of the 20th century, who specializes in the Spanish Civil War. As a historian and a Benedictine monk at Catalonia's most famous shrine, he is an inevitable media choice when it comes to debating the more controversial historical issues that involve the Church. As they say in Catalan, 'he has no hairs on his tongue' when it comes to criticizing the current Spanish Church leaders, and resents their ongoing obsession with beatifying priests and nuns killed in the Civil War. He has had a running battle with an official Church historian, Vicente Cárcel—son of a Spanish policeman, no less—and bitterly opposes attempts to present the deaths of these victims as having been caused by official Republican persecution. 'They were not what I understand to be martyrs,' he insists. 'Martyrs give their lives for Christ and their faith, and most of the priests were killed because they were regarded as representatives of a Church that had most decidedly taken up arms in the conflict.' He says the revolutionaries attacked what they felt to be political enemies, not holders of the faith. He supports his argument by pointing out that the statue of Jacint Verdaguer[4] in Barcelona was not torn down by the anticlerical anarchists even in the bitterest days of the Civil War. 'He was their hero, too,' he adds with pride. Indeed, he believes that the extremist political position adopted by many Church leaders also led to much bloodshed. He is also adamant about the ongoing political implications this has had since the war, and denounces the Spanish Church for not having raised a finger to honour priests persecuted and executed by Franco.

Hilari, why might the Catalan issue be of interest to non-Catalans?

Let me just repeat what the cellist Pau Casals once said on that score: 'We are a peaceful nation. We do not seek to colonize anyone. All we want is to live in peace and contribute to the cause of world solidarity.'

In your opinion, what makes Catalonia a nation?

I think the awareness that one is a nation, and the will to be one, must be seen as the essential factors involved. Anyway, the fact that Spanish politicians are so obsessed with opposing our nationhood is the surest sign that we are one! They don't bother to go on about Murcia or Cantabria not being nations, because everyone knows they are not, and have no wish to be. As they say in Spanish, 'If the river sounds loud, it's because there's water in it…' The opinion of the locals must surely be the key factor here, and not that of occupiers and outside observers. We are a nation because we have decided to be one despite Spain's insistence that it is in Madrid and Seville that our fate is to be decided. In the past, we haven't snapped up our chances to become independent. All we need now is to believe in our own strength and one day—who knows?—maybe we'll regain our freedom again.

What is your verdict on the Transition period?

In the first place, one cannot forget that it was a very difficult time. The Franco regime was still firmly entrenched. There were lots of vested interests. The ever-present army showed a huge aversion to change. So I personally approve of the cautious way the Transition was conducted. However, I do not feel in any way tied down by agreements made by the Catalan politicians who took part in drawing up the 1978 Constitution. As has been revealed, fear of the military dominated the talks.

Has the Franco regime been sufficiently reprimanded?

As of now, over thirty years later, almost no-one is calling for trials against Francoists. And there is no way that the vast fortunes made during the regime will be investigated! Today, all we want is to know the truth, however much some people insist that to do so is to kick up trouble. The fact is, they have been bombarding us for so long with a false view of history.

Do you have memories of the war?

Yes, indeed. I remember the beginning of the Civil War. I was a student at the Blanquerna School.[5] During the air raids we kids were told to stand alongside the building's strongest walls. I remember one girl who was paralysed with fear. The teacher took her in her arms and said, 'Come on, dear, cry as much as you can, my little one!' Which of course she did! I couldn't understand why she was making her cry. Later on I understood that she was saving her from suffering a trauma later on in life. For me that little girl is a paradigm of a whole country that still needs to cry. For the truth is that there are people who are still afraid to speak.

Why was it not until the 1990s that the darkest side of the Franco regime began to be revealed in some parts of Spain?

And so undramatically! I am proud to say that many of the film-makers and authors who have exposed the truth behind the Francoist repression are Catalans. Maybe that is because here the suffering caused by the war was twofold: as a nation and as a democracy. Very late in the day there were those who claimed that there were anti-Francoists in the Church too, as if they were ashamed to admit that the Church openly supported Franco! Anti-Francoism within the Church in Spain only really began with the Second Vatican Council under Pope Paul VI in 1963. In contrast with much of Spain, however, the darkest facets of Francoism began to be exposed in Catalonia many years ago. This is because we have got a solid historiographical tradition. Excellent documentary films and books have been coming out for years. In this regard the books of Josep Benet, Josep Maria Solé i Sabaté and Joan Villaroya stand out, as do the TV documentaries of Montserrat Armengou *(see page 170)*, Ricard Belis, and Dolors Genovès.

What are your thoughts on the current make-up of the Catholic Church leadership in Spain?

The Spanish Church is quite divided. In the re-election of Antonio María Rouco Varela as president of the Bishops' Conference, the result was touch and go. It was only because a nephew of his and his own secretary had been made bishops that he scraped in. The only thing the Spanish Church seems to be unanimous about is slapping down us Catalans! In 2006, when the Catalan Statute of Autonomy was being debated in the Catalan and Spanish parliaments, they actually brought out a document which defined the unity of Spain as a 'moral asset' *(bien moral)*. And yet they spend their time complaining about the 'politicisation' of religious and social life! The fact that they keep on insisting on the beatification of 'martyrs' killed during the war means that they still haven't moved on.

Why have British and American historians taken relatively little interest in the Catalan issue during the Republican years and under the Franco regime?

That's a good question. I remember when Hugh Thomas' book on the Civil War came out, Josep Benet[6] said to me, 'This fine historian, who's come out with this wonderful book—mainly using written sources, rather than interviews, mind you—has based his analysis on the memoirs and writings of people on both sides. He seems to have assumed that what matches in both accounts must be the truth.' However, Francoists and Republicans may often be found to agree over things that Catalans don't agree with at all! So we're often just left out of the picture. Neither side respected us, so the historians who wrote about them didn't either. Remember the phrase about Spain attributed to José Calvo Sotelo,[7] *'¡Antes roja que rota!'* (Better red than broken up). Good old Josep Pla,[8] Catalonia's greatest 20th-century prose writer, said that nothing resembles a Spanish rightwinger so much as a Spanish leftwinger. What they cannot stomach is a Catalan view of things. There must only be a Spanish one.

Can the same be said of the war period?

The Civil War, among a good many other causes, was a war waged against Catalan separatism. Some historians, such as Santos Juliá,[9] strongly deny that. But I am convinced it's true. The Catalan Statute, which President Azaña[10] had been obliged to back in return for Catalonia's support for the Republic, was one target the military had in their sights. The funny thing is that even Catalan Francoists were treated differently to Spanish ones. For instance, when they arrived to enrol at the Fascist HQ in Burgos, their oaths of allegiance were nearly always regarded with suspicion. They needed to be fully repentant about their whole Catalan background. Serrano Sunyer even changed his name to Serrano Súñer![11] But, going back to your question about the apparent lack of English and American interest in the Catalan issue, I would say that Orwell's *Homage to Catalonia* is anything but homage to Catalonia! I think he had no real idea what country he had come to fight in!

As a historian, do you think Catalonia and the Republic were unfairly abandoned by France, Britain, and the USA in 1936 and 1945?

Haven't British politics always been marked by a pronounced sense of what is practical and empirical? In Churchill's history of the Second World War, I sense a distinct 'I'm all right, Jack' syndrome. This is pushed home by the constant complaints of Australian and New Zealand generals about their troops being constantly thrown into front-line commitments while the Brits rested in the rear! As regards abandoning the Republic, I go along with Paul Preston and Enrique Moradiellos,[12] who see France as very much under British pressure in the enforcement of non-intervention. For Britain what mattered was to maintain the Munich policy of not upsetting Hitler under any circumstances. It was an absurd form of pacifism that did nothing to avoid the war. All it did was allow Hitler and Fascism time to reap their first victories and try out new weapons and military strategies.

Individual Catalan contributions to the Allied cause only rarely seem to have been acknowledged. The spy Joan Pujol,[13] the photographer of Mauthausen,[14] the escape lines for Allied pilots through the Pyrenees. None of that seems to have been added up in Catalonia's favour...

I think that's largely true. Even Churchill's praise for the bravery of the people of Barcelona in the face of massive Italian bombing raids—in a speech he made in the House of Commons in 1940 no less—was erased from Hansard so as not to upset Franco and persuade him not to join the war on Hitler's side. Neither then nor now is it considered a good idea for the British Government to praise Catalonia in any way because it would immediately cause trouble with Spain. There are countless examples. It's that pathetic! After the war, we pro-British Catalans thought our overt support for the Allied cause would in some way be rewarded. But this was not to be. In 2008, the French and German Consuls-General in Barcelona apologized for French and German cooperation in arresting and handing over President Lluís Companys to certain death at Franco's hands.[15] Yet no apology has been forthcoming from Britain for impounding Pau Casals' British bank account in the early years of the war. Little did it matter that this world class cellist—then termed an 'alien'—had been the all-time favourite of Royal Albert Hall audiences. Nor was Professor Trueta[16] ever officially honoured for having brought medical know-how to Britain that saved the lives of tens of thousands of Allied wounded during the war. The British Establishment never ceased to consider Casals and Trueta as 'Reds', even though they were probably not a shade darker than pink.

Were Catalans disappointed with Britain's lack of interest?

Catalan democrats certainly were. Lots of them had been in touch with the British Consulate and provided information for the Allies throughout the war.[17] They thought their commitment would be acknowledged. Things were looking up when the United Nations proposed condemning Franco in 1946. Catalan anglophiles thought this would lead to Allied intervention against Franco. But the veto enforced by the British representative, Alexander Cadogan, prevented the resolution being passed in the interests of ensuring 'allies against Russia'. Catalans were thus to be early but lasting victims of the Cold War. Later the Americans became strategically blind to Franco's crimes for the same reason. No attention whatever was paid to the cause of Catalonia, or indeed to that of democracy in Spain! In that sense I do admire professor Paul Preston for sticking his neck out in backing causes such as the 'Salamanca Papers' issue.[18] I'm sure it must have caused him no little discomfort when dealing with certain Spanish historians and institutions.

In 2014, Catalonia will be commemorating the 300th anniversary of her defeat in the War of the Spanish Succession, as a result of which she effectively lost her statehood. Some attribute that defeat to the British. Is that fair?

Well, let's look at the facts. The Catalans had signed the Treaty of Genoa with Britain on June 20, 1705,[19] thus allowing British troops to disembark on the Catalan coast. In exchange, the British promised to support Catalonia's national rights, whatever the outcome of the war. But they completely failed to comply with that. Why? Because the balance of power in Europe had changed with the death of the Austrian emperor. The Catalans were left to their fate, and had to face the joint armies of Spain and France alone. Even then, they held out for a good year. The persecution suffered by Catalonia in the wake of that defeat was remarkable, though quite unknown to Europe. The inhabitants of Barcelona were forced to pull down the whole of the centre of their own city. All the country's universities were closed down, and the executions and punishments that took place went on for years. That led to a wave of sympathy across Britain. The Whigs, then in opposition, were very critical of the Tories for abandoning Catalonia, as is witnessed by the pamphlets "The Deplorable History of the Catalans" and "The Case of the Catalans Considered" (both from 1714), the latter of which—I seem to remember—opens with a quotation from William Congreve: 'You gain your ends, and damn them when you've done.'

Empar Salvador comes from a Republican working-class background. Born in the Spanish-speaking Valencian hinterland, as a child she was interned in an institution that was theoretically a convent school, but which she prefers to refer to as 'a Francoist concentration camp'. There she was made to work her knuckles to the bone, as were the other girls, but she was never taught to read or write. The nuns told her she had been abandoned by her parents, and that she 'had the devil in her' because they were 'Reds'. 'That is such a grievous sin,' she recalls being told, 'that God cannot forgive it.' Her internment and the harsh treatment she received had been prescribed as a means towards the 'miracle' of her redemption.

When asked why she has Republican sympathies today, she says that years of questioning herself about why she had been 'abandoned' and why she had received such treatment lie at the heart of it. It was not until years later, once her family had managed to be reunited, that she discovered the truth. She had never been abandoned at all. She had been separated from her mother while her father was in hiding. 'I remember that I sometimes used to hear my father sobbing at night, when I thought everyone was asleep.' She later found out that her father and other members of the family had been anarchists. 'I suppose realizing they'd been Republicans influenced me a lot. But I can't remember the actual moment I became a Republican too. I suppose I became what those who ill-treated me hated most.'

Today, at 62, Empar Salvador is one of those Valencian grandmas who just won't take 'No' for an answer. In 1974, during the bitter last years of the Franco regime, she had to go into hiding in Valladolid, in north-western Castile, where car-factory workers took her in and protected her. Those were years of strife and repression at the hands of the police and the Falangists. 'I went into hiding where they least expected to find me,' she points out with a smile. A rebel and a die-hard anti-Francoist, she speaks with vehemence and idealism—in Catalan and Spanish—about the ongoing need to uncover the crimes committed by the regime, insisting that Spain is 'the last corner of Europe where Fascism has yet to be overcome'.

Faithful to her restless search for justice, she caught the public's eye in 2005 after 'sticking my nose'—as she says in Catalan—'where no one had asked me to'. She had heard on the grapevine that the Valencia city cemetery held dark secrets from the grim post-Civil War days. She came up with one of the most shocking discoveries made in recent years about the Franco regime. In some dusty old cemetery registers that some Francoist civil servant had carelessly left undestroyed, she found lists with the names of 23,661 men, women, and children who had been executed—or simply allowed to die through exposure to disease and starvation—in the city's improvised jails between 1939 and 1945. She managed to discover the ways in which the prisoners had been killed and buried in mass graves in the city's cemetery. In 2009 Empar Salvador took a documentary film about the Valencian mass graves on an international tour which met with great interest in Europe and South America.

In your opinion, has justice been done to the victims of Franco and the Civil War?

I'm not sure I like the term 'Civil War' to define what happened in 1936. It shouldn't be called 'Civil' when one of the sides received the combined support of Nazi Germany, the Italian Fascists, and North African and Portuguese mercenary troops. It was rather the first phase of a long international war of resistance against Fascism. Justice has certainly not been done to the victims of that war, because they have not been legally rehabilitated. Nor were the criminals involved ever brought to justice. Nothing has been done to prosecute—nor even morally condemn—those responsible for the Francoist genocide nor those who collaborated with it and became rich thanks to repression. This also applies to the Catholic Church, which was directly involved in the kidnapping and sale of the offspring of women prisoners. It is also true of those firms that exploited prisoners to death through forced labour, thus totally disregarding the Geneva Convention.

You are critical of the agreements the Spanish Socialists and Communists made with the heirs of the dictatorship after Franco's death.

Very much so. They allowed the Francoists to grant themselves an amnesty so that they could never be made responsible—then or at any time—for what they had done. They cooperated fully in the operation, along with the major trade unions. In the Transition agreements, known as the 'Moncloa Pact',[1] the left signed an agreement with the Fascists to silence the crimes, forget the victims, and destroy all proof of the Francoist genocide. This ensured the impunity of those responsible for it.

What do you think about the 'Law on Historical Memory'?

Despite its apparently good intentions, the bottom line is that it contributes to ensuring this impunity. It effectively declares the crimes to be nullified because so much time has gone by. They seem to forget that crimes against humanity do not have an expiry date. The law completely ignores the years of work carried out by a wide range of anti-Fascist organizations that have strived to ensure that the crimes are not forgotten. Neither does it legally rehabilitate the victims, nor does it annul the summary courts-martial and repair the damage caused by other forms of repressive legislation. It even discriminates between the victims of Franco and other victims such as those affected by terrorism. In this regard, for example, it offers indemnities of €9,616.18 for victims of acts prior to 1 January 1968—the most numerous, since they correspond to the severest period of the Franco regime—but ones of €130,000 for victims of incidents during the period between 1 January 1968 and 6 October 1977, who are far fewer. I think it is a law that should be internationally repudiated and repealed.

What exactly did you find in that Valencian cemetery in the winter of 2005?

I found evidence of the existence of six mass graves with a total surface area of 40,000 square metres. They have been considered by Francesco Cossiga and Joan Garcés[2] to be among the largest mass graves in 20th-century Europe. They were in use between April 1, 1939 and October 19, 1950. I also found the Valencia General Cemetery's registry of burials, in which I was able to identify the names of 23,661 people piled into these graves between April 1, 1939 and December 31, 1945. They include babies, children, and adolescents, as well as men and women of all ages and conditions. A lot of them were executed without trial. Others died from the terrible conditions the Francoists imposed on the Republican population that survived the war. All the data was written in code and, naturally, there was no clear reference to people being thrown into these mass graves. But, in time, I managed to decipher the code. Studying the registers with care also enabled us to discover that only some of the deaths were recorded in them. Several thousand were not registered at all. We will probably never know the exact number of those buried in the graves. A full list of those registered is contained in a book we published in 2008.[3] It's important to bear in mind that, in the post-war period, the population of Valencia was under 400,000. That's the first thing that struck me. How could such a relatively small city

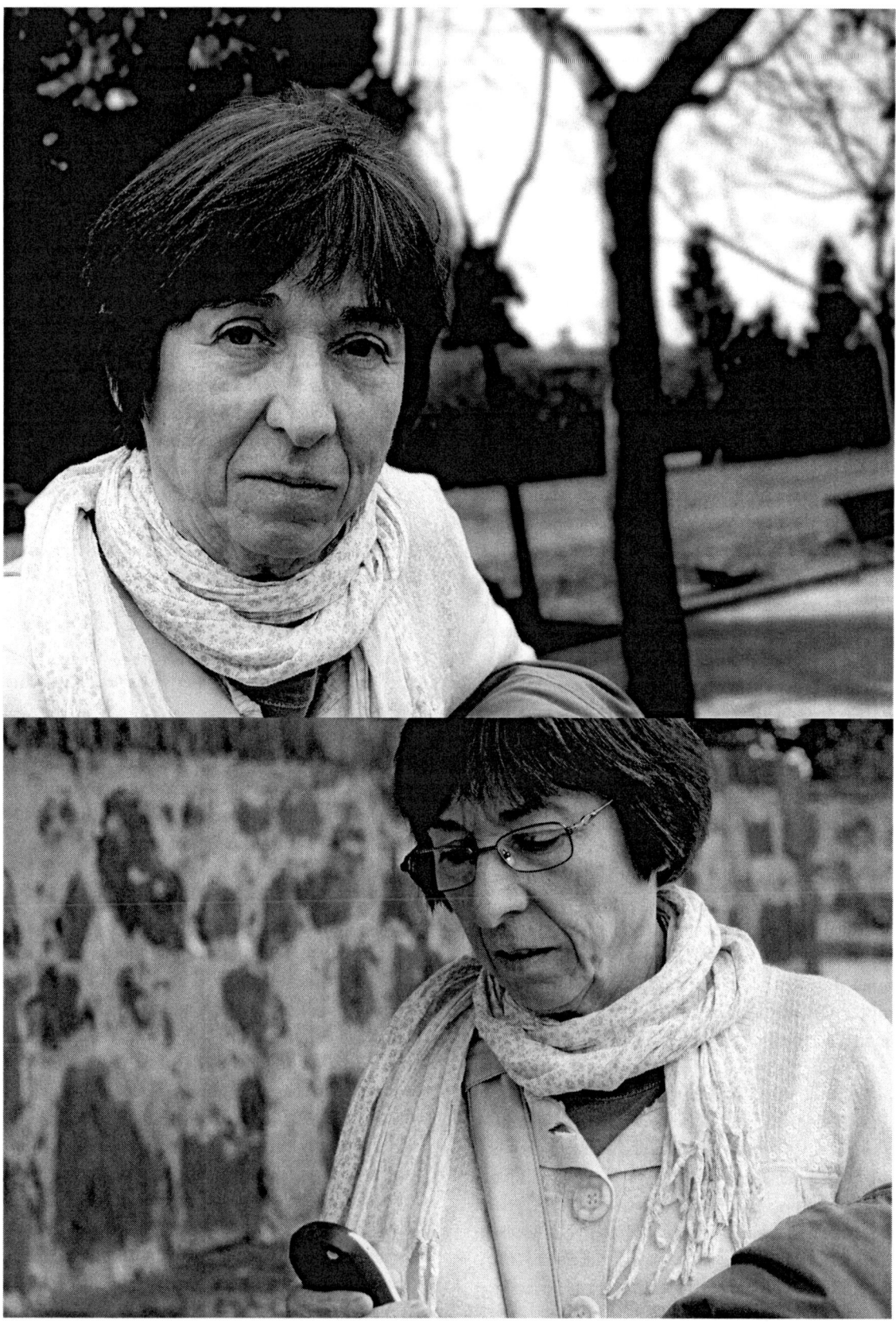

house such huge mass graves? It's simply hair-raising. It is obvious that they made Valencia pay for resisting so long, and for being the last big city to fall. Franco's troops entered the city on March 30, 1939, and April 1st was declared 'Victory Day'. For the Republicans of Valencia it was more a day of terror.

How did the authorities react to your discovery?

The Valencia City Council, presided over by Partido Popular Mayor Rita Barberà, tried to destroy the only grave that still remained intact. They drew up plans to build 1,030 new grave niches slap on top of it! We had to go to court to stop that. Meanwhile, the Council actually tried to sell the earth extracted from the grave for reconstruction work near Sagunt castle, to the north of Valencia. That came to light when piles of bones emerged from the material that was transported there. There was also a rumour that the registers we found were going to be removed from the cemetery outhouse. So we had a notary make an official record of their existence and had them photographed. As they were not officially catalogued, we were afraid they would be made to vanish. We managed to stop the works and protect the books. Although I made the existence of the graves and the registers known, Valencia City Council has always tried to keep them secret, even though they have never dared deny the validity of our findings.

Why was the *Comissió de la Veritat* (Truth Commission) set up in February 2007?

It was created at a time of great despair. The news reached us that, despite the judicial order that interrupted the works at the cemetery, an attempt might be made to destroy the last grave. We needed to protect it at any price. We thought the best way would be to make the Valencia findings known to international organizations such as UNESCO and the Council of Europe. All this was a lot more complicated than you might imagine. There was, and still is, a pact of silence regarding those graves. There seemed to be general agreement to keep the affair a secret. No previous City Council, not even left-wing ones, had mentioned them and only local editions of the press ever referred to the affair. So almost nothing was known about them. We asked the European Commission to help us. Much to our surprise, Vice-President Franco Frattini—much impressed by the facts—agreed to preside over the Commission at the congress we organized in Valencia's main conference hall to present the case. You can get some idea just how extreme the media blackout was from the fact that, despite the 1,700-strong international audience attending,[4] the leading Madrid newspapers—including the Socialist paper *El País*—failed to even mention the event! The congress was nevertheless important because we managed to publicize the existence of the mass graves before both the Council of Europe and UNESCO. This had been our main objective, although we were fully aware that it would take more to make the shit hit the fan. Today things continue to be more or less the same. But at least everyone now knows the story.

How does Spain compare with Argentina, South Africa, or Germany in the way it has dealt with its Fascist past?

Those countries condemned the dictatorships that ravaged them. Spain has not yet done so. With a greater or lesser degree of success, those countries conducted processes whereby victims were legally reinstated and those responsible for crimes and repression were tried or morally reprimanded. But in Spain no-one has been tried for the crimes of the dictatorship. Neither have the victims been well and truly reinstated. You could almost say that in Spain practicing genocide was good business. They did not even have to return the goods and property they stole! In this sense I remember one international human rights official saying in 2007 that Spain's record was comparable to that of El Salvador. And I think that's true. By whitewashing and banalising history, the system has actually been able to incorporate all this into what is seen as Spanish 'tradition'. How else could they have been able to save the image of Prince—later King—Juan Carlos, who, as Franco's heir, had sworn allegiance to the basic principles of the Falangist Movement. Which of his promises are we to believe?

The worst thing is perhaps that most young people have no idea of what really happened. There has hence been little—if any—'inoculation' effect.

What do you think should be done to put the dictatorship into the past?

We need to keep on looking for ways of overcoming the official media's ongoing refusal to face up to the real nature of Francoism. It is only thanks to private organizations and individuals who suffered under Franco that any form of critical historical memory has been made available. Officially only the most glaring evidence has been acknowledged. To all the rest the most blind of eyes has been turned. State policy goes no further than focusing attention on particular cases that have no bearing on those responsible nor their heirs. There are occasionally innocuous tributes, sometimes to the dead of both sides. Can you imagine that happening in Germany? The State also funds exhumations conducted by families or by associations that the more progressive judges authorize locally. Otherwise the State does all it can to shirk the responsibility it has to dig out the truth behind the mass burials.

Hasn't this been denounced internationally?

Who by? All right, Amnesty International has denounced Spain for its practice of conceding impunity. Yet some experts say allowing untrained volunteers to conduct exhumations may just be a ploy to bring about the unwitting destruction of key evidence. Who knows? What is called for is the full legal reinstatement of the victims, the annulment of the penalties and the condemnation—albeit only in a moral sense—of those responsible for the crimes. However, I fear it will be impossible to do justice until Spanish society formally renounces Francoism. That is why associations such as the one I preside over *(Fòrum per la Memòria del País Valencià)* want to take this issue before the International Courts. We have been struggling for years to obtain the justice that is simply not forthcoming from Spanish courts. Anyone who may harbour doubts about this should consider the fate suffered by Judge Baltasar Garzón, the only one who in 2008 dared raise the possibility of trying the crimes of the Franco regime.[5] Soon after he was suspended and had to find a job abroad at the International Criminal Court in The Hague. Could the same happen to a German or Italian judge proposing to investigate the crimes of Hitler or Mussolini today? It is difficult to imagine. As a Francoist slogan proclaimed in the sixties, *'España es diferente'*.

Eugeni Casanova and Jordi Llisterri

A church in search of identity

Religion may not be what makes most young people tick in today's Catalonia. But, the Roman Catholic Church has its followers. Like so many other fields, religion, too, seems to be inextricably linked up with the whole issue of identity. I met Jordi Llisterri and Eugeni Casanova—authors of excellent books on religious issues in Catalonia—on the steps of Barcelona's Sagrada Família, the most-visited creation of cult architect Antoni Gaudí. Trying to find them in the milling crowd of journalists and tourists—largely Japanese and Croatian—wasn't easy. Incidentally, that day the Barcelona press was again full of the controversy regarding Madrid's plans to construct a high-speed train tunnel only centimetres beneath the southernmost part of the amazing temple's foundations, a plan that has predictably raised the almost unanimous protest of Catalan believers and nonbelievers alike.[1]

Eugeni Casanova, born in Lleida in 1958, is a journalist and writer. He has worked for the press (television, radio, and the internet) as well as in advertising. For years he specialized in international journalism, and worked in over thirty countries. In the nineties he covered almost all the major conflicts that occurred worldwide. He has published a dozen books, which often combine a basic journalistic approach with historical research, travel, and current affairs. In November 2008 he published El Complot: La trama en la segregació del bisbat de Lleida i el litigi de les obres d'art [The Plot: The division of the Lleida Diocese and the dispute over works of art] *in which he studied the complex relations between the Church and Catalan society. The central issue dealt with in the book is the conflict that arose between the Catalan and Spanish churches over the emblematic division of the diocese of Lleida in the 1990s, and the subsequent dispute over the treasures in its museum.[2] It led him to carry out research at the Vatican and produced fascinating data regarding the leadership of the Catholic Church in the world today.*

Jordi Llisterri, born in Barcelona in 1972, is editor of Foc Nou [New Fire], *a magazine of religious ideas with a title that conjures up an image midway between Pentecostal tongues of flame and —for Catalan-speakers—the idea of a 'fresh start'. Since the early nineties, he has worked as a journalist in the field of religious affairs. He has also been on the staff of the Tarragona Archbishopric's press office. In 2005 he published the interesting book* Les Ferides de l'Església catalana: La divisió de la diòcesi de Barcelona i els bisbes imposats [The Wounds of the Catalan Church: The division of the diocese of Barcelona and the imposed bishops][3] *which examines the struggle between those in favour of maintaining the identity of the Catalan Church and those intent on dissolving it within the Spanish Church.*

Is the practice of religion the same in Catalonia as it is in Spain?

JL:[4] I think it's not exactly the same, as it tends not to be in countries that have different cultures. Catalan culture is different to Spanish culture and this makes itself felt in religion. Both in the past and today, I think a more private and less ostentatious form of religious practice is to be found in Catalonia. There are fewer processions and mass pilgrimages, for example. Catalan Catholicism has always had a leaning towards the French tradition in this sense. In Catalonia, the Second Vatican Council of 1962–65 has always been very much a reference point as regards the great change that occurred in the Church at that time. The development towards a more open, inclusive, and progressive form of Church was adopted much more quickly in Catalonia than in Spain. And I think a lot of this spirit still remains today.

EC:[5] I would like to point out that religion and politics are two fields that have long been deliberately muddled together in Spain. In this regard the Church in Catalonia has always been quite different, in the sense that it is open and decidedly partial to freedom of thought. In Spain this has not been the case, and I think it is no exaggeration to say that the Church there was intimately wound up in Francoist politics and with fascism in general. This is still visible today in the way the Spanish Church's leadership identifies with authoritarianism. One has only to hear the COPE radio station, which is owned by the Church. However, the Spanish Church does try to use the Catalan Church as a means of alienation. Not only in the times of Franco, but even today. Any candidate to become a Catalan bishop with even an inkling of a Catalanist CV is automatically discarded. They decided that Bishop Deig of Solsona (1990–2001) was to be the last of the 'separatist' bishops. Since then the Vatican and the State have been hard at work to reduce the presence of Catalanists in the Catalan Church hierarchy. And, needless to say—despite popular protest—they have been mightily successful.

What has the attitude of the Catalan Church been towards the language?

JL: The Catalan church has always headed the movement in favour of recovering the Catalan language. After the loss of the Catalan state in 1714, it was in the churches that the language was maintained. In family life and in church, catechism classes were conducted in Catalan so that kids would understand them. Again, when the *Renaixença* movement[6] arose, many of its most enthusiastic pioneers were clergymen. They were not just the sector of society that had kept up the use of the language, but also the one that had the fullest access to culture. In the Francoist period, the same phenomenon occurred. Whatever their position may have been during the problematic period of the Civil War, when the followers of the Catalan Church saw that the Franco regime was antidemocratic and had no respect for human dignity, many of them opposed it. Within this movement against the dictatorship, the defence of the Catalan language and identity played a key role. The vast majority of the Catalan church, both at a lay and clergy level, maintains its commitment to Catalan culture today.

What about the relationship between the Catalan and Spanish churches in recent years?

EC: The Church was one of the first instruments that Castile—by means of the Royal Council—brought into action to try and make Catalonia Spanish. Leading this operation was the Inquisition, in the times of the so-called Catholic Monarchs, Isabella and Ferdinand, who united the kingdoms of Castile and Catalonia-Aragon in the 15th century.[7] There are documents that show that even at this early stage, victims exposed to torture were forced to speak in Castilian even though they might not have spoken the language. In the 16th Century, the Spanish Church made every attempt to water down the Catalan church, and actually brought in Castilian monks from Valladolid to Catalonia's most sacred shrine—the monastery at Montserrat—with the clear aim of swamping its Catalan component. The appointment of Castilian bishops to Catalan bishoprics, while expatriating Catalan ones, also formed part of this operation. This

policy was—and still is—made possible thanks to the influence the Spanish Church and Government exert on the Vatican. In this sense it is significant that the Pope does not include Catalan among the scores of languages in which he gives the official Christmas greetings from Saint Peter's Square. This is clearly due to the veto imposed by the Spanish ambassador to the Vatican. This worrying fact was personally confirmed to me by former president Jordi Pujol[8] last year. As a further example of this attitude, we cannot forget the example of Bishop Antoni Deig. He formed part of a generation of Catalan priests who were committed to the idea of a Catalan Church. When he died in 2003, they actually boycotted his funeral ceremony! The current Bishop of Solsona did not allow his body to be publicly honoured by the enormous mass of people that had come to do so. No one was allowed to speak in his favour, as generally occurs at such ceremonies.

JL: Although I would not express things in the exact terms that Eugeni does, I think it is vital to point out that much of this problem arises from the fact that the Vatican deals with states, and Catalonia is not a state. As long as this situation does not change, things will continue in the same way. It is a situation suffered by all countries that have no state.

EC: That's not exactly true. Scotland has managed to have its Catholic Bishops' Conference acknowledged by the Vatican. In our case, many Catalan bishops have striven for years to have a Catalan Bishops' Conference acknowledged. But the Spanish Bishops' Conference systematically boycotts all Catalan initiatives in the Vatican. The leadership of the Spanish Church is profoundly anti-Catalan. To some it may seem excessive to say so, but the facts are there. They can only admit us as a provincial backwater of the Spanish church without an identity and history of our own, let alone any form of power or international projection of any kind. When the Catalan bishops saw that the Spanish Church would not accept a Catalan Bishops' Conference, they thought of another formula, that of a Catalan Episcopal Region. But the Spanish Church, which had to convey the petition to Rome, took years to do so. Despite the Vatican's eventual approval of the formula, the whole process has been held up to this day. No one has the political will to execute this measure.

JL: I think Scotland is respected because it forms part of a 'United Kingdom', which reflects the political structure of the State. We are not a 'United Kingdom'. If we were, we might have the same structure today. One can say that the Spanish Church is yet another of the tools the Spanish State has for the homogenization process that is conducted from Madrid. If we could cut ties with Madrid, this would no longer be so. We would be like the Portuguese, who enjoy complete independence as a national Church and suffer no Spanish intervention. Portugal, therefore, is our model. But we should also be self-critical, because to some extent we have been excessively trusting of the role we thought the Vatican would play in this. We believed that, because we were Catalans, because we are 'good Catholics', we were going to be respected. And this has not been the case. On the contrary, we have had many lobbies working against us.

EC: As regards Spanish participation, the Vatican is well and truly in the hands of people who profess a National-Catholic ideology. Antonio María Rouco Varela, president of the Spanish Bishops' Conference, is one of the seven or eight most influential men in the Church. Other very influential Spanish conservative figures in the Vatican are Antonio Cañizares, currently Prefect of the Congregation for Divine Worship and Cardinal Martínez Somalo[9]—who has been number three in the Vatican hierarchy—not to mention the influence wielded by the *Opus Dei*[10] since John Paul II's day. Together they have exerted a combined effort in countering all initiatives in favour of the Catalan Church, and progressive thought within the Church in general. They fought hammer and tongs against Liberation Theology and changed as many bishops as they could during the papacy of John Paul II, very much with a conservative agenda in mind. In Spain they annulled much of the work done in the progressive period associated with Cardinal Tarancón,[11] with a severe swing to the right under the auspices of Cardinal Suquía,[12] himself a follower of *Opus Dei*. The fact they have even done away with the catechism in

Catalan shows there is a conscious effort to mop up all that remains of the Catalan Church and its spirit. Behind this there is quite definitely the support of the Spanish Government, with the backing of secret services when necessary.

What about the changes imposed regarding the territorial boundaries of the Catalan Church?

JL: In 1953 the Concordat between the Franco regime and the Church determined that ecclesiastical borders should be redesigned to be made to fit in with civil boundaries where possible, although respect for tradition and culture was said to be an aspect that also had to be given great consideration. Oddly enough, in Spain this process has only been applied in Catalonia, where the territories of the western strip of the diocese of Lleida have been carved away and given to Aragon, where they belong in terms of political boundaries, but not from the point of view of tradition, language, and history. This had seemed to be exactly the kind of change the Concordat had warned against! Another worrying factor, as regards the cohesion of the Catalan Church, is that for the first time since 1964 it does not depend on one single juridical body, as it has done historically. With the promotion of the Barcelona Archdiocese, the Catalan Church now has two 'heads', one at Barcelona and the other at Tarragona, the age-old seat of the Catalan Church since Roman times.[13] This is a new problem for our internal unity and organisational cohesion.

EC: I would add that a lot of the setbacks suffered by the Catalan Church are no accident. They are entirely contrived. If you observe the steps that are being taken, the victims are always the same: the integrity of the Catalan Church, Catalan culture, and Catalanism. It turns out that the diocese of Lleida had to adapt to the borders of autonomous Spain. This is done by splitting the age-old diocese of Lleida and giving half of it to Barbastro, a step clearly taken to please the *Opus Dei*.[14] In the process they are even trying to deprive Lleida's Diocesan Museum of 113 of its pieces—of which it is the legal owner—on the grounds that they originated in Aragon. But it is the Lleida diocese that rightfully owns them, because it bought them. Besides, under the same premise, half the Vatican Museum would have to be dispersed. Now what is quite clear for all to see is that the Spanish Church has not pushed for any boundary changes other than one that affects Catalonia. Why don't they change other boundary anomalies, such as those that we see at Jaca—also a part of Aragon—which forms part of the bishopric of Pamplona?

JL: There's an easy answer to that. If they gave Jaca back to the Aragonese Church, then they would be forced to resolve the whole question of the Basque Church, another area where they are quite clearly maintaining divisions to favour Spanish interests. Even a child can see that! To avoid changes in one area, they will bend over backwards to maintain another. Needless to say, all this policy obtains the unfailing support of the Papal Nuncio, who not only lives in Madrid and reads the Madrid press daily, but is also most chummy with the all-powerful Archbishops of Madrid and Toledo.

EC: Indeed, the Spanish ecclesiastical lobby has managed to make the Vatican think that Catalan nationalism and the secularisation process of Catalan civil society are two sides of the same coin. They point to the relatively high divorce and abortion figures there are for Catalonia—as there are in so many advanced societies—and go so far as to push the 'argument' that what many Catalans are after is the destruction of the Catholic Church! After years of this absurd discourse, one finds that in the Vatican they often associate Catalanism with depravity and collusion with the devil. They see us as 'infidels' from a separatist territory. This is the image that the leadership of the Spanish Church gives of Catalonia. It's a little bit like what occurred in the Republic and during the Civil War.

Culture

Jennifer Berengueras
Campaigner against bullfighting

Jennifer Berengueras is an Anglo-Catalan member of the Prou [Enough] *antibullfighting platform. On July 28, 2010 this group brought off the feat of getting the Catalan Parliament to abolish this blood sport for good. A year earlier, in 2009, the Platform had presented a Popular Legislative Initiative which raised the support of 180,000 signatures in favour of the ban.[1] There are to be no more corridas in the country as of January 1, 2012.*

Berengueras' determination to campaign for animals' rights stems from her childhood, when she was regularly besieged by images of bulls being tortured on TV. She remembers regularly bursting into tears 'with a sense of rage and frustration' after such scenes. Years later, when she went to University, she decided to study a subject connected with animals and nature. But it turned out not to be veterinary surgery, because, as she confesses, she didn't have 'the stomach' to wield a vet's scalpel on a pet. So she read Environmental Studies instead, specialising in ecology and the conservation of wildlife. Predictably, though, her more specific concern was for animals that suffer at the hands of humans in practices such as bullfighting and vivisection. Now she doesn't cry when she sees images of cruelty to animals. Instead, she thinks of effective ways of getting it stopped.

Wednesday July 28, 2010 was a special day in your life.

It certainly was. On that day the Catalan Parliament put an end to five centuries of torture to bulls. By doing so I think our MPs not only showed respect for animals but also brought in a wave of democratic health for our nation. It was a day of great satisfaction and acknowledgement for the campaigning many people had been involved in for so many years. Nevertheless we cannot claim that our campaigning work is over. To achieve the complete abolition of bullfighting, there is still plenty to do. This is only the beginning of the end for this cruel practice.

What does the July 28th vote effectively mean?

It means that after January 1, 2012, bullfights will no longer be held in Catalonia. I am happy to say that an ample majority of Catalan MPs voted in favour of the bill. Perhaps what most moved me was the fact that after the vote, a good many of them actually stood and applauded us. I think it is a sign that Catalans—like the majority of Spaniards as well—are ashamed to be associated with this kind of activity. It is now time to evolve and to introduce ethical criteria when approaching the question of our traditions. The debate has boosted an awareness of the need to prevent cruelty to animals both at home and abroad. Indeed, the international support for our campaign was vital.

Deep down, what motivated you to campaign for an end to bullfighting?

Unfortunately, there are cruel animal-baiting traditions almost everywhere in the world. Even in civilized Denmark there is a tradition which involves bludgeoning dolphins to death![2] In Spain foreign tourists often go to bullfights because they have no idea what's involved. You see them leave the arena after the slaughter of the first (of six) bulls and you hear them rage, 'I didn't know they killed the poor animal!' What they had seen in tourist brochures and TV publicity was the cocky matador swishing his gaily-coloured cape around his head, and they thought they'd love it. They had not been shown shots of the bull belching blood and falling to its knees with gore pouring off its back. I've seen whole groups of distressed foreign tourists leaving Barcelona's Monumental bullring, some clearly in tears.

***Aficionados*[3] say bullfighting takes place on private premises, and accuse campaigners for prohibition of behaving like the Inquisition.**

Every year they come up with some new argument. To insist on 'respect for minorities'—as they now seem to do—is all very well. But that cannot entail tolerating the death, torture, and ill-treatment of animals. Frankly I don't see myself as an inquisitor. But common sense and respect should put the idea of hurting other beings out of the question. It's the same kind of case as paedophilia. Respect for minorities is fine as long as it doesn't involve unnecessary harm to others, be they human or animal.

Aficionados also give 'ecological' reasons for preserving bullfighting.

Yes. Last year they came up with the notion that bullfighting helps conserve bull-breeding habitats. Aficionados insist that it's thanks to bullfighting that the *dehesa* (the rolling grassland habitat scattered with holm oaks, typical of central and southern Spain) is conserved. I had the opportunity to speak before a European Parliament commission on this issue. The *dehesa* is not really a natural environment at all. It's man-made. All right, it's worth conserving. But bull-raising has almost no part in this, since it accounts for less than 5% of the whole *dehesa* area. The rest is protected by special measures that do not depend on bull-raising at all. In fact, the over-grazing, destruction of young trees, and disturbance to the subsoil associated with intensive bull raising is anything but ecological. And the claim that bullfighting 'saves the species' is absurd. The *toro de lidia*, or fighting bull, is not a species at all. It's just another version of *bos taurus*. There are some six billion of them in the world. So I don't think they're in any imminent danger of extinction.

What is the EU's position on this issue?

The EU tends to stay neutral when so-called 'traditions' and religious beliefs are involved and yet, the EU is indirectly funding bullfighting. Some of the cattle farmers it funds rear bulls for bullfighting. Worse still, Regional Development Funds have been used to refurbish bullrings, as in the case of the ring at Haro in the Rioja region. Our organization is pressing for a ban on funding for activities involving cruelty to animals.

What shape has your campaign before the EU taken?

In 2008 we staged a protest to counter an aficionado bid to promote bullfighting with an exhibition at the European Parliament. In response, we outflanked them by placing a life-size white fibreglass bull at the entrance to the building. We asked MEPs to sign their names on it in support for a ban on bullfights. Three hundred MEPs signed, as did over two-thirds of the Parliament's Brussels-based civil servants! We were amazed at our success. In contrast, only seven MEPs attended the pro-bulls show: five were Spanish, one was French and another Belgian. On the blog of the latter MEP there was soon an irritated comment about how he had been 'hoodwinked' into attending. The video presented at the event showed no gore, and made bullfighting look like courtly pageantry. Everyone knows the truth is different.

How strong is the anti-bullfighting movement in Catalonia?

People may think it's a passing fad. But we have been on the road for over a hundred years. This can be seen by poring through the early 20th-century press. For years we have drawn up manifestos, sent protest postcards to institutions, and organized press campaigns and demonstrations of all shapes and sizes. But we realized this was not effective. We saw we had to make politicians change the law. The strength of our movement made them see they had to take us into account. So we decided to present what's called a Popular Legislative Initiative (PLI) in the Catalan Parliament. This had never been done before anywhere in the Spanish State. And we won!

What did the PLI involve?

In June 2009 we got the 50,000 signatures we needed for the bill. They were officially validated, but the truth is we had another 130,000 in reserve. The truth is we had 180,000. Proportionally, it was like presenting 1,200,000 signatures in the UK. Then the Initiative followed the same course as any other bill presented in the Catalan Parliament. At first we hoped it would be voted on before Christmas 2009. But, this didn't happen until seven months or so later. As regards party support, all we asked was that the opinion of the Catalan people should be fully reflected. So we banked on the parliamentarians prohibiting bullfighting, which is what the vast majority of Catalans want. As regards parties that have got a policy on this issue, ERC and ICV have abolition on their programs. The Catalan branch of the Partido Popular, on the other hand, openly backs bullfights. In the end, the Socialists (PSC) and CiU allowed their MPs to vote freely. We knew there was one staunch pro-bullfighting MP in the PSC, David Pérez—he has even promoted bullfighting internationally—but in both parties there were known to be MPs in favour, against, and undecided. We were right in thinking that the latter would end up voting in accordance with the will of the Catalan people.

What about the position of Barcelona City Council?

It actually declared Barcelona to be a 'bullfighting-free' city in 2004, coinciding with the *Fòrum de les Cultures*.[4] Some over-optimistic citizens assumed that this meant that bullfighting had been banned from our city forever. Unfortunately, though, this motion was altogether useless, because the city had no real powers and competencies on this kind of issue. So bullfighting continued to limp on unhindered in the city. It was the Catalan Parliament, which deals with matters of animal protection and public spectacles, that had the key. And this is why we had to create the *Prou* Platform and take the matter before the Parliament.

Almost all of the city councils that have passed anti-bullfighting motions in the State and abroad seem to be in Catalonia.

Yes. To express opposition to what in Spain they call the 'National Festival' is much less of a taboo here than it is in Spain. Maybe because we are more European... But people are now beginning to campaign in Spain, too. There too, a large majority of citizens also feel embarrassment about bullfighting. Gallup did a rather conservative survey on this in 2007 and found that 73% of Catalans were clearly opposed to bullfighting. Other surveys over the years have given figures of 80% and 90%. Even in Andalusia, normally thought of as the heart of 'bullfighting Spain', 68% of the population now reject bullfighting outright! In South America anti-bullfighting feeling is as widespread as in Spain. Aficionados are in fact a minority everywhere, even in toreador territory. Bullfighting was banned in the Canary Isles in 1991 and nobody even noticed. Abolishing this practice in Catalonia has raised fury of a suspiciously political hue.

What do you make of the role played by 'cult' bullfighter José Tomás in recent bullfights in Barcelona?[5]

Tomás' bullfights were staged in Barcelona's Monumental bullring with a specific strategy behind them. They started just after the city had been declared 'bullfighting-free'. In 2004, the owner of the ring, bullfighting *empresario* Sr. Balañá, had declared that he was fed up with losing so much money on the bulls. Other *empresarios* elsewhere grew afraid the closure of the Monumental might lead to a domino-effect closure of others in Spain. So they began to invest heavily in Barcelona. They had the brilliant idea of bringing back José Tomás, a retired torero who was game to making a much awaited come-back—in Barcelona of all places—as marketing strategy. Bus-loads of regular aficionados were brought in from all over Spain, while special planes were laid on for Madrid's jet set. The media and the Ministry of Culture, which subsidizes bullfighting handsomely, did their bit. OK, admittedly there were Catalan aficionados at the José Tomás fights. But the whole affair had a decidedly crusading air to it. In any case, the bull lobby's claim that it was the aficionados of Catalonia who had filled the arena was quite absurd. At Tomás' latest corrida in Barcelona, we actually watched arena officials give out handfuls of free tickets at the door. But the official line given in Madrid papers spoke of all tickets having been 'sold out in 50 minutes on-line!' The funny thing is that José Tomás ended up publicly scrapping with dramatist Albert Boadella,[6] one of those most intent on using him for political purposes.

I gather aficionados take a poor view of your protests at the bullring gates.

Yes, before we opted for the ILP strategy, we used to protest at the gates of bullrings. We were generally hailed with all kinds of insults. At one corrida a man came up to me brandishing a coin with the face of Franco on it, and shouting, 'The Generalísimo would put you in your place for sure.' Another time a short-haired girl and I were holding a banner and a gentleman came up to us yelling, 'You're nothing but red lesbians!' Incidentally, very rarely are we insulted in Catalan. A survey carried out by *El Mundo* newspaper published a photofit picture of the typical aficionado: male, over 65, Partido Popular-supporting with a marked preference for blondes!

What do they actually do to the bulls before the fight?

We used to base a lot of our campaigning on explaining the really sordid things they do. But just seeing what happens during the fight is quite enough. Apart from that, aficionados can always claim that those unseen practices are pure invention. They generally file down the bulls' horns to make them less of a threat. But of course that also affects their sense of distance. What they do to the bulls in the ring should suffice to sicken normal people. Sticking the *banderilla* darts in the bull's back,[7] piercing its lungs with a sword, and then using the cape to swing its head around to cause further injury... All the actions carried out in a corrida are designed to destroy a bull in the most cruel fashion imaginable.

Bernat Joan
The gentle linguist from Eivissa

Dr. Bernat Joan i Marí is a former MEP who currently holds the post of Secretary for Language Policy for the Catalan Generalitat Government. Running a potentially controversial department that deals with a tricky issue, you'd expect to see him regularly besmirched with red paint on the part-Berlusconi-owned Spanish channel Telecinco. Yet he has been relatively lucky as there has been little of that. As an affable, highly cultured, and easy-going man, with plenty of books to his name, he's managed to steer clear of the aggro. Joan is probably the last person you would associate with that clichéd image of his birthplace Eivissa—Ibiza—the 'crazy island of sin and drugs'. In fact, the locals don't often have much to do with the more excitable and rowdy specimens who stream onto the island in the boisterous summer months. He was born there in 1960. As he says, the island offers lots of surprises to the truly uninitiated, starting with its surprisingly unspoiled scenery. Its name also contains a secret. For what to almost all visitors is 'Ibiza' is just a Hispanified version of the island's real name, Eivissa in Catalan, which is the local language there, as it is in mainland Catalonia and Valencia.

Eivissencs—the people of Eivissa like Bernat Joan—speak a marvellously mild and melodious form of Catalan, a petrified version of the language originally brought to the islands by 13th-century Catalan settlers. The seductive soft s sound of what is termed the 'salty' feminine definite article—sa instead of mainland la—gives the language a vaguely exotic flavour. Bearing in its DNA the gentle pace of the generally unruffled nature of the Mediterranean—which does, however, have its moments of fury—it's a dialect that's quite unsuited to expressing ill-temper or impatience.

As a youngster, the repression exercised by the Francoist regime made Bernat Joan take an early interest in left-wing politics. However, as he says, the 'discovery' of the Catalan language and its literature 'opened up a new vista that had been completely hidden from me', and which was to change his life. As well as being a linguist, Bernat Joan is a compulsive writer. For years he has written as many as half a dozen articles a week, for a variety of magazines and websites. He also keeps up a diary he started in 1984—'no particular homage to George Orwell', as he points out. Like so many islanders involved in business or politics, he leads a nomadic life. He spends three or four nights a week away from the island, mainly at the Language Policy office in Barcelona where he works. So too does his wife—Esperança Marí—who is an MP in the Balearic Parliament in Palma, on neighbouring Mallorca. They have two daughters, one an expert in Asian Studies, the other a musician. 'We get together at home in Eivissa whenever we can. But we're also happy to do so in other places in the Catalan Countries.'

Spanish politicians and journalists often complain about Catalan language policy, as if Spanish were in danger of disappearing in Catalonia. What do you make of that?

Opinions of that sort make no sense at all. They can only be the result of misinformation or bad faith. Spanish is thriving in Catalonia. In fact, it's the mother tongue of almost half the population. All locals and almost all immigrants speak it. To suggest that language policy in Catalonia is aimed at 'impeding the presence of Spanish' is just absurd. Spanish is by far the most widely used language in Catalonia, and the Generalitat Government is responsible for trying to ensure that Catalan plays the role of what we call the 'common language' within the context of multilingualism. Catalan and Spanish are the two official languages.

Are there any differences between the language policy of the first Catalan CiU governments from 1980 to 2003 and that of the Tripartit coalition governments of 2003–10?[1]

The language policy of the current Generalitat is a continuation of the policy that was implemented by the governments of *Convergència i Unió*. Essentially, we go along with the steps taken by Aina Moll, the first CiU director of Language Policy. I was younger then, and very critical of some of her measures. Today we face new challenges. For instance, between 2003 and 2009 we have had to multiply the budget of the Language Normalization Consortium by four to meet the needs of recent immigrants. We have also developed very successful volunteer teaching programs. However, as a member of a party (ERC) which voted against the Language Policy Law,[2] I believe we are being hampered by legal measures that are not strong enough to ensure the full recovery of Catalan as the common language, although, to be fair, a lot of progress has been made lately. We now have far more powerful tools, such as language consulting services, automatic translators, and the very practical *parla.com* on-line learning method.

Recently immigration has quadrupled. Is that a threat to the survival of the Catalan language?

Immigration is not a threat, so long as we can enable it to enjoy a normal existence. Under normal conditions, when people migrate, they learn the language of their new country. Only in extraordinary circumstances is that not the case. If we were an independent State, we would not even have to think about the question. It isn't immigration that threatens the language, but the language's insufficient legal status. There is also the problem of the weak attitude we often find among Catalan-speakers. New immigration gives us a fresh opportunity to turn Catalan into a more vigorous language, spoken by many more people. Historically, Catalonia has tended to be a country that assimilates growing numbers of speakers.

Are language policies the same in all the Catalan-speaking territories?

Catalan must be one of the most divided languages in the world, as regards its administrative status, second only perhaps to Kurdish! We have the full range of circumstances: from the optimal situation of a small Pyrenean State—Andorra—where Catalan is the only official language, to situations such as in Catalonia and the Balearic Islands, where bilingualism is official with Catalan acting as the acknowledged 'territorial' language. But we also have situations in which bilingualism is official on paper, but where Catalan is not recognized as the territorial language. Sometimes it is even given a different name! This is the case in Valencia, where the language is officially called *Valencian*. In other Catalan-speaking areas the language has no official status at all, as in French (or North) Catalonia, L'Alguer in Sardinia and the Franja de Ponent area of Aragon.[3]

What about the role of the Spanish State as regards the use of Catalan? Hasn't the Council of Europe been critical on that score?

Historically, the policy of the Spanish State has been to promote a unitary State with one language which is considered superior. The others are treated as superfluous, decorative leftovers. One of the basic features of Francoism was its attempt to wipe out

Catalan, Galician, and Basque. Things have now changed. The presence of what they call 'autonomic' languages is admittedly more visible in the websites and documents of the State's central bodies. Yet these languages still enjoy little more than a token presence, with 'Catalan' and 'Valencian' being treated as if they were two different languages! Some attitudes are patronizing, even preposterous. For example, Catalan, Basque, and Galician can be used in the Senate on one token day in the year. It could be called National Derelict Languages Day! On that day the Senate hires one translator for Catalan and another for Valencian, as if they were not one and the same language. Can you imagine the House of Lords hiring separate interpreters for speakers from Lancashire and Yorkshire? So on the one hand they are really restrictive about the use of languages, but in another way they are amazingly generous, in hiring two translators for one language on a particular day![4]

So the State's attitude to minority languages has not changed that much…

The State ought to acknowledge Galician, Basque, and Catalan as official State languages alongside Spanish. Why don't they do the same as Switzerland, Belgium, or Finland, and recognize that there is no one single language that is peculiar to the State, and that all of them have the same status? If the State fails to acknowledge even that, how can Catalans be expected to feel comfortable in a State which, linguistically speaking, treats the majority as first-class citizens and the rest as rabble?

Are the public services (in the post office, railways, airports, etc.) made available in Catalan?

The public services in Catalonia tend to be bilingual as far as signposting is concerned. But Catalan is often not available when it comes to customer service. The telephone companies are particularly bad here. There is simply no willingness to implement a comprehensive language policy. On the contrary, the State keeps on implying that Spanish is the important language, the rest superfluous, a sort of nuisance they just have to put up with. The Spanish philosopher and politician José Ortega y Gasset, seeing that it was impossible to eliminate non-Castilian identity around the State, came up with the 'magic' formula of *conllevancia*.[5] It suggested simply replacing the active persecution and elimination of rival identities with a long-term policy of ignoring, cold-shouldering, and dwarfing them.

Catalans and the Catalan language are often treated with contempt in the Spanish media and on the internet. Is that fair?

Obviously not. Some months ago the Madrid newspaper *El Mundo* conducted an acritical opinion poll that asked people if they felt hatred against Catalonia. I think it would have been unthinkable anywhere else in the EU. I'm sure it's in line with the kind of hate-stirring Serbian newspapers carried out before the last Balkan war. The use of the Catalan language is another favourite bugbear. I'm sure that if we had given up Catalan, Catalanophobia would have disappeared years ago. They know that our fundamental trait as a people is our distinctive language. They cannot understand that speaking a different language does not mean renouncing Spanish. We don't prevent anyone from learning Catalan. Anyone who speaks Catalan is considered one of us, even if he was born in Central Africa or has no residence permit. Maybe that's why Catalan is considered such a nuisance by Spanish racists. I hope the Human Rights Court in Strasbourg will one day do something about such racist practices in the Spanish media.

Catalonia, Valencia and the Balearic Islands are among Europe's most massive tourist destinations. Are tourists aware that Catalan is spoken there?

It depends where they go. Londoners who spend their holidays in discotheques in Eivissa or on the Costa Blanca won't have a clue that Catalan even exists (or Spanish, for that matter!). However, if they travel to the interior of Mallorca, or most of Catalonia proper, they can't miss it. However, when all's said and done, the important thing is to change the attitude of Catalan-speakers. They often seem afraid to let on that they speak Catalan. Takes this case: on a bus ride, I once heard an English tourist ask another what Eivissa meant. The answer he got was, 'Don't you know? It's Spanish for *Ibiza*.' In other words, *Ibiza* wasn't Spanish, but English! Being the nut I am, I took the trouble to explain to them that Eivissa was in fact Catalan. I just couldn't hold back! 'Attitude' is, I think, what Americans call it!

Opponents of Catalan—political parties, institutions and the media—complain about it being the 'vehicular language' of education. They say, 'They don't let us educate our children in Spanish!'

At the beginning of the Transition to democracy, it was decided that there would not be a dual education system. If we live together, if we want social cohesion, then we must have one single homogeneous education system. That was decided on even before we knew which language was to be used. Later it was decided it should be Catalan. Why? In order to ensure that what is laid down in the law is fulfilled: that, at the end of their school education, all students should be fluent in both Catalan and Spanish. To see the wisdom of that decision, you only need to look at what's happening in Valencia, where there are two educational models. Pupils who study in Catalan end up knowing both the official languages perfectly. But those who study in Spanish, and only do Catalan as an extra subject, end up with a very poor knowledge of Catalan. To make opportunities equal in our society, we must encourage fluency in both languages. That can only be achieved if education has Catalan as the core language. Up to a point, as far as language is concerned, education corrects social inequalities. It is incomprehensible that some parents use their children as weapons against the Generalitat's language policy. They are harming their offspring, and pushing them into marginalisation. This is something I would never dream of doing to my daughters who, needless to say, have a perfect fluency in Spanish, as do all kids.

Yet, on this issue, some foreign media have taken sides with those wanting education in Spanish...

Students receive much of their education in Spanish. The problem is the poor information some foreign correspondents have about the question. That's not surprising, since they generally live in Madrid where they absorb an atmosphere that is hostile to Catalonia. They often fail to verify any information they are fed. Lots of these misunderstandings undoubtedly occur because Catalonia is a nation without a State. It is thus seen as essentially bereft of legal rights. Catalans are often accused of being unwilling to cooperate with the State. On the other hand, I am quite sure that, when we achieve independence, people will regard it as perfectly normal that we should use our language in all fields and at all levels of education. Nobody is shocked that the Danes use Danish to educate children in Denmark!

Jordi Portabella
To kill bulls, or to kill bullfighting?

One day in the late 1960s, when he was still a boy, Jordi Portabella looked down a microscope. He suddenly realized that there were a lot more worlds than he had previously imagined. He remembers acquiring, at that very moment, an unquenchable interest in the world and its inhabitants, huge or tiny. Later on, when he went to university, he had no doubts about choosing biology, which he studied in his home city of Barcelona. He specialized in ecology, and then went on to do an MA in environmental engineering. In 1983 he became an active member of the Crida de la Solidaritat [Call for Solidarity], a nationalist movement working to protect the language and culture of Catalonia. He coordinated the group's Ecological Platform, which aimed to create a greater ecological awareness in the country and cooperate with other green movements.

In 1987 he joined the historic Esquerra Republicana de Catalunya (ERC),[1] a Catalan left-wing party, at a time when fellow Crida member Àngel Colom was planning to run for the post of party Secretary-General. Until 1992 he held a seat in the Catalan Parliament, in the fourth and fifth legislatures, taking a particular interest in environmental issues: animals, energy, mobility, and regional policy.

In 1999 he headed his party's candidature in the elections to the Barcelona City Council (Ajuntament), and subsequently held the post of Deputy Mayor until 2007, in a coalition administration headed by the Socialists. During that period he was in charge of the city's Finance Department, as well as chairing the board of Barcelona City Zoo. He contributed to developing education and research policies there, as well as favouring a program aimed at reintroducing species to their natural environment. He did a great deal for the conservation of species close to extinction, as well as promoting environmental legislation for animals, in both commercial and private ownership, and played a part in restricting the use of animals in circuses and on the stage.

In 2004, by means of a secret vote taken by the City Council, he contributed to having Barcelona declared a 'bullfight-free city', a step that anticipated the 2010 abolition of this practice in Catalonia. In 2007 he resigned from the city administration and took up a new role in the ranks of the municipal opposition. This is a task he now combines with various kinds of creative activities connected with the environment.

You contributed greatly to the ban on bullfighting in Catalonia. You must be satisfied with the abolition of this practice by the Catalan Parliament.

It has been a very long and taxing struggle. Some media speak of the ban as a sort of flash in the pan. But I like to see it as a further step in a movement that started up in most of Europe two centuries ago. The Enlightenment saw bullfighting banned in several countries, such as England, where 'Martin's Act' was passed in 1822. It banned several blood sports involving animals. Indeed, an amendment made to it soon got bullfighting prohibited too. Few people know that there were bullrings in England as well. The followers of Wilberforce did not only do away with slavery. They also had blood sports banned if they involved the death of animals. These two issues divided Whigs and Tories. The latter were opposed to banning either practice. In Europe a similar debate was being conducted at the time. It is wrong to think of Spain as the only place bullfights have existed, although it's one of the few—along with Portugal and the South of France—where they have carried on unhindered. Almost everywhere else in Europe the practice has disappeared, and often failed to leave any lasting mark on historical memory. In Spain it has been regulated, going through periods of greater and lesser popularity. Under Franco, however, bullfighting received widespread official backing, and was proclaimed to be the *Fiesta nacional*.

Wasn't it seen as a 'National Fiesta' before?

Not exactly. In fact, the whole phenomenon of bullfighting, as we know it today, is much more recent than people think. Although animal-baiting and athletic activities involving animals go back to the times of Minoan culture in Crete, the first modern bullfights as such did not take place until the mid-18th century. Successive Spanish governments have almost always backed the activity, whereas in France it was no more than tolerated—and not regulated—until 1951. So the idea of bullfighting as an unchanging, 'age-old tradition' is quite definitely a hoax. The practice goes back in time, but has had very different formats. Essentially they involved carnivalesque, circus-like acrobatics. But not the death of the animal, which is the crux of the issue.

Is bullfighting 'un-Catalan', in your opinion?

In relation to this question, I think there are a number of myths that need to be dispelled. For example, Barcelona is said to have had as many as three bullrings. What they do not say is that one of them was a temporary one. Several of the bullrings built in Catalonia are known to have been constructed on the initiative of the military. At present there is only one bullring in Barcelona, and it is the only functioning one left in the whole of Catalonia. So it would be an exaggeration to suggest that there is wide support for bullfighting or that it has a strong tradition in Catalonia. Bullfighting as we know it today was in fact born in Andalusia, in the south of Spain, and exported from there. The tradition is therefore Andalusian, not Catalan.

Just how strong is the anti-bullfighting lobby in Catalonia today?

In April 2004, the city was symbolically declared to be against bullfighting by the City Council. I think this links us to a strong humanistic spirit, opposed to the cruelty to animals, which goes back to Barcelona's mayor in the 1890s, Dr. Robert. He called for the abolition of bullfighting in the Spanish Parliament. No trustworthy survey conducted in Catalonia has ever shown less than 60% opposition to the practice. Now it is nearer 80%. Increasing concern for animals and ecology means that bullfighting fans are waning in numbers, and the average age of those attending bullfights is steadily rising. Abolitionism has clearly got time on its side. The most influential lobby in favour of bullfighting is made up of those who live off it: mainly bullring *empresarios* and bull-breeders. In some areas it is big business, and profitable, because there are generous subsidies from the local and even the European administrations.

Can I ask you how the disappearance of bullfighting in 2012 might affect the image of Catalonia in the eyes of tourists?

Well it may not do at all, because bullfighting has already been almost completely phased out. Out of the roughly twelve bullfights there are every year, there is an average attendance of about 5,000 people, except for the famous José Tomás corrida, which was obviously a 'special event'. So that means there is an attendance of about 25% of the ring's capacity, of which about 30% are tourists. The Barcelona Tourist Board has never based the city's appeal on the image of bullfighting. So those tourists who do go to the bullfights are either basically off-beat or else hoodwinked into taking in a bullfight as part of some special offer. The Catalan government does not promote bullfighting in any way. So the demand for it is minimal, if you set it beside the two and a half million tourists who visit the *Sagrada Família*—just a few blocks away from the Monumental—or the million or so who visit FC Barcelona's Nou Camp stadium or the Picasso Museum.

In spite of what you say about the low profile bullfighting is given by the City Council, do you think tourists in Barcelona get a clear idea that they are visiting a Catalan city?

I think it is fairly easy to perceive the Catalan character of our city as if it were something in the past. What is a lot more difficult is for visitors to see that Barcelona is a primarily Catalan city today. They see the Gothic architecture and the Modernist (Catalan Art Nouveau) buildings, and they know that this is something Catalan. But it's hard for foreigners to appreciate a distinctively Catalan spirit in contemporary Barcelona. However, is enough done to promote modern Catalan culture as an element of interest for tourists? Not at all. And I reckon that's a serious mistake. If we promoted a Catalan city, it would be nothing more than what other cities do. That is, to use local culture as a basis at every level short of the international dimension. The problem is that *prêt-à-porter* cosmopolitan products require no particular commitment, and are easier to push. To opt for them is a decidedly provincial decision. Being 'provincial' often stems from not being confident enough about one's own culture. Barcelona fails to act as the capital of a culture such as Paris, Rome, Prague, and Athens do. In the future, we must become more universal and operate on the basis of our own culture.

Oleguer Presas
A committed defender

'Oo, oo Oleguer'[1] was one of the favourite chants of FC Barcelona and Catalan national team supporters at matches during and around the 2005–6 season. Strange though it was that the hard-to-impress Barça terraces should hail a defender—hat-tricks by Argentinians or Brazilians usually being more in line for cheering—Barça fans had a soft spot for this rather shy but very committed central defender from Sabadell. Oddly enough, Oleguer Presas had not been brought up in Barça's famous Masia football nursery but joined Barça's junior team at the age of 21, after playing for a number of second- and third-division sides. In the 2002–3 season, Dutch coach Louis Van Gaal spotted him and promoted him to the first team. Oleguer made his first-team debut in a Joan Gamper trophy match against Red Star Belgrade.

At first, he had to contend for a place in the defence with world-class players such as the Dutch national team captain Frank de Boer. By the 2004–5 season, he had won the confidence of the new coach—another Dutchman, Frank Rijkaard—and played 36 matches. It was Oleguer's best period as a player. He contributed to winning the 2004–5 and 2005–6 Spanish League titles, two Spanish Supercups (2005 and 2006), three Catalan Cups and—most importantly—Barça's second European Champions League trophy (2005–6). An untimely hand injury in the 2007–8 season, as well as the arrival of vintage Juventus star Gianluca Zambrotta—signed for free—reduced Oleguer's first-team presence somewhat. This may have led to his decision to move on in summer 2008 to Holland's Ajax, where in his first season he played twenty-seven matches. As regards his qualities, most experts point to a cool head and a capacity for concentration as his major assets. He has always been quick to cut off the progress of attackers, and his height ensures he can head off dangerous centres into the area.

Some people think that the Madrid media's bias against Oleguer's ideological stance—clearly left-wing and in favour of Catalan independence—may have contributed to his move to Holland. The fact remains that Oleguer's popularity at home contrasted sharply with the abuse he had to put up with on many grounds around Spain. In 2006 he published a book, Camí d'Ítaca [Road to Ithaca],[2] together with fellow Sabadell writer Roc Casagran. The book reflects on the success of FC Barcelona in earlier seasons, and also serves to air Oleguer's views on the struggle against Francoism, the Iraq war (which was then underway), and other contradictions generated by the current economic and social system. Oleguer contributed part of the profits from the book to the Bressola Catalan schools in the northern part of Catalonia under French administration. When Oleguer received €25,000 by winning the President Companys Prize in 2006 for his support for the Catalan national football team, he contributed the prize money to a project run by Escola Valenciana, to promote education in Catalan in Valencia.

You have sometimes described the situation of your country as 'abnormal'. In what sense?

For more than three hundred years Catalonia has been attacked from all sides. It hasn't been able to become a 'normal' country, like so many others around us. Although people say that we have got home rule, we cannot run our own affairs at all! Our country's politics depend on the degree of autonomy the Spanish State is willing to concede to us. That makes all sorts of decisions hard and slow to take, over and above the fact that it cuts down on our rights. This has had fatal consequences for our chances of enjoying a normal social and cultural status. We are not allowed to govern ourselves, and suffer constant external interference. Attempts have repeatedly been made over the course of history to wipe out our country's identity and symbols. Even in today's Catalonia, to lead one's life in Catalan is by no means easy. The fact that everyday life—going to the cinema or to university, the law courts or the pub—involves having constantly to change languages means that things are far from normal.

Would you put this down to immigration?

Some may say that our language is losing out socially due to the arrival of immigrants. But that is by no means the only reason. I think immigration is good for the economy, and it also provides cultural and social enrichment. I don't mind speaking to newcomers in other languages to make myself understood. But it's a different matter when your language is a less widely-spoken one that survives under the heel of a stronger one that enjoys the support of the state. Special attention is required on the part of our government to prevent a process of language substitution, and it's often lacking. And that's what has happened with all the governments that there have been in the Spanish State up till now. One sometimes wonders how our language has managed to survive.

Some media say the Catalan language is 'imposed' on non-Catalan speakers.

But the truth is that the Catalan language is clearly discriminated against in almost all areas of public life! As a language with fewer speakers, it needs the support of public institutions to guarantee its use. That support takes the form of obligatory schooling in Catalan and the need for public sector workers to know the language to be able to attend Catalan-speakers in their own language. Taken out of context—as so often happens—this compulsory requirement for the language (which I see as vital, but which is often not respected) can give outsiders a completely false idea. Catalan is the official language of the Catalan Countries. It is official everywhere, except in North Catalonia, which is under French administration. What the Catalan institutions do is legislate regarding its usage, just as Swedish institutions do with Swedish or French ones with regard to French. In those cases, no-one talks about imposing anything. What we need is a situation in which it is seen as normal for a person who comes to lives in Barcelona to learn Catalan.[3] To give you an example, at FC Barcelona, all our training sessions were conducted in Spanish, whereas in the Netherlands all our training sessions are conducted in Dutch. And so they should be, because when a player moves to a new country he ought to adapt to his new surroundings. Only someone who has been misinformed can swallow the idea that Catalan is imposed on anyone in Catalonia.

What about your experience at Barça? Did players coming to play there from other countries identify with the club's Catalan spirit?

I think it very much depends on the individual player involved. Football players are really quite normal people, whatever people may imagine! They are just like anyone else. Getting to know and identifying with the spirit of the place you are now living in largely depends on your character, on the way you see things. Players sensitive to this tend to soak it up. However, if our country were 'normal,' these things would not be a problem. Doubts about what language to learn

or what codes of behaviour are prevalent around one wouldn't even arise. One wouldn't have to spend so much time trying to 'enlighten' newcomers!

What would happen to the Spanish Football League if Catalonia were to become independent?

That's a question that bothers a few people. I think it needs to be put in the right context. Nowadays, the tendency is for frontiers to be opened up. What is at the heart of the debate is the need for a European League. On the other hand, I don't think that becoming independent would automatically imply breaking off all relations with other countries. No way. In this particular context we have the precedent of an Andorran team that plays in the Spanish League. When I think of an independent country, at no time do I imagine an autarchic and isolated State, but rather a sovereign State with the capacity to adapt to daily issues and the needs of its citizens, showing a will to cooperate at all times with other nations.

What are your feelings when you play for the Catalan national team?[4]

To tell you the truth, I have mixed feelings on that score. On the one hand there's the pride and pleasure you feel when you play for your national team. Match days are major events. The atmosphere at the stadium is electric, and there are lots of positive aspects that make it a special day. On the other hand there are serious limitations. You can't help remembering that you are only competing at an unofficial level. Indeed, the Catalan team is only allowed to play Christmas-time friendlies.[5] So you end up asking yourself why you can't compete on an official basis, which, at the end of the day, is what makes sport tick. It's what the fans want. It is official championship participation that is missing. And that is what a lot of we players have come out for. Serious steps need to be taken to make our national side official in the not too distant future.

Do you think Catalonia's political demands are understood abroad?

The mass media fail to be neutral anywhere. So it's probably not that surprising that not a lot of coverage is given to our demands. When dealing with international issues, such as ours, they tend to rely on press agencies that are of course not neutral. They often make unrealistic generalizations about the issue, because they don't have first-hand sources. This means that only exaggerated or controversial news items appear, usually quite out of context. Journalists almost always respond to specific political interests. In the case of Catalonia, and due to the pressure exerted by the Spanish political and economic establishment, the international media often give a biased and deformed view of what we demand. Maybe it's our fault, and we haven't done enough to explain things. In that sense I'm absolutely in favour of taking as educational an approach as possible. However, it is often quite difficult to do so when one is the underdog with no international representation and without the support of a government which has this as a priority. That is our situation right now.

Some media are critical of those sportsmen and women who publicly take on political commitments. What do you think about that?

I think it's quite natural that sportsmen, like anyone else for that matter, should feel they have the right to give their opinions. Some in the media criticize sportsmen and women who speak up on particular issues. But this generally occurs because those media represent interests that are opposed to these views. They probably would not do so if they agreed with them. The truth is that almost all the world of sport is politicized. There are big companies with major interests in the world of sport, and their participation in politics is often as significant as it is unnoticed. The same media fail to see anything odd in that. Yet they deny individual sportsmen the right to give their opinions. It's quite hypocritical really.

Even some sectors of our own Catalan press seem hostile towards sportsmen who express certain political views…

Indeed, it's sometimes difficult to know just what we mean by 'our own press'. But the Catalan press behaves much like the others, really. Nowadays all the major media form part of great economic lobbies. I understand that, if discordant opinions squeeze their way into some area of the media, it's because there is public demand for them. We should not forget that, for them, the Catalan language represents a potential market of ten million consumers. That makes these large media groups put up with possible ideological contradictions. Although they would naturally tend to shun Catalan, their economic interests lead them to want to control that market too. What made the owners of RAC1 (a radio station) and the newspaper *El Periódico* opt for Catalan,[6] for example? Quite clearly the fact that there is a market for it.

What is it like for a Catalan to play abroad?

Living away from home is a very enriching experience for anyone. You have to start from scratch in completely unknown surroundings. Customs and the way people go about things are completely different. It makes you see that there are lots of different ways of doing things. You learn how to take in new ideas, and how to respect differences. In my own case, I've come across people who have no idea about what goes on in the Spanish State. People ask me if Catalan and Spanish are the same language! They are surprised when I tell them that ten million people speak our language. But isn't that pretty much what happens to us? Catalans normally have no idea about the Frisian Islands. Maybe they ring a bell. But generally we have no idea that they have a language of their own or what degree of autonomy they enjoy, if any. So it isn't so strange. People the world over tend to know very little about other countries, especially if it's a question of national minorities. It's a shame. It arises from a situation in which people are exposed to a limited set of ideas, and in which information is controlled by a powerful minority.

Joan Solà
The power of Catalan

Professor Joan Solà, Emeritus Professor of Linguistics at Barcelona University, was one of the leading homenots *of Catalonia at the time of his sad death in 2010.[1] He leapt into the public eye when he was awarded the prestigious Premi d'Honor de les Lletres Catalanes (Honour Prize of Catalan Letters) in 2009. Soon afterwards he had the honour of becoming the first person of a non-political background to be invited to address the Catalan Parliament. Or was the honour for the Parliament? Whatever the case, his brave speech warning of the dangers facing the future of the Catalan language is already regarded as a classic.*

Solà was born in 1940 in Bell-lloc d'Urgell, on the plains of Urgell in western Catalonia, an area popularly known as the Terra Ferma or hard, firm lands. With its almost unpronounceable triple palatal letter 'l'—the first two pairs of which 'geminate',[2] a curious capacity of the single and double 'l' in Catalan—it seems like the perfect birthplace for a philologist. In the late 1950s he left his staunchly Catalan-speaking home town to go and study at a Catholic seminary, as did so many Catalan young men of the period. At a rather sinister religious institution in Lleida he was shocked to find that Catalan was all but outlawed. One of the few teachers Solà got on with was an Aragonese liberal who taught Latin, and with whom he also discussed literature. One day his teacher said that the true epic of Hispanic literature was not the Poem of the Cid, as was generally supposed, but a poem in Catalan called Atlàntida.[3] Solà, who was only fourteen at the time, had never even heard of it, nor of its author, a priest-poet named Jacint Verdaguer. Curiosity got the better of him, and he went out of his way to get a copy from outside the seminary, where books in Catalan were frowned upon. The young student read those magic verses, but understood nothing of the legends involved. He was also baffled by much of the vocabulary. However, he was bowled over by the brilliance he had seen his own language capable of attaining.

The discovery of Verdaguer, the 19th-century prince of Catalan Romantic literature, was to be the turning point in Solà's life. When, some years later, he read Carles Riba's magnificent Catalan translation of the Odyssey—*a work he describes as his* Treasure Island—*his fate was sealed. He would never cease to admire the immense power of Catalan, a language which as a youngster he had seen as little more than a farmer's dialect. As he used to say, the spell cast on him by Verdaguer and Riba as a young man had yet to be broken. Self-taught in Catalan, due to the ban on the language in schools during his youth he could not even spell his own brother's name!—it mattered little to him that he was severely reprimanded by his philosophy teacher for writing his answers to an exam in Catalan. Later he studied day and night to become an academic, and in time was appointed professor of Catalan linguistics at Barcelona University. 'For my sins',—as he put it—in the years before his death he was one of the most interviewed and outspoken of Catalan intellectuals.*

What is your opinion of the fact that Catalan is often portrayed as an 'imposed' language, and Spanish as an endangered one?

First of all, I think that trying to contest such ludicrous claims is an utter waste of time. However, I sometimes dream that common sense may one day prevail. I would like to bring together a couple of politicians from each political party who might be interested in starting up a new system of interpersonal relationships in Spain. We have suffered so many centuries of senseless conflict! But it's just a dream. We cannot come to an understanding with our opponents. They start from the premise that the State is the all-important thing and that everything that defies that framework, as is our case, is a nuisance. Readers of *The Economist* or the *New York Times* don't even know where Catalonia is. They couldn't care a damn about us! Why should they? All they see is the Spanish State, Zapatero, the King and the flashy aeroplanes Iberia sends over to them from Madrid. We are seen as absurd flies that they cannot swat fast enough! In that context, telling people in London or Madrid about our worries is pointless. But we could certainly do with more international journalists with less anti-Catalan bias.

In what ways do you see Catalan as a language that is still oppressed?

I'm not too keen on giving particular examples, because people can claim that they are exceptions, or unimportant. I prefer going to the root of the matter. But, if you insist, I will give you a couple of examples anyway, the first from the popular world of sport. As everyone knows, Barcelona Football Club is a massive social phenomenon. It is one of the largest sports clubs in Europe. It has also had a great run recently, winning six State and international championships in the 2008–9 season. Well, I think some of those critics should know that none of the key matches involved were available for TV viewers in Catalan. Only in Spanish. Does this sort of thing happen to sports enthusiasts in other countries? I mean, do Manchester United supporters have to watch their matches in another language? No. Well, that's what happens to FCB fans. What's more, Spanish is absolutely the dominant language in sport, be it in the swimming-pools of Barcelona or on the ski slopes of La Molina:[4] almost all coaching is given exclusively in Spanish! So, may I ask, which is the language that is being 'imposed'?

Then there is the question of the law courts. Lots of lawyers I know feel obliged to warn their clients not to use Catalan in front of certain judges in order not to hamper their chances of a favourable sentence. Can you imagine? And then there's the world of medicine. A few months ago a doctor friend of mine died, embittered and depressed. He told me that in his department, all records and written work were conducted in Spanish, even though all the staff were Catalan. This hadn't happened even under Franco! I have been going to the famous Sant Pau Hospital for treatment. OK, all the signs and notices there are in Catalan, and maybe in Spanish and Arabic too. But the five or six medical teams I have seen, each of them made up of six to eight doctors, almost all of them Catalan-speakers, conduct virtually all their business in Spanish. The loudspeaker announcements, the case histories, the records and archives are all in Spanish. The idea, I suppose, is that if one day a non-Catalan substitute is called in, he or she will be able to read the case histories in Spanish. So what is the bottom line to all this? Well, frankly, it's a death sentence for our language. When I argue with friends, some of them say, 'Come on, Joan, stop going on like this all the time!' As I see it what they really mean is, 'Stop complaining about trivialities, because it's as much as the hospital can do to cure people!' In what countries is a question as vital as language seen as a 'triviality'? There are two issues involved here that must not be confused: language and power. We cannot do the same as politicians do, mixing them up for the sake of quick solutions. Otherwise, we can say goodbye to the age-old language of Catalonia that survived Franco but not democratic Spain.

Lots of Catalan youngsters seem to be using more and more Spanish. Why is that so?

That's an easy question to ask and a hard one to answer. The Catalan government has a language department which is run by people who feel for our language but who fail to come up with the magic formula to persuade young Catalans to use it. There is an enormous inertia in favour of Spanish, which makes the recovery of Catalan a colossal task. Even some Catalan-speakers cower when they see us coming. They seem to be saying, 'Oh no, here come those bores who want to break up our comfy use of Spanish!' They see us as disrupters of the New Order, so to speak. 'Don't go telling that poor shopkeeper who's struggling to stay open that now he's got to put up his shop signs in Catalan! Poor man, he's never had the chance to study the language!' What has happened to us over the ages? We have a weak language. We carry on our shoulders an age-old sense of unease and shame regarding our language, so we keep on slipping into Spanish. The fact is that we actually know more Spanish than ever. So to many it may seem redundant—damned nearly heroic!—to want to keep up another language in the face of so many social and political difficulties, not the least of which is immigration. In my opinion, the fact that the two languages have not been given an equal status by virtue of a Constitutional Court ruling should be a *causus belli* for our Government. Our opponents are very powerful, and have brute force on their side. But, as Unamuno said, 'You may win, but you will not convince.' Acting against the Catalan language, they have made things easier for Spanish-speakers. And it's no use occasionally parading the odd Catalan-speaking immigrant on the television, because that's cheating. There's one in a thousand! The vast majority couldn't care two hoots about Catalan! Nothing will change until everyone—immigrants and locals alike—see that Catalan is as important a language as the other one. Our Government ought to be instilling in us the belief that we must fight to make the two languages equal. And that needs to be done here, not in Madrid or Brussels. Catalan must be accepted here first, then elsewhere. I live out in a district of Barcelona where Catalan is the majority language. But in central Barcelona, Catalan is being pushed out. That's where I'd like to see those journalists who keep going on about 'Spanish disappearing' in Catalonia. Only an idiot could write something like that! The fact is that it's impossible to live in Catalan in Catalonia today, not to mention in other supposedly Catalan-speaking territories. We live in a state of absolute schizophrenia. We read reviews in Catalan on films that we have to see in Spanish. On the radio, we hear cuts from American films in Spanish. We imagine Paul Newman is a gentleman from Madrid. However, if we do things in Catalan, they accuse us of being 'political' and imposing our language!

In some Catalan-speaking territories, there is sometimes the claim that it is another language that is spoken…

Yes. I have thought a lot about that problem, although I'm not a specialist in sociolinguistics. I cannot see an obvious answer, but it seems to me that the problem is basically political. This summer I read some novels by Baltasar Porcel.[5] He often harps on the apparently conservative idea that you cannot change your destiny. If you are a slave, then don't try and stone your boss, because he'll have you hanged. Maybe we should be pragmatic, not make a fuss and accept our lot without any form of ambition. But the thing is that the politicians who are striving to do away with Catalan in Valencia and Mallorca operate quite openly. They are perfectly explicit about their phobias! Defenders of Catalan, however, seem to find it much harder to agree, although I must say I am impressed by the number of organizations working to promote Catalan in Valencia and the Balearic Islands. I've got no solutions for the problem, other than to suggest that it's better not to close in on ourselves like besieged hedgehogs. We cannot claim to possess the whole truth. We must be open to negotiation and use our imagination. Open warfare against the opponents of Catalan is hopeless, because they've got the power, they've got the army, and we've got nothing.

How do you think immigration affects the prospects of Catalan?

I sometimes travel to Italy, and I feel real envy when I see groups of Arab and Turkish kids playing in Italian in the Piazza Navona. Italian is not an important language internationally, but all the immigrants arriving in Italy pick it up in no time. The reason is that people address them in Italian from the word go. That is not the case here.

What do you think about the fact that some observers talk about a 'radicalisation' of Catalan politics in recent times?

In the face of new and particularly powerful political attacks, I think we Catalans must adopt a very firm attitude. Every day brings fresh confirmation of the fact that Spain refuses to accept diversity. I am convinced that Spain will never accept our differences, or any kind of multicultural formula. Spaniards are allergic to our language, for goodness' sake! The big parties, the Partido Popular and the Socialist PSOE, always aim to get more votes by appealing to the Spanish flag and language, casting us Catalans as the principal targets. I think the unanimous reaction of the Catalans, starting with President Montilla[6]—since he has said he wants to exert his right to head a protest, whatever that means—must be to protest wholeheartedly. We want equality, that's all. No more rhetoric, please! What we are calling for can be written down in two lines. However, I very much doubt whether Montilla will protest, and I don't think the Catalan people will revolt, because I think we are a bit fed up with revolting. We have done it too many times in the past. It is Montilla who ought to take the initiative. If our rights as Catalans are rejected, surely our President and his government ought to act first. Demonstrations and popular referendums alone will not achieve much.

You seem to be alternately pessimistic and optimistic about the future of Catalonia…

My head is not God's head. But I sometimes think about a phrase spoken by a linguist, 'How to do things with words'. Saying a word causes things to happen! It's like saying, 'Son, I forgive your sins.' Good Lord! How strange! God must think and act all at once. My head is not like that. It's incapable of doing miracles. All I see are problems and contradictions. Even so, my attitude—though many people may not see this—is not pessimistic. What I refuse to do is to be lied to. What I will never be prepared to admit, as some people insist we should, is that there's nothing wrong, that there is what some people call 'Linguistic Peace'. That just isn't true! It's a terrible lie, and it does us a lot of harm, because it forces us to give in. We are the only ones who give in! Spanish speakers, and those who feel Spanish, are in a much stronger position than we are. They have the State on their side. So I won't accept lies or weak excuses, especially from our own government. Really, I'm an optimist! I see that there are still plenty of young people active on many fronts. For example, on the internet I think we can talk about a tidal wave of activity in Catalan, in spite of some doubtful spelling and syntax! In the last two or three years we have seen that there are plenty of people who don't want to give in. Although our Government keeps trying to put a brake on the movement, plenty of people are responding to the need to stop Spain ill-treating us any further. Of course, our Government has to deny this. Why? Because they are mostly members of the same party as the one that rules in Madrid! President Montilla said some months ago that 'Catalonia is more important for us than Zapatero or Spain'. No-one can take that seriously, least of all him and his Government. They do not act as if they took it seriously. And some very serious action is now called for if Catalonia and its language are to survive as they have until today.

Xavier Vinyals
In search of Olympic recognition

Xavier Vinyals, born in Barcelona in 1967, is the President of the Platform in support of Catalan National Sports Teams, an independent organization with Catalan Government funding. Its objective is to achieve the full international recognition of Catalonia as a sporting nation. Until 1993 Vinyals was also the first Director General of the Catalan Olympic Committee, an organization created in the 1980s in response to the desire of many Catalans to gain official status for Catalan Olympic sport. There had been a similar organization in the 1920s, prior to the military coup of General Primo de Rivera in 1923. Professionally, Vinyals is a lawyer and historian, though he is also the Consul-General of the Republic of Latvia in Catalonia. He is proud to have taken part in the 1992 Barcelona Olympic Games opening ceremony at the invitation of the Lithuanian National Olympic Team, which was taking part in its first Olympics. As part of the delegation, he carried a Catalan flag in his capacity of Director General of the Catalan Olympic Committee, much to the glee of the Catalans present in the Montjuïc Olympic Stadium. It was the only Catalan flag in the whole flag-laden parade.

Before the Games, back in 1988, Vinyals had been responsible for the creation of the acronym CAT to identify Catalonia. It took the place of a simple 'C', which had been used until then. Amongst other things, CAT is now used as a Catalan internet distinction tag for e-mail and web addresses, as well as an unofficial nationality sticker on cars. When asked why he has dedicated so many years—since he was 18 years old—to voluntary work in aid of the internationalization of Catalan sport, he says it is a question of 'national consciousness'. 'I could not, and cannot, envisage my country as one eternally engaged in regional sport as part of Spain.' Sport is the trench he has chosen to stand in to defend his country's interests.

How did the movement in favour of the internationalization of Catalan sport begin?

The movement did not appear out of the blue. There was a social demand for it because Catalonia is a nation. Nations need their icons and emblems to identify themselves internationally. In the modern world, sport is one of the most important of these emblems, and increasingly so. So it is logical that Catalans should want to have their own sides and national teams. Doesn't everyone want the same in their country? What countries in the world are dismantling the ones they have nowadays? None I fear! Some very thoughtfully and impartially conducted polls have been carried out to measure the degree of support there is for this in our country, and I would say it is overwhelming. No fewer than 80% of the population of Catalonia want national sides to compete officially at an international level.

So this movement is neither a flash in the pan nor something recent.

Exactly. You might not think so, but the tradition of international sport in Catalonia is one of the oldest in Southern Europe. Indeed, almost from the very start there was the idea that sport had to be associated with an idea of model citizenship. Different sports sprang up in the late 19th and early 20th centuries, as they did in much of Northern Europe. Catalan society soon went in for all kinds of sports, and this new activity was almost always linked to such values as social integration, democratic and ethical ideals, and other civic qualities. One of Barcelona's leading sports papers bore the subtitle 'Sport and Citizenship' beneath its masthead. Catalonia had a developed sports culture at a time when in Madrid show-jumping—practiced exclusively by the military—was practically the only sport. In contrast, Catalan sports enthusiasts had shared the values and been at the heart of the Olympic movement, in full communication with Baron Coubertin, from the very start. The Olympic movement speaks in its documents of 'sporting nations', and not of States. Catalonia was due to have its own Olympic Committee at the beginning of the 1920s, and created the Olympic Association of Catalonia, long before the Spanish Olympic committee even existed. Our country was awarded the Olympic Cup by the International Olympic Committee in 1923, just before the military coup of Primo de Rivera. This military general and dictator largely put an end to this movement. FC Barcelona was even banned in 1925! Then, in the Republic, when the Olympic Games were awarded to Hitler's Berlin in 1936, the Catalan Government organized an alternative Games in Barcelona, where many athletes of democratic ideas intended to compete after refusing to attend a Games presented by the Nazis. Things were at their worst, however, in the Franco years, when the Falangist movement had a big hand in sport, and used it to cultivate fascist propaganda. Things did not pick up again until the arrival of democracy. But no one seems to remember our traditional position and our record as a democratic sporting nation from the beginning.

Does Catalonia compete officially in any sports?

Yes, but only in very few sports, minor ones mainly. In the sports where recognition has been attained, this has clearly been as the result of an intelligent and sustained effort to achieve recognition through the different international federations involved. For example, Catalonia was a founding member of the International Rugby Federation long before any oblong ball had bounced in Madrid! It would perhaps be more difficult to understand the success there has been in different sports if Catalonia had not had a very long and rich tradition in the sport concerned. This is why one does not find the same demand in, say, communities such as La Rioja or Cantabria, where the practice of certain sports may go well back in time, but where the context in which it has been symbolically rooted is clearly Spanish in orientation. Unlike us, they do not see a need for the creation of national teams because they already have the Spanish one.

If each autonomous community were to demand a national team, wouldn't that mean 17 new national teams in European sports?

There is no way all the autonomous communities are going to opt for that. They may have their own regional sides, but the vast majority of sportsmen and

women from these communities identify 100% with the Spanish side. As a democrat, I would not dream of preventing anyone from having a national side if they wanted one. But you cannot compare the sporting tradition of Catalonia with, say, that of Rioja, Cantabria, or Extremadura. There they have the Spanish team deep in their hearts. They do not see themselves as being 'deprived' of a national side like we do. In Catalonia, the feeling we have for our national team is a deep and widely-shared one, as well. It has nothing to do with political opinion or concepts like sovereignty or anything like that. There are many people, even among those who do not use the Catalan language on a daily basis, who want Catalonia to compete with her own teams anywhere in the world. It's that simple. It's not a move designed to go against Spain. Like the Scots and Welsh, we want our own teams, that's all.

So it is basically a question of feeling, of identification?

That's right. I think that everywhere you go, people identify with certain colours and flags over and above other forms of political allegiance. We are talking about what people feel deep down. And there are a lot of Catalans who do not identify with the Spanish football team. They do not feel it is their team. Some even see it as a rival. Others have mixed feelings, but don't actually mind when Spain wins. Nevertheless, the polls reveal that at a sociological level, most Catalans want the official recognition of their national teams. This occurs because the world of sport has a sentimental and symbolic side to it which helps people to take root in countries. This can easily be perceived when people from other countries come to live in a place and identify with a particular sports club there. It is a way of ensuring quick identification with their new country. How many Arsenal supporters are non-white or are of immigrant origin today? This identification is currently impossible to achieve among newcomers in Catalonia, because official Catalan teams don't exist as such.

Would having official teams have any other advantages?

It would be a major step forward for Catalan sport, and it would enable more players to have an international status. It would be an obvious boost for the standard of our football at home. From the point of view of clubs and federations it would also be a vital step forward, permitting the consolidation and expansion of many different sports and teams that now have a more fragile existence. There is also the question of the economic impact. Catalonia, as a sports brand, is quite unknown at an international level. We simply do not exist. The internationalization of our sport would lead to the promotion of the brand 'Catalonia'. Competing in the world would be a magnificent way of making ourselves known. How often do we hear of countries lacking independence participating in official sport? Almost never. To a large extent, it is thanks to sport that we know about some countries at all!

What is your attitude to the Spanish teams?

We have nothing against them. But they are not the ones we identify with because they are not our teams. In fact, we are very much made to feel they are not ours. Former president Pujol,[1] in April 2010, spoke of the pressure exerted by certain official institutions on Catalan sportsmen—he mentioned the Spanish administration, and even the King—to encourage them to 'disguise' their Catalan identity as sportsmen. Though this may sound ludicrous to some, they know what they are up to. Suffice it to say, though, that in sports where Catalans make up most—or even all—of the Spanish side (roller hockey or water polo, for example), the use of Catalan by their coaches has been publicly denounced in the Spanish media. The Spanish Administration makes no attempt to correct such attitudes. But we do not oppose the Spanish teams. We simply demand our own. We would love to be able to play against Spanish teams. But we know that the very idea of it is taboo for many Spaniards.

You mention the language question. But does the Spanish Administration actually obstruct the possibilities of official Catalan sport existing?

This needs some explaining, for the situation is both complex and contradictory. In theory at least, Catalonia has exclusive powers and jurisdiction in the field of sport. This is so according to the previous Statute of Autonomy and also the one in force now. Catalonia has thus developed its own model of sports organization. Taking part in Catalan sport is run on a private and not on a public basis. The Catalan federations are private bodies according to the law. The clubs and federations were created independently and run themselves. In theory that is. However, the current Sports Law goes beyond the limits laid down by the current Spanish Constitution. Together with Italy—where it is an inheritance from the Mussolini era—Spain is the only country in the world where sports people are actually forced to take part in the national teams in all sports if selected. If not, they can be fined. Elsewhere international sport is in the hands of national federations, which are private entities. They do not depend on the government or the State. They are independent, so they establish their own rules and regulations. In Spain all federations are now subject to State intervention. Hence, they effectively prevent Catalan Federations obtaining international recognition. But this power is not always the determining factor. For example, the Catalan Bowling Federation has recently won international recognition after winning a vote against the Spanish Federation. The Spanish Sports Council—that is, the Spanish Government—took this decision to the international Court of Arbitration for Sport at Lausanne. And Catalonia won her case. This has created a precedent which is a breakthrough, and which will I hope be of use to other Catalan sports. In the past, the Spanish Government has prevented Catalonia participating in sports such as roller hockey, a prohibition which may well have deprived the world of an international champion side in this sport. They used all their international influence to make other countries' federations vote against Catalan participation. But we feel sure one day Catalan sport will get universal recognition. Even a man as opposed to Catalan rights as Juan Antonio Samaranch is on record as admitting that the day Catalans really put their minds to it, there would be no stopping their path to official international status.

What happens to individual players who refuse to play for Spain?

There have been several cases. They make things impossible for them! It is the case of Oleguer Presas,[2] an FC Barcelona defender who was the pet enemy of the Spanish media and bawled at at all the non-Catalan grounds he played on. However, such was the pressure applied against him that some say his move to Dutch football may have been caused by it. But his is not the only case. There are others too. There are players in various sports who have refused to play for the Spanish team and have suffered sanctions for doing so. Not to play for Spain can jeopardize a player's entire career. So the accusation that it is us who politicize things is quite absurd.

Media

Montserrat Armengou
A TV documentarist who denounces Franco

When TV documentary-makers Montserrat Armengou and Ricard Belis went to Argentina to show their latest film on political repression in Franco's Spain, Armengou found herself wondering 'who on earth is going to take an interest in a film like ours in a country with a dictatorial record as bleak as Argentina's?' Despite her fears, the response to their film Els Nens Perduts del Franquisme (titled Franco's Forgotten Children in English) was overwhelming. 'Indian community chiefs and Argentinian mothers of the disappeared, with their white scarves on their heads, queued up for an hour to embrace us,' she remembers, with more than a trace of emotion in her eye. 'They saw that the forced adoption and disappearance of the children of victims which they had suffered in South and Central America had occurred on an incomparably wider scale in Franco's Spain.' Since then their films have had a major impact on the political documentary scene worldwide: 'Les grands documentaires de la petite télévision catalane' was the way one Le Monde journalist described their work.

Armengou sees it as 'a great privilege' to have gotten to know the people she has met making her films. One of her only regrets, on that score, is that the British Isles has not been as receptive as others, particularly with regard to the excellent film she and her colleague Ricard Belis made about Ramon Parera, the remarkable Catalan engineer who built the world's first purpose-built civilian air-raid shelters in Catalonia during the Civil War. Why should that interest Britons? Because during the Blitz, his deep air-raid shelter project was unwisely shelved by the Churchill government in favour of the smaller Anderson shelters, even though these were little more than corrugated-iron sheds planted in people's back gardens! One American journalist claimed at the time that 'they wouldn't protect Londoners against flying marrows'. How many lives did the abandoning of Parera's project cost? And all because—as the film reveals—the Conservative element in the War Cabinet feared that collective underground shelters might encourage negative group dynamics, such as the contagion of despair, or even the spread of subversive left-wing ideas.

Armengou had always wanted to be a journalist. She says she would have loved to have lived during the Second Republic and Civil War period. She sees herself as forming part of a group that has a 'mission', which is to draw people's attention to the fact that the transition from dictatorship in Spain was in no way the profound process it had been in South Africa, Italy, Argentina, or Germany. 'Why was Spain's case so different?' she asks wryly. 'Why were those responsible for a cruel dictatorship not only forgiven but also permitted to lead the process of democratization in their own interest?' Armengou is aware of the 'nuisance' her work represents today for the heirs of the Francoist regime who still yield so much power in Spain. 'It gives people a new dimension through which to perceive the present,' she points out. 'In question-and-answer sessions after screenings, the debate often revolves around why so little has been done to change things,' she adds, tongue in cheek. In reply, she often resorts to fumbled 'excuses' about the nature of the Transición, a period of change she judges to be have been pitifully short-lived.

Would your work as a documentary film-maker have been the same if you had been born in a more 'normal' country?

Almost certainly not. If things had been otherwise, I might have done research into the lost tribes of the Amazon, or the latest advances in malaria vaccination! The absence of State policies regarding the Transition from dictatorship, the amnesia regarding that period and the lack of justice, truth and redress for victims, is what has made some independent associations, concerned journalists, and forensic experts take on the role of historical 'fire-fighters'. It's what the French call *le devoir du mémoire*. And that task has largely been undertaken from Catalonia because, although the Historical Memory people are powerful throughout the State, the only TV channel that has promoted investigative journalism on our recent past is Televisió de Catalunya (TV3).[1] Spanish public TV (TVE) has more often obstructed it! When we produced *Franco's Forgotten Children*, the Spanish Parliament's TV control commission debated whether the documentary ought to be broadcast State-wide, and decided against it. OK, this was in a tough period, when the Partido Popular was in government. They said they had 'better things to broadcast!' And they did. For example, a documentary on the issue of 'exile' made by the Pablo Iglesias Foundation.[2] When an exhibition was organized in parallel to that documentary, the King himself was asked to inaugurate it, as he too was considered to have been an 'exile'![3] What more need I say?

An Argentinian journalist jokingly accused you of 'endeavouring to break the Agreement of the Transition'.

Argentinians do tend to be very verbose and flattering! Ricard Belis and I have often thought that the launch of *Franco's Forgotten Children*, in January 2002, marked a turning point in this regard. Its success was due to the fact that it appeared at the right time and in the right place, as well as to the magnificent work carried out by historians showing that the repression on one side and the other had not been the same. Francoist repression was far greater, in all senses, both during the war itself and after it. Just weeks before Franco died, death sentences were still being carried out against political dissidents. No-one was talking yet in terms of 'recovering historical memory', an expression used then only by a handful of specialists. Our documentary opened a Pandora's box regarding Francoist repression. I think we brought the stark truth into viewers' sitting-rooms. As far as I am concerned, it was fascist repression from beginning to end. With our first documentary we let rip, enabling our audiences to know that the kind of things we had associated with distant Argentina—events that made us sob on our sofas at home—had actually occurred in our own back yard, and on a much greater scale!

We have always seen ourselves as free journalists selling exclusive reports. Nowadays exclusive reports have lost most of their moral character. They tend to centre on photographs of naked starlets on remote beaches. We plugged into a different line of exclusive journalism. In *Franco's Forgotten Children* we set out to show that the regime kidnapped children, and in *El Comboi dels 927 (927 on the Train to Hell)* we revealed, as a scoop, the fact that the very first Nazi train that took family-loads of prisoners to a concentration camp in Western Europe was not one carrying Jews, as might have been imagined, but Spanish Republicans, many of whom were Catalans. And when we brought out the documentary on Ramon Parera, we were the first to show that, when Britain was threatened by the Blitz, civil defence was largely ignored. It is in this sense that we hold up the documentary as a means of recovering historical memory.

How has this involvement with the Civil War affected you as a person?

Intensely. I had always been rather cocksure about my 'professional detachment' from things like suffering. I thought I could see things like a doctor who, after surgery hours, can just switch off from all the blood and gore. How wrong I was! I have only recently understood the emotional burden that this job heaps on you when you come into contact with victims of dictatorship or their relatives. It came home to me with a vengeance last year when I suddenly collapsed with a fierce bout of anaemia. I realized that unveiling

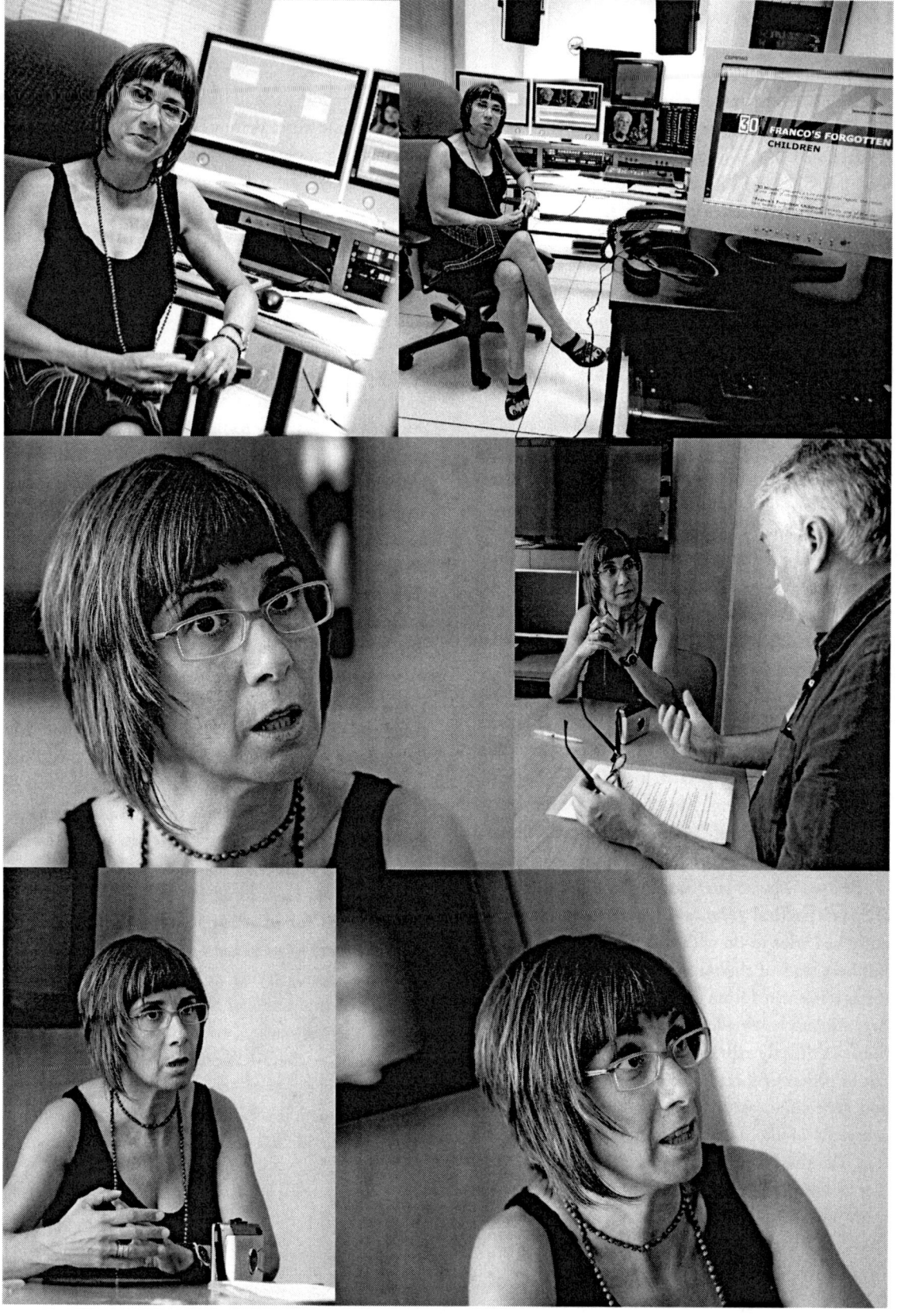

so many personal tragedies was not something that came free of charge! Despite side effects like that, the satisfaction I feel is immense. I think we've done a good job. The pain I have seen at the graveside when people recover relatives they lost seventy years ago is something indescribable. They are often humble, simple people, politically very unaware, yet capable of expressing a moving language of justice and forgiveness. I have learnt so much from them. What is sad is that redress is so desperately slow that I'm afraid a lot of the last survivors will be dead before they obtain any real satisfaction.

Why did the wave of documentaries on Francoism come so late, over twenty-five years after the dictator's death?

The fact that TV3 took it upon itself to go for that kind of programme was a key factor. Although it was risky for a relatively small television producer to approach the question of historical memory, audiences for which were thought to be limited, Catalan television went for it. TV3 has also backed this line of documentary with the work of Dolors Genovès, Josep Rovira, Felip Solé, Montserrat Besses and others. Many of our programs have had audiences five times larger than had been expected. Joan Salvat—currently head of the documentary section and my immediate superior as director of *30 Minuts*, the programme I work for—has given us unfailing support in this.

But yes, why so late? Bearing in mind the nature of Spain's political *Transición*, ignorance and fear obviously had a lot to do with this. Catalonia and Spain still bear scars of the trauma they were put through. It was transmitted from generation to generation. The Argentinians know a lot about that. The first generation was directly repressed by Franco: exterminated, put in prison or forced into exile or hiding. The second generation, apart from families who were fully conscious of the situation, grew up in silence and fear. The third and fourth generations are the ones that have started to scratch the surface in search of the truth. But there is still a tremendous amount of pain, and the feeling prevails that the truth could once again become a synonym of danger, even death. I've interviewed people too paralysed to utter a word, even quite recently. Then there are people who just can't stop weeping. Some elderly people tell you that they are not afraid for themselves but for their children. And lots of people have recognized themselves as victims within the context of the documentary. Some had spent years blaming themselves for what happened—the deaths of their fathers, the shaven heads of their mothers, their offspring constantly insulted and looked down on at school—and when they see the documentary they realize that their experience was not unique, that it was shared by people with different ideologies and circumstances around the whole State. They suddenly understand that they formed part of a systematic plan which involved extermination and persecution. That obviously has not brought back their lost father, who lies in some unmarked grave, but it makes them see that they were victims of repression, not mere victims of the whims of 'that Falangist we were unlucky enough to have in our village'. But I've also come across sadder cases: people who indirectly end up blaming their father or grandfather: 'My father was a good man, but he did insist on meddling in politics. My mother warned him "You keep out of trouble!" And then, of course, they took him away, and just look what became of the rest of us.' In the end, that schoolteacher or trade unionist father—who may even have stood in elections—was all too often blamed for what happened, incredible though that may seem to us today. I'm astounded when I see Spain desperately trying to be accepted as a normal member of international forums and conventions—such as the G8—when, to all intents and purposes, it's a country where fear still exists and where such basic human rights as access to knowledge about a recent dictatorship are still vetoed, not to mention the refusal to provide full redress for its victims.

Some people say that all those things ought to be forgotten.

Yesterday I was phoned by a journalist from *The Times* who asked me just that, saying 'Why do people want to know what happened? Isn't it better to forget?' Well, I'm not sure if yesterday wasn't my day, or what, but I just came right out with this answer, which took the form of a question: 'Can you imagine a society, such as Britain, in which, years after a period marked by mass executions by the roadsides, no-one wished to find out what happened and who was responsible?' It did the trick. He really had no answer. Here we live just a bit to the south of Britain but we too are human beings. So it shouldn't be that surprising that we too should want to know about our past and find out what happened. It is a vital step if wounds are ever to be healed.

Does the education system inform young Catalans adequately about their history and the significance of the Civil War?

Catalonia is a country where primary school children are virtually clueless regarding the Republic, the Civil War, and the Franco regime. At best, the issues are dealt with in passing, very superficially. They may get better coverage in some secondary schools, where project work may occasionally be done if teachers are so inclined. Survivors of these periods may even be brought into class to tell their stories. But in general there's much more of a tendency to dwell on the Roman Empire than on the Second Republic, and that's a real shame, because you need to understand the Republic in order to understand our current democracy and all its shortcomings.

What about the role of the Spanish media?

I often wonder what European or American viewers think when in our films we show snippets of debates recorded in Madrid and broadcast on Spanish radio or television. They hear hacks saying that Spanish has been banned in Catalonia, that children are prevented from learning Spanish at school and therefore cannot understand the language… all sorts of rubbish. I think we should be implacable. Take them to court over it! The trouble is we take it lying down. We behave as if it didn't bother us. We ought to be a lot more belligerent.

Josep Gifreu
Catalan media expert

Josep Gifreu is Emeritus Professor of Communications at the Pompeu Fabra University (UPF) in Barcelona. An expert on the mass media, he is a member of the Philological Section of the Institute of Catalan Studies, the most prestigious academic institution in the country.[1] As a researcher and senior adviser on communication and culture, Gifreu's views are much sought after by politicians and those running the mass media. He has written prolifically, especially on the difficulties involved in recreating a communication system associated with a stateless and persecuted language like Catalan. El meu país: Narratives i combats per la identitat [My Country: Narratives and arguments for identity] (2001) *stands out as a more personal and political take on the issue. Gifreu writes regularly for the Catalan language dailies* Avui *and* El Punt, *as well as for the weekly* El Temps. *He is also an avid reader of newspapers. 'Preferably American,' he states, 'but hardly ever Spanish.'*

Josep Gifreu was brought up in the 'province'[2] of Girona, on a farm near Banyoles, the city where the 1992 Olympic rowing events were held. As a young man he opted for Barcelona, a city he is in love with. 'It's big enough to be cosmopolitan,' he insists, 'yet small enough for you to feel at home in.' As he has grown older, he has tended to 'go back to the land', and loves to hike in the mountains whenever possible. He loves 'hunting' mushrooms—as they say in the Girona area—a national passion among Catalans. He pleads a distaste for the sea, which he rejects as 'treacherous', in contrast with high mountains, which he sees as 'solid and safe'. He includes music, the cinema, and creative writing among his frustrated vocations, although he doesn't rule out the possibility of one day trying his hand at writing a 'short' novel. As regards other pastimes, he proclaims himself to be a devout polytheist, professing complete devotion to the Holy Trinity: Bach the father, Beethoven the son, and Mozart the Holy Spirit.

What might foreign observers find interesting about the question of communications and the mass media in Catalonia?

Over and above the difficulties Catalonia has in controlling her own mass media, any democrat might well feel a certain degree of discomfort in observing the democratic deficit that this field suffers from here. Catalonia, unlike all member States of the EU, in general lacks the instruments with which to create its own natural communications environment.

What effects does this have?

It greatly impedes the possibilities of allowing people to feel part of a normal community. This would serve as a necessary common starting point. Let's call it 'Point Zero'. Starting out from Point Zero, when you are surrounded by masses of people with all kinds of allegiances to different national identities—as well as doubts about the community itself—would help put an end to a situation in which so many people feel either excluded or schizophrenic.

Schizophrenic, did you say?

Indeed. Plenty of Catalans suffer from schizophrenia. We feel part of a national community, and yet we have to make a huge effort to find our footing in the real world we live in. We are therefore far removed from the Point Zero that other Europeans start out from quite naturally. It's hard not to feel bitter about the lack of normality. That applies even to things as apparently innocuous as advertising. As soon as it made its appearance on Spanish public television (TVE) in the Sixties, it became a major tool in the homogenization of the population. It got a twenty-year start on advertising in other languages, such as Catalan. The structure of the large mass media in Spain is an inheritance from the Franco period. The language of advertising has never been normalized. Catalan TV (TV3)[3] is peppered daily, even today, with commercials in Spanish. Yet no ads in Catalan can be shown on any Spanish channel.

What other negative effects does this lack of control cause?

There are several major ones. One is them is the fact that we have no say in the regulation of the frequency spectrum or in the structure of the State-wide television channels. The Catalan-speaking countries are 'occupied' by a series of Madrid-based TV channels which have Spanish as their only language which account for 80% of the audience. For years, Spanish law prevented the creation of private TV channels in Catalan, which was not the case for channels in Spanish.

Why did that happen?

The Catalan parties really failed to see how important it was to control the media framework for the recovery of our national culture. A key question in the future will be the ability to create audiovisual products and other key elements in the vast digital TV industry. If we cannot adequately produce and distribute digital TV, our future will be bleak. The competition we are going to face is ferocious. That goes for the hugely popular video games sector, too. Today nearly the whole of the market is covered by products in Spanish or English. TV production requires hefty resources. At present we have a situation in which, although 90% of the population of Catalonia understands Catalan, viewers have to do 80% of their TV viewing in Spanish. The claims of the Rodríguez Zapatero government that it supports the linguistic and cultural pluralism of the State can only be seen as a joke. It was only recently, with the introduction of Digital Terrestrial TV, that any licences were granted for the creation of autonomous channels in Catalan. Canal 8 was created, although its contents are by no means all in Catalan.[4] But the head-start obtained by other private channels has made it hard for such products to compete.

How do you think Digital Terrestrial TV will affect Catalan television and the normalization of the language?

DTT has been sold as a step towards a wider range of programming, with a far better signal and screen definition. But it basically means more efficient use

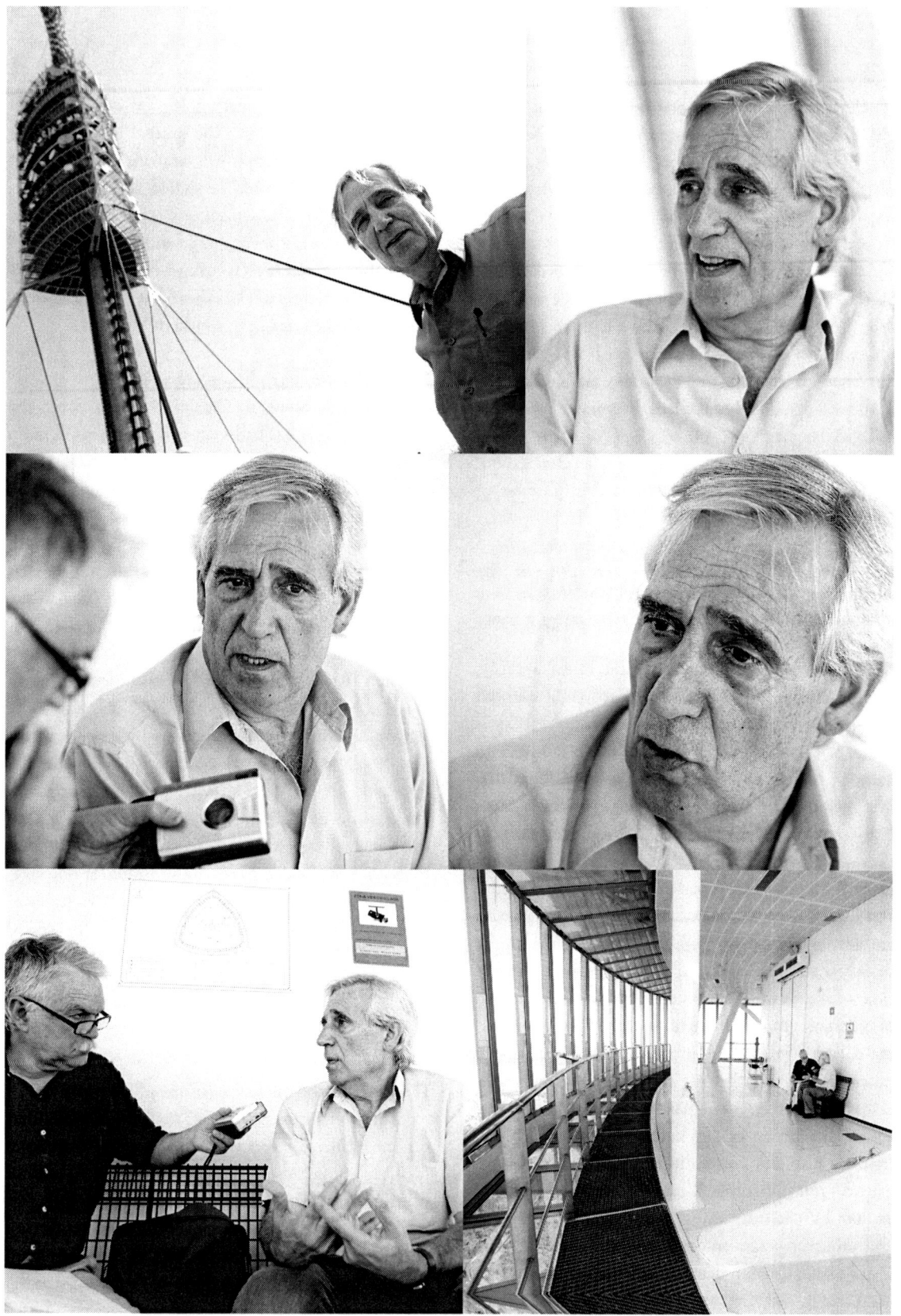

of television space by the State channels. For example, people in the Pyrenean counties of Catalonia may have had trouble receiving some of the State and conventional channels in the recent past, perhaps getting only six or seven, of which three were in Catalan. Now they'll receive over thirty, with excellent quality, and almost all of them will be in Spanish or English. So the proportion available in Catalan will suddenly drop from 40% to 10%. Disney Channel, in Spanish, will get universal coverage and will compete directly with the children's programs on Catalan TV. If there are suddenly excellent alternatives available in other languages, people may opt for them. When these changes were discussed and policies decided on, no attention whatever was paid to the question of our language.

You have maintained that the creation of the autonomous regions in the 1978 Constitution may have obstructed the chances of recovering a more unified Catalan identity…

Although it may seem paradoxical, I think it's true. The territorial model introduced in 1978 allowed for—and even encouraged—the creation of 'ministates' within the State that were often tempted to 'tamper' with their historical and cultural identities. The regions were given considerable powers in areas like language, education, culture and communication—fields very much associated with the expression of local identity. On paper that may sound all right. But these powers were often exploited by autonomous authorities for strictly political reasons, such as the desire to place new-fangled 'identities' in confrontation with each other, in order to prevent the creation of common ground. In the case of the Catalan-speaking countries, this phenomenon largely impaired the possibility of coordinating differing historical traditions, the kind of step that is necessary to achieve the normalization of any culture if it is to prosper. In both new and conventional media creation, this caused great difficulties. Currently there are as many as 200 TV channels available for viewers in Spanish and other languages throughout the State. But there is not one in Catalan that can be watched throughout the Catalan-speaking countries. As a result, Catalans have very little idea what's going on in Valencia or Mallorca, and vice versa. The mutual ignorance that prevailed under Franco is still rampant today. TV and radio stations that could be shared with other Catalan-speaking areas have been systematically prevented by the State, using a number of different ploys. Currently the *Guardia Civil* is being sent in at the order of conservative judges to close down the booster stations offering TV in Catalan to southern Valencia.

Is the situation in radio as bad as in TV?

It's a little better in Catalonia-proper. Since the 1980s Catalonia has had increasingly successful radio stations, both private and public. Their share of the market comes close to 50%, which is remarkable. This is due to the fact that the Catalan government is responsible for granting a number of wavelength licenses. The positive figures for radio indicate that the low figures for TV consumption in Catalan are due to the appalling communication model that is applied. The range of programmes offered by radio is much larger, and so too are the audiences. Radio is a much cheaper medium than TV. It is also more successful than the written press, which accounts for just 20–25% of the market share. The situation has improved greatly thanks to the launch of the Catalan editions of *El Periódico* and *La Vanguardia*, and the Catalan-only edition of *Ara*.[5] The weeklies and monthlies in Catalan have a lot of room for improvement. The newsstands offer pitifully few publications in Catalan. The popular sports dailies *Sport* and *Mundo Deportivo* are only available in Spanish. There is also a sports daily in Catalan called *El 9* which is sold independently, but also as part of *El Punt* and *Avui* dailies.

What about the on-line editions of newspapers?

These offer better prospects than TV. The fact that on-line readership seems to be the trend is positive for Catalan, because it doesn't involve the expense of printing and distributing paper editions. In fact, this is probably what kept *La Vanguardia* from producing an edition in Catalan for so long. It is encouraging that on-line access to the website of *El Periódico* in the two languages is roughly fifty-fifty. That's good news, because it means the potential market for readers of the press in Catalan is considerable when quality options are available. The number of on-line readers of *Avui* has also grown in recent years. There are other successful on-line general information websites in Catalan, such as *VilaWeb*, *El Racó Català*, *Singular Digital*, and *El Debat*, which are well established. Catalan television's web page, the most popular of all, has about a million visits a month. There are other internet sectors that are almost completely normalized, such as the websites of all the universities in the Catalan-speaking countries. This would have been unimaginable ten years ago. In addition, countless small enterprises and individuals are creating their own blogs and web pages in Catalan. This is a positive development for a lesser-spoken language, as it is for lower-budget enterprises that can thus afford to make a contribution to normalization.

What threats do the media in Catalan face?

The threats and limitations to Catalan in the media are varied. Sadly, some must be considered more or less irreversible. Others depend on conditions laid down in Spanish law. You often hear people saying that the problem is the 'free market'. But the market isn't free! The communications market—both public and private—and the market for cultural products and their distribution are 100% regulated by the State. As for cyberspace, although Catalan has a very strong foothold, globalization and the presence of other languages and newcomer cultures in our midst make the operation much more complicated than could have been expected a few years back. As regards the mass immigration of non-Catalan speakers, the need to make our language and culture visible and useful to them is a major challenge. There are two tools currently available to confront this: education and the media. But whereas schooling and language 'immersion' campaigns in Catalan seem to ensure the initial integration of newcomers, the question is whether the media will be able to continue making Catalan visible and attractive to them after they leave school. In that sense, Spanish, with its limitless resources, is a serious threat. This is one of the big problems we must face, and one in which the media in Catalan will have to play a decisive role. But the State does nothing to help. On the contrary.

You've often spoken about an emotional deficit that Catalans suffer from because they have not been able to access some cultural areas in their own language.

The question of emotions and passions associated with nations or communities is something that is now being researched and has become quite fashionable. I have written about this subject. It is important in the creation of the collective imagination, and public opinion. Catalans are at a great disadvantage in this sense, compared to other Europeans. For example, Catalans are forced to experience films by linguistic 'proxy', because we can hardly ever see films in our own language as most Europeans do in theirs. We have had to watch almost all of them in Spanish, usually through dubbing rather than the more civilized use of subtitles. So in our experience, Paul Newman is a Spanish-speaker! So normally we only experience real-life situations in Catalan, but not those on cinema screens or, until relatively recently, on TV. Apart from the odd film in Catalan, the first real chance we had to enjoy TV fiction in Catalan was with *Dallas* in 1983, when other Europeans had been doing so for decades. This means that immigrants who seek incorporation into our culture have an added problem. But going back to your question, the nation is basically a 'religious' community, in the sense that it involves ingredients like identification, loyalty and automatic responses. Albert Camus—who incidentally seems to have had Catalan ancestry—used to say that captains and soldiers are equals before the nation. Nations make people equal in feelings and in their sense of identification. Emotions play an important role in identity. More so, perhaps, than reason. So the importance of being brave and going into this question is obvious if clichés are to be challenged and solutions for identity issues are to be found.

Pedro Morón de la Fuente
An Andalusian-born Catalanist

Pedro Morón de la Fuente, born in Granada in 1951, is one of over a million Andalusian-born citizens of Catalonia. His home is in Sant Boi de Llobregat, a satellite city just south of Barcelona that is famous for two things: Rugby football—it is the home of the Santboiana team—and the revered burial place of Rafael de Casanova, the last defender of Catalonia in the famous 1714 siege of Barcelona that marked the end of the War of the Spanish Succession. He was the Chief Councillor of Catalonia's capital when the city fell to the joint armies of Castile and France. The subsequent installation of the Bourbon dynasty on the Spanish throne spelled disaster for the Catalan nation and its age-old institutions, which were largely dismantled as thousands were forced into exile. Sant Boi de Llobregat was not surprisingly chosen as the venue for the first post-Franco Diada[1] rally, less than a year after the dictator's death. On that day, September 11, 1976, some 60,000 demonstrators defied the threatening utterances made by the still-intact Francoist nomenklatura and gathered there, an event that many remember with nostalgia. Pedro Morón—twenty-five years old at the time—is one of them.

With a Catalan wife and two children, Morón's family is typical of many that bring together Catalan and Andalusian spouses. He has worked as a journalist for newspapers, radio, and television, and immigration is one of his pet subjects. He is the author of several books about Andalusians in Catalonia, the most well-known of which is probably Els altres andalusos, la qüestió nacional de Catalunya [The Other Andalusians, the Catalan National Question], *the title of which recalls that of the most famous book on immigration in Catalonia:* Els altres catalans [The Other Catalans] *by Francesc Candel, published in 1964.[2] Pedro Morón is also the founder and editor of the magazine* Nas de Barraca, *president of the Sant Boi 'House of Andalusia', and runs an association called Catalònia Acord. Both the latter organizations have the central aim of encouraging a deeper understanding between Catalans and Andalusians in Catalonia.*

You were born in Andalusia and yet you consider yourself a Catalanist. How come?

When I arrived in Catalonia I was just ten. I was virtually illiterate but I was sent to school here. I have always lived in suburban towns with large immigrant populations, and I've come to understand why many of my fellow Andalusians fail to fully integrate despite the many years—in many cases, over fifty—they have lived here. Over the years, I've also become very well acquainted with the kind of bias some immigrants have against almost everything that is Catalan. It's an attitude I have come to see as something clearly fostered in Madrid. It's sad, but there are Andalusians living in the suburbs who have been receptive to anti-Catalan feeling. It is a phenomenon that is not always dealt with properly by some local institutions and parties, may I add. There always seems to be someone at hand to whisper 'we're in Spain!' into their ears. Being aware of that has instilled in me a strong sense of solidarity with the Catalan people. It is a feeling that has been nurtured in me as I have become more acquainted with the country's age-old history, and by a growing awareness of how the Catalans lost their rights, *manu militari*, some three hundred years ago. But that kind of information is not always available for people. Needless to say, I feel Andalusian too. And I believe the country I was born in also deserves to be independent if it so chooses.

Are there many Andalusians in Catalonia who feel the same way as you do?

I believe that there are more than some opinion polls might lead you to believe. There are plenty of 'New Catalans'—a term used to describe those born outside Catalonia—who are fed up with the treatment Catalonia is getting in some Spanish media. They perceive how, year after year, the State budget investments announced for Catalonia are either scandalously low or simply not fulfilled. They also see how Catalans keep on losing purchasing power with respect to other regions, while the taxes they pay are lavishly handed over to these regions in the name of 'solidarity'. All too often it is the governing party in Madrid that reaps the benefit from this practice, while Catalonia continues to be portrayed as a mean, spoilt region. Though quite unjust, it is a view that is intensely cultivated in Spanish media while the Spanish government does little, if anything, to put things straight. Now I am proud to say more and more Andalusian-born Catalans are 'coming out of the closet' and joining other Catalans in complaining about this kind of treatment. Today they are not so worried about sticking their necks out, even if it means being criticized by fellow Andalusians. Indeed, many of us have become confident enough to take part in the local Referendums for Independence held in 2009 and 2010. The truth is that more and more of us see Catalonia as our homeland.

You mention institutions and parties that have the wrong attitude on immigration. What do you mean exactly?

In my view there are some institutions and parties that go to suspiciously great lengths to promote and reinforce the old cultural and emotional ties of immigrants from other parts of Spain to their places of birth. I say 'suspiciously' because in my view they do so for political reasons that have little to do with Catalanism and integration. It is particularly true of some municipal councils. The Baix Llobregat area, south of Barcelona, could be described as a large-scale laboratory set up to experiment with anti-integration policies. It's hard not to see this as a strategy aimed at preventing the natural incorporation into the country of the very large number of immigrants from other areas in Spain who settled here in the period between 1950 and 1980. This suspicion is reinforced when we see this practice is more or less openly funded by the more neo-Lerrouxist[3] wing of the Socialist party, associated with leaders such as José Bono, Juan Carlos Rodríguez Ibarra, Alfonso Guerra, and Manuel Chaves.[4] On the ground, Josep Maria Sala has for years been responsible for implementing these policies, which are now being applied with new, non-EU immigrants.[5] The party is now organizing various groups based on all the countries of origin of the new immigrants (North Africa, South America, Eastern Europe, Sub-Saharan Africa, etc.) with the objective of continuing to divide the Catalan people and thus reinforce Spanish identity and the Spanish party

system. It's as clear as that. The idea is to surreptitiously isolate them from what they term 'Catalan nationalism'. They do so under the cover of the apparently attractive concept of 'multiculturalism', one of the major promoters of which is one *Col.lectiu Crisol*, which for years took absolutely no interest in Catalan culture whatsoever.[6] Yet it is the PSC's reference point as regards popular culture.

One ex-secretary general of the PSC, Raimon Obiols,[7] warned that the Catalan socialist party was running the risk of becoming a Peña Rociera.[8] What do you think he meant by that?

Well maybe you should ask him! But it's perfectly true. Since the arrival of democracy in 1975, the once Catalanist PSC has slowly but surely metamorphosed into the Spanish PSOE. The Catalanists in the party have steadily lost power since the seventies. In the Barcelona metropolitan region, where the Socialists have almost total hegemony, it is the Spanish wing of the PSC that is now all-powerful. The Catalan PSC practically disappeared with the underhand dismissal—for dismissal it was, disguised or not—of Catalan president Pasqual Maragall in 2006. At the 2004 Sitges Congress, the more Catalanist leaders of the PSC had already been ousted from the key posts of responsibility by their PSOE counterparts. So it's hardly surprising that Obiols should have expressed his worries about the future of the party. The PSC's obsession is that Andalusia- or Extremadura-born 'clients' must be kept happy in order to maintain power and votes in Catalonia. Hence the constellation of Rociero festivals, *Ferias de Abril* and Holy Week processions—completely Andalusian in spirit—that are fostered throughout Catalonia. This is clearly done to ensure an on-going 'captive vote' of Andalusian immigrants. Now that non-Spanish immigration is taking its place, we may well soon be seeing these same Socialist politicians dancing sambas, sirtakis, the dance of the seven veils, or whatever—anything except the Catalan *sardana* of course—with a view to keeping the votes pouring in.

You seem to be particularly critical of the *Feria de Abril*, the large-scale Andalusian festival held in the Barcelona area every spring?[9]

I have never been against the celebration of the *Feria de Abril* in Catalonia. What I have been against, for over thirty years now, is that it should have become a private business exploited by very few people at great profit. I'm by no means alone in feeling unhappy about this particular event today. But for years to criticize it publicly meant being black-listed while crying in the wilderness. Some people used to regard me as a renegade and politically incorrect for thinking as I do and speaking my mind. But now such criticism has even reached the mainstream media.

Can you give me more details?

Certainly. I think it is relevant to point out that the man running this whole show, one Francisco García Prieto, President of FECAC (the *Federación de Entidades Culturales Andaluzas en Cataluña*, or Federation of Andalusian Cultural Entities in Catalonia), does so in a very peculiar way, and enjoys an uncanny degree of influence in Catalan society. I would even speak of impunity. The business monopoly he holds over the event has been criticized by various Catalan institutions. The mass media, too, have at times denounced his intrigues and the shady business interests involved. García Prieto, however, appears to be untouchable, and enjoys a position of immunity and absolute power as the head of what some call 'the Andalusian community of Catalonia'. This is a 'post' he has held for over fifty years, though no-one remembers his ever being voted into it. He is generally thought to enjoy protection in high places. No politician would dream of meddling with him for fear of losing cart-loads of votes. The result is that he receives vast subsidies and handles budgets of gigantic proportions to run an Andalusian fair that lasts even longer than the Seville fair it purports to emulate! The million-dollar question is, why does all this happen in Barcelona and not, say, in Madrid, where there are also plenty of Andalusians? Excuse me for asking, but might it not have something to do with sidelining Catalan culture?

As an Andalusian, what do you think of the fact that the vehicular language of education of Catalonia is Catalan? What about those who would rather it were Castilian?

Maybe one should start by saying that Catalan is the language of Catalonia in the same way that Spanish is that of Andalusia. In this regard let me ask you what the British Government would answer if people demanded their education in French because they were of French origin? Need I answer? Catalan needs to be rescued from centuries of being overshadowed by the Spanish language and downtrodden by the Spanish ruling class. Physically and psychologically. It was forbidden in Franco's day, and today it still very much suffers the consequences. Can you image what the situation of English would be today if it had been forbidden for most of the last century? It is logical that Catalans should feel that the recovery of their language is one of their main priorities. A great deal has been done to bring back the language and the results are, on the whole, quite satisfactory. Catalan literature has never been as widely available as it is today. Catalan has never been more widely spoken, in terms of numbers of speakers. Likewise, protests about education in Catalan are minimal, almost anecdotal. So results are being achieved.

An Andalusian-born Socialist has presided over the Catalan Generalitat Government.[10] As an Andalusian yourself, what do you feel about that?

The fact is that anyone who lives in this small country can become president of the Catalan Government. That is the basis of the democracy we enjoy and it's protected by law. So, logically, José Montilla had every right to stand as a candidate for the presidency of the Catalan Government. He even went to some lengths to learn to speak Catalan properly. But it cannot be overlooked that Catalonia is a nation without a State, with a whole range of issues that need resolving in order to bring things back to normal. In this sense, we might well ask ourselves whether Sr. Montilla—who in 2005 denied that Catalonia had historic national rights—is the most appropriate person to lead the country at a time like this. Not because he is not capable of doing so, but because the party to which the Catalan Socialists are inextricably bound (the PSOE) is clearly opposed to Catalan identity and self-government in all but a token way. I have a friend who says that the situation is a little bit like giving a nurse with a vampire husband responsibility for a hospital blood bank! But I have nothing personal against Montilla. In fact, I often used to think that a political profile like his might one day enable him to attain the post he now holds.

Vicent Partal
"A language is a dialect with Google coverage"

Vicent Partal Montesinos, born in Bétera, not far north of the city of Valencia, in 1960, is a Valencian journalist based in Barcelona. He is the current director of VilaWeb, the largest and most influential online newspaper in the Catalan language. Partal has also worked for other media outlets such as El Temps, the Diari de Barcelona, TVE, Catalunya Ràdio, El Punt and La Vanguardia, amongst others. He now presents L'Internauta, a programme that is a must for those wanting to update their knowledge about cutting-edge information technology and communications in Catalonia.

Partal is considered one of the pioneers of the Internet in the Catalan Countries. In 1994 he created what he terms 'the first online information system south of the Pyrenees' with the magazine El Temps, which was given the name El Temps Online (www.eltemps.net). The following year he founded Partal, Maresma & Associats, a pioneer consulting company specialising in the use of the Internet and facilitating access to it. This company gave rise to the Catalan web directory Infopista, which in 1996 led to the appearance of the so-called 'Catalan highway', which now has over fifty editions worldwide. Partal has been awarded the Catalan National Journalism Prize, the Barcelona City Journalism Prize and the Jaume I Honour Prize, among others, for the pioneering work he has undertaken in the field of digital journalism. He has also written several books on international politics and the Internet, and in addition he holds the post of vice-president of the European Journalism Centre.

Catalan is a surprisingly widely-used language on the Internet. Isn't this odd for a 'minority' culture without a State of its own?

I think there are several reasons to explain this. First I think we must start off by saying that, in general, Catalans have a flair, almost an obsession, for what is modern and new. The Internet was fascinating to us from day one. In addition, because the Internet is an instrument that suffers much less from political and economic restrictions than conventional mass media did in the past, it is particularly attractive and useful to cultures such as ours. It enables popular initiatives to prosper. For example, although at present there are very few magazines and no daily newspapers printed in Catalan in Valencia, there is an impressive array of websites in Catalan throughout the region. Many of them are first-rate. The Internet enables what is natural to flourish, because the economic requirements are not so demanding. It for the first time enables Catalan-speakers who live abroad to be informed in Catalan and live part of their lives in our language. And this change is making a very substantial mark on things. The Internet is one area of Catalan life that has made huge progress and that contributes to raising the morale of many Catalans throughout the world. It is said that over half of the Internet communication in our country is conducted in Catalan. Google is one of the most well-informed enterprises in the world, and they have always gone for Catalan in a big way. It is one of the fifty languages they operate in. Indeed, Catalan was the first 'Stateless language' that got Google coverage. This was largely thanks to the extraordinary contribution made by Lluís Izaguirre in developing a formula for applying Catalan to the Internet.

The introduction of the domain '.cat' has also been a major success.

You can say that again. This was the idea of a lawyer called Amadeu Abril. The fact that the first 'culture' as such in the world to have its own domain accepted on the Internet should have been ours is an extraordinary feat. Previously there had been an attempt to have the domain '.ct' accepted for Catalonia as a country, an initiative that the Catalan Parliament backed but which was not successful. The obstacles for this were immense and clearly political. But Abril had a brainwave, which was to bypass the political difficulties involved in getting a national domain and get a language domain. He focused his attention on a category of domains that grouped together not national communities but other sorts of homogeneous communities. For example, there is one for museums and another for education. Abril argued that if these communities had domains, maybe the Catalan-speaking community could too. An association of five people was created to promote this idea. They had to act in an almost clandestine manner, with only indirect support from the institutions. All parties involved fulfilled their roles to perfection, and cooperation between all concerned was magnificent. The technological requirements were quite a challenge, but we managed to cope.

Were there obstacles to this process?

Yes indeed. Our greatest obstacle was, of course, the Spanish administration. But luckily they were slow to react, and only did so at the last moment when it was too late. They never thought we would be able to pull it off. There came a moment when ICANN[1] had to ask those governments involved (Spain, France, Andorra and Italy, all of which have Catalan-speaking regions) if they had anything against the creation of the '.cat' domain. Although at first they came out saying it was a private matter on which they had no objections, the truth is that they secretly put pressure on the US Government to get it stopped. But the US Government, in true American style, asked the Spanish Government for a written complaint. They thought better of it and backed down. Opposition to our '.cat' domain also came from those who said we wanted to make a domain for cats. The animal that is! They wanted to prevent cats appearing in the domain! At first we accepted. But in the end we even managed to convince the party concerned that there were cats who spoke Catalan. They asked us, quite seriously it seems, 'how do we know if a cat speaks Catalan?' Our answer was that if a cat's owner spoke to it in Catalan, it was proof that the animal understood the

language. Not only have we achieved a way of identifying an independent Catalan Internet system, but also acknowledgement for the fact that cats can speak Catalan! All in all, the '.cat' domain, with over 50,000 users today, is a major step forward for our acknowledgement as a nation.

You are the creator of Catalonia's major on-line newspaper, VilaWeb…

Yes. We started up 15 years ago. In fact I started it up with my wife, Assumpció Maresma, who was then editor of *El Temps* magazine. Providing a solid journalistic product in Catalan was our target. We saw that the Internet might offer us new opportunities. At first we weren't even sure how! Our success can be rated by the fact that we now have 370,000 readers, according to the Nielsen research group. We are also a very respected media outlet, having won the Catalan National Journalism Prize in 2004, among others. Sometimes the mind boggles when you see how far we have come. I suppose being pioneers was important. But I also consider that we have put a lot of work into this, and have faced challenges as they cropped up. Perhaps the strangest thing about us is that we have lasted 15 years in a market where products tend to burn out pretty fast, or are pushed out of the market by competition. Perhaps the best thing about online journalism is that the whole concept of competition changes. No-one reads just one online paper. People look around, and so it makes for much more plural information-seeking habits. Another positive factor is that the Catalan online news community gets along well, and cooperation is constant.

What sort of a role can the Internet play as regards the integration of immigrants into the Catalan-speaking community?

Well, I would like to start by saying that we must have a historical perspective when looking at this question. Inevitably it will be the second or third generation born of those who come to live among us who will be prepared to use our language. I really do not see anything to be worried about here, and I think it's just a question of patience and time.

What challenges face the Catalan Internet in the future?

I think there will be major changes in the future. The Internet is now turning into the television of the future. In this sense there have been interesting developments recently. Apple, a central player in this sector, has announced that after this summer (2010), all its products will be available in Catalan. Version 4 of its mobile operating system will be available in 36 world languages, including Catalan. Google presented the Catalan version of YouTube in January, 2011 and has always been considerate towards our language. Making sure Catalan is fully available in all those areas is our most important future challenge now. We must take full advantage of the important opportunities that are now available to us, including Google's video subtitling technology. It is excellent, and if we can get Catalans used to watching subtitled films,[2] then we will be able to offer as much television as we feel like. And what's more, it's free! Maybe one day technology will provide us with immediate high-quality voice dubbing of an adequate nature.

What about the introduction of Digital Terrestrial TV?

This is a major setback for Catalan. Many experts had warned from the beginning that this was not advantageous for us. It has made the range of TV available in Spanish enormous, while the equivalent in Catalan is proportionally much smaller. In other words, it introduces a huge amount of channels in Spanish and pitifully few in Catalan. I think now is the moment to decide exactly what role Catalan is to have in the future. Despite our current political dependence, our language can compare favourably with Dutch, Finnish, Danish, Slovenian, and Hungarian, for example. We cannot expect to compete with Spanish. It is in another division. Spanish is—as I always say to tease my Spanish friends—a great American language spoken by a few Europeans. So we cannot compete with it. Neither can we compete with English, which is the only truly global language. We must also accept that we live in a multilingual world in which the romantic idea of 'one country, one language' has vanished for good. We are a country where

200 languages are spoken, and in which Catalan must aspire to being the language of national cohesion alongside others that are also spoken in our midst.

What is it that needs to be done to make a place for Catalan in the globalized world?

What we need to establish are the conditions a lesser language such as ours needs to survive in a context marked by new technologies such as the Internet and so on. We must find a new role for our language within the global framework. We should be able to offer everything that people need to participate in and feel part of the global world. We cannot afford to lag behind in any respect. For example, we must make available a view of what is going on in the world to people whose main language is Catalan. Our Internet system must give Catalans the tools with which to know about literature in Mali and current affairs in North Korea—say—at the touch of a key.

And can the Internet help to achieve this?

What the Internet currently enables us to do is to live our lives fully in Catalan. This by no means implies that we must live our lives only in Catalan. Nowadays it's absurd to aspire to living just in one language, be it Catalan, Danish, or Spanish. Perhaps this is only possible in English, and even then, I'm not too sure. So we must be prepared to accept that, though in our daily lives the use of our language is sufficient, we may have to use other languages when we need to aspire to other levels of knowledge. For leisure, work, travel, for whatever activity we engage in. So what are the basic requirements we are calling for as regards Catalan? Well, firstly, an official status for the language we speak, making it the country's common language. It must have all the attributes that make a language global today: influential mass media, education at all levels, Internet coverage—and here we even have our own domain—and high culture and universities. It is in this last field that I see the greatest threats today. But in general, I think we are doing pretty well. If the linguist Max Weinreich once said that 'a language is a dialect with an army', I now insist that a language is a dialect with Google and an Internet domain. Fortunately we now have both.

You say you are worried about the use of Catalan at the university.

I think that there is a worrying misconception about what it means to 'widen the market', so to speak, a tendency some think involves leaving Catalan out. I think it should be possible to teach all subjects in Catalan. We cannot afford to lose out on the resource of having all areas of high knowledge covered in our language. This would be a mistake. Even Cambó[3] was aware of this, dedicating great sums of money—both private and public—to having all kinds of academic texts translated into Catalan. I'm not saying some subjects may not also be studied in other languages such as English. But Catalan should be the principal language of education in our country, as Danish is in Denmark.

Are you optimistic about the future?

Yes I am. Especially if our country becomes independent, a step I think may not be as far away as some believe. Today we can say that, in contrast with other 'less-spoken' languages, Catalan is a fully global language. And this is so because Catalans are capable of fully interpreting global reality through the use of our own language. We do not need an auxiliary language to get a picture of what is going on in the world. And it is in this sense that I think Catalan has qualified as a global language in a time of huge changes. Although at times I'm not sure that Catalan society is fully aware of the vital steps that have been taken, nor of the strength of our current position.

Vicent Sanchis Llàcer was born in Valencia in 1961, and is one of many influential Valencians who have made it to the top in Barcelona.[1] *He graduated in Communication Studies from the Universitat Autònoma de Barcelona, and currently teaches journalism at the city's Universitat Ramon Llull. He is also vice-president of the prestigious 20,000-member strong cultural association Òmnium Cultural, an organization which, as its motto says, 'works for the country, the language and the culture of the Catalans'. Òmnium was responsible for convoking the million-strong July 10th demonstration in 2010. Sanchis was certainly one of the visible faces behind the march's success.*

Sanchis has been the editor, among other publications, of the magazine El Temps *and the newspaper* Avui, *both of which were founded after Franco's death. He currently heads the television channel of FC Barcelona, Barça TV, and contributes to a number of publications. He would love to hear more Catalan spoken in the streets of his home city, Valencia, like when he was a boy. 'But that's just a dream,' he fears, 'as it has been replaced by Spanish, and it would seem the process is irreversible.' It was with an essay entitled "Franco against Flash Gordon" that he won the last Joan Fuster prize, one of the most prestigious in the Catalan literary world. It deals with two issues that he is fascinated by: the censorship of comics and Francoism.*

What is the best attitude foreign observers can adopt when approaching the Catalan issue?

I think it is useful to see the Iberian Peninsula as a reality built around two states. One 'pure' state—linguistically and culturally speaking—which is Portugal, and another, more complex one, Spain, with four major cultural and political components: Catalonia, Galicia, the Basque Country, and Castile, the latter representing officialdom and doing its best to impose itself on the others. Some European countries—for instance, Great Britain and France—went to great lengths to homogenize and unify their territories. They are probably more than satisfied with what they did. And yet, in many cases, they did a lot of damage, too, and often quite brutally—for example to the Scots, the Corsicans, the North American Indians, and vast tracts of the Third World. The Castilians are doing much the same to us.

The international media do not seem to share that view.

No. When foreign correspondents come to Spain, they are automatically based in Madrid, so they tend to live fully immersed in the paranoia, the complexes, the angers and delights of the State capital. They rarely go out of their way to get 'decontaminated'. When they're told that something is white, it's white. And when they are told that separatism and nationalism are terrible problems, they fail to see they are being told this by people who are really practising their own brand of nationalism. Their lack of professionalism often prevents them from analysing what is going on, so they convey a warped vision of our country to international public opinion. They are often writing for countries that have the same kind of 'problems', and where the 'solutions' are often construed in the way Castilians do: with an obsession with assimilation, and a complete lack of respect for our differences. With regard to Barcelona—a city that for decades was the non-administrative capital of Spain, but which has been turned 'provincial'—it is normal that this development should be perceived with concern. We need to explain that the story they are being fed in Madrid is untrue, because it only reflects one side of the picture. However, the less official role played by the Internet is becoming increasingly important and positive, and it's free of censorship. Web surfers perceive that lots of Catalans staunchly contest the views put out from Madrid. In fact, odd as it may seem to some people, Catalan has become one of the world's thirty most-used languages on the Internet.

The resilience of Catalan on the Internet contrasts with the poorer showing of the written press in Catalan.

Yes. The reasons for that are complex. From 1939 to 1975 Catalonia was turned into a media desert, as regards Catalan. In the heyday of the comic, Catalan was an outlawed language! The Falangist party, responsible for media control after the Civil War, only gave a couple of licences for the publication of comics in Catalan in all that period. And once they were awarded, the Civil Governor of Barcelona had them withdrawn! No normal Catalan comics were ever allowed. To get out of a historical black hole like this one is not a simple matter. On top of that, the market is unfair to small languages—not just Catalan, but even Spanish, compared to English. Besides, plenty of businessmen, many of whom are Catalans, see Catalan as a nuisance. However, the introduction of a few simple changes can sometimes affect the market quite a bit. For example, when *El Periódico* brought out its Catalan edition, the percentage of the daily press sold in Catalan leaped overnight from around 15% to 25%. Now that *La Vanguardia* has also brought out a Catalan edition, that could bring us close to the 40% mark.[2] What is more worrying is the situation of magazines. If you scan the newsagents' shelves, you can easily end up in tears.

The cultural and information industries in Catalonia are often perceived as being buoyant. Yet the 'Catalan-ness' of their owners is questionable.

The priority, both in Spain and worldwide, is business concentration. Ten years ago you often heard the prophecy, 'In five years' time, the whole sector will be concentrated in Madrid'. Well, Catalonia has been able to turn the tables on that, despite the very hostile legal and administrative context. Telefónica is no longer a key communications group, and Prisa is on

the verge of bankruptcy. Against all the odds, in Catalonia there are two, maybe even three, major communication groups that are alive and kicking: the Planeta group, MediaPro, and, to a lesser extent, Prensa Ibérica. Our hope, as Catalans, is that one day a Catalan group could make it on the international scene.[3]

You have been director of Barça TV, the television channel run by FC Barcelona. What new perspectives does that open up?

Barça TV is a thematic channel in Catalan. When the digital TV (DTT) explosion hit Catalonia and Spain, we were worried. Lots of channels were allotted to companies that had no interest whatever in Catalonia or the Catalan language. But the only entirely new DTT channels with good content and powerful structures were Disney Channel and Barça TV. FC Barcelona competes in a wide variety of sports and sustains a whole range of parallel activities, as well as three foundations that are continually generating news and events. Barça TV broadcasts free-to-air on DTT and is trying to make its product attractive to the whole family, not just to Barça fanatics. This means being involved in social welfare programs, as epitomized by Barça's support for UNICEF, and believing in the country from a national point of view. Whichever way DTT develops, it cannot be worse than the situation we have left behind us, dominated by six analogue channels in Spanish and just two and a half in Catalan.[4]

As a Valencian living in Barcelona, why do you think national consciousness is much greater in Catalonia than in Valencia?

I think Valencians who feel different from Spaniards—those who feel entirely Valencian, or Valencian-cum-Catalan—are fighting a losing battle. We simply haven't made it in time to win back a national consciousness for our country. The Castilian colonization of Valencia, at all levels, began at least as early as the 16th century. The War of the Reapers (1640–1659), between Castile-Spain and Catalonia, involved Catalonia, France, and Spain, almost on level terms, and it gave the Catalans a clear awareness of their national status. That happened again in the War of the Spanish Succession (1701–1714).[5] As for Valencia, every war served to integrate Valencia deeper into the Castilian national culture. Now Madrid-based tourism has made the Valencian coast its favourite option, and the city of Valencia has become dependent on Madrid. When, in the 1960s, there was an attempt to counter all that, led by Joan Fuster,[6] Valencian society was already so Castilianised that his ideas met fierce opposition. The two leading parties in Valencia (the Partido Popular and the PSPV, the local branch of the Socialist PSOE) are now 100% Spanish. So, much though it breaks my heart, I can only say that the battle is pretty much lost.

Why hasn't this provincialisation process affected Catalonia so much?

The attitude in Madrid towards the autonomous regions—and they're always thinking in terms of Basques and Catalans—is, 'we've already given those people far too much!' One key objective in Madrid is to cut Barcelona down to size. They see it as a city which could become the capital of a new European State. When the Catalan President, Pasqual Maragall, suggested moving the Spanish Senate to Barcelona, in Madrid they joked about him having gone mad. They want to concentrate all the financial institutions, the major mass media, the energy sector, and the major privatized enterprises in Madrid, because they know that he who controls power controls history. The day that La Caixa,[7] *La Vanguardia*, or Mediapro disappear, we'll begin to look like Valencia.

Lots of Catalans were upset when *Avui*[8] was taken over by the Godó group. They were afraid that might lead to its disappearance, or its ideological prostitution.

A few very powerful enterprises control almost the entire market, and they know they need to trim their ideological preferences and allegiances in order to reach different kinds of audiences. The private radio station RAC1 is a case in point. It should be seen as a victory for the Catalan movement, because it has recently overtaken official Catalunya Ràdio in audience ratings, and even in Catalanist commitment. But, RAC1 also belongs to the Godó group, which is not at all Catalanist! Success stories such as that are sometimes possible because Catalanists have made concessions.

What do you think about the closing of the TV3 booster stations, which prevents Valencians seeing Catalan TV?

The Valencian government had no problem closing down Catalan television, which was broadcasting to Valencia via booster stations set up by private initiative which had no legal backing. Autonomous governments have resources for closing down TV channels that are considered 'harmful' for the community. Why did the Valencian government opt for this measure? One portion of the Partido Popular's electorate, both in Madrid and Valencia, is defined by its stark anti-Catalanism. So closing down a Catalan TV channel was received very well by that sector, especially in Valencia, where hostile media were encouraged to give the whole affair full coverage. However, opposition to the closure is being led by the very active organization *Acció Cultural del País Valencià*, which gathered hundreds of thousands of signatures in favour of a parliamentary motion to save TV3 in Valencia. It would also be a good idea if Catalan and Valencian MEPs who believe in our culture did something useful for a change on this issue!

Some years ago Valencians with a national consciousness seemed to have no problem about calling the language they use 'Catalan'. Now, however, everyone seems to use the term 'Valencian'. Isn't that a sign of surrender?

I would need five hours to answer that one! But there is one thing in relation to this that worries me greatly. The linguistic schema that emerged from the 1978 Constitution is one in which, apart from Spanish, there are what are called 'autonomic languages'. That's a totally perverse term, because it starts out from the notion that every autonomous region has a language of its own, and that just is not the case. Those 'autonomic languages' were conceived of as being for use within the region, and therefore only of concern at a regional level. Unfortunately, that has ended up reinforcing an old tradition, which was to call our language 'Valencian', although that did not mean that it was seen as different from Catalan, to which it is practically identical. But the Spanish and Valencian administrative set-ups found an excellent excuse for saying, 'Our autonomic language is called Valencian. It's ours, not yours!'[9]

In effect, the law splits the Catalan language up into three 'autonomic' lingos, while enforcing the use of Spanish between our territories. It's quite a crazy situation. And it happens even though High Court rulings state that Catalan and Valencian are 'one and the same language'. That leads to absurd situations, like when we are presented with the option of choosing between 'Valencian' and 'Catalan' on ATM machines at banks.

What do you think of the general indifference a lot of Catalans feel towards the negative way things are turning out in Valencia?

I'm fed up with hearing Catalans saying that the situation in Valencia has 'nothing to do with us', or that what is going on 'won't affect the future of Catalan'. Catalans who say that are either partial to suicide or simply stupid. They can't see that all the artillery that's been used against Valencia will be turned against them once they have obliterated us. Catalans have never been geared up to that kind of solidarity. Valencia and the Balearic Islands have always been a sort of nuisance for Catalonia. 'It's difficult enough for us as it is, without you adding to our problems!', is what they seem to be saying. You won't find many clearer cases of a linguistic nation than the Catalan Countries—Catalonia, Valencia, and the Balearic Islands—unprotected as they are. Acting together would be perfectly legitimate, as well as vital for survival. Like it or not, we have the truth about our language on our side. It is one language, damn it! And it is one culture we share. No Romance Languages Department at any university in the world would deny that.

Foreign insights

Helena Buffery
Teaching Catalan in Birmingham and Cork

Dr. Helena Buffery is the only one among this book's interviewees who does not actually live in Catalonia. She is now a lecturer at University College Cork, where she teaches students about Catalan language and culture in the Hispanic Studies Department, but until 2010 worked with students of Catalan at the University of Birmingham. She admits that she is not a 'real outsider' to the Catalan issue, because her maternal grandparents lived in Barcelona for most of their lives. Dr. Buffery regrets having gone through most of her pre-undergraduate life without knowing much about Catalan identity at all. However, her Aragonese-born grandfather was pleased when she started to learn Catalan, despite the fact that the only words he could be heard to utter in that language were: Què collons![1] Helena Buffery came to Catalan via Oxford University, and elected to spend her year abroad in Barcelona. It wasn't long after that that she discovered that her own grandmother was a Catalan-speaker! As far as most people were concerned, Helena points out, her grandmother just spoke xapurreau, the uncultivated 'village dialect', and she did not see herself as a native Catalan speaker... Helena remembers reading Mercè Rodoreda,[2] and asking her grandmother the meaning of words she couldn't find in the dictionary. She was amazed to see she knew every one of them!

Dr. Buffery is critical of the fact that Catalan is taught at more British universities than Spanish ones, although she also points out that teaching Catalan in Hispanic Studies Departments is not always that easy: 'Departments of Spanish aren't always particularly pro-Catalan.' When she advises students prior to their Erasmus courses at Barcelona's Autonomous University, she is careful to prepare them for the sociolinguistic and sociocultural situation they will find there. She recommends that all students learn some Catalan before going to the Autònoma, and she is critical of some Erasmus tutors at other European Universities who are 'unsupportive of the fact that so much Catalan is spoken there'. However, she is also worried by present trends, because increasingly students do not go on to study advanced Catalan in their final year, choosing other options instead. This happens because the impression they get is that they do not really need to use the language, since their fellow-students in Barcelona speak to them in Spanish. This hampers their chances of getting as high a grade in Catalan as they might have done otherwise.

You sometimes complain that teaching Catalan at an English university was not always easy. Why is that?

I have encountered problematic attitudes from the very beginning of my career, when I was doing a PhD on a Catalan-related topic. There is a whole range of negative reactions, which go from my Head of Department always teasing me by saying *els nostres clàssics*[3] in a kind of jokey way, to finding people who are always on about the time they went to a museum in Catalonia and couldn't find leaflets or guidebooks in Spanish. I generally reply by asking them how often scholars coming to the UK find equivalent documents translated into other languages. Why does it make people feel so defensive? Why does it make them so angry? The answer is because of their expectation that Spanish was going to be their passport to the entire world, instead of seeing that learning a different language and coming to grips with a different culture is actually something positive, whatever the language. That's what I tell them. It's vital to be as open as possible, and to show that there are lots of positive aspects to Catalan culture. I just keep to my work and try to show them that there is really nothing to be afraid of.

You mention the need to 'explain' Catalonia. Is that something Catalans need to do?

Yes, all too often. But when it comes to explaining, I'm not particularly into the 'victimism' line.[4] It can often be counterproductive. It can mean that discourse gets stuck in a rut, where it's a question of Catalonia versus Spain all the time. That is not a strategy I use. The way I explain Catalan culture to newcomers varies a lot according to who they are and what their interests are. And lots of Catalans do likewise. Using varied approaches can help to avoid perpetuating misconceptions about the social and political reality of Catalonia. I try to practice cultural diplomacy in order to create a common ground on which cultural dialogue can take place. In some ways that's easier from the outside; however it is true that there are often many layers of preconceptions to be dealt with. In part this is due to inadequate media coverage of the Catalan question, both in Spain and internationally.

Equally problematic is some of the rhetoric used to 'sell' Catalonia abroad. It can sometimes be perceived as excessively arrogant.

Some people criticize Catalans for an excess of self-esteem, some for a lack of it.

Yes, I think that is part and parcel of the political situation in which Catalonia finds itself. That is, forming part of a nation-state in which it is not fully represented. I think Josep-Anton Fernández's book *El malestar en la cultura catalana (The Unease in Catalan Culture)* describes that syndrome perfectly. If you are unable to see your reflection at a political level, then you tend to overcompensate for what you feel you lack. Otherwise, Catalans tend to fall into a state of melancholy or a sense that they are hitting their heads against a brick wall all the time. There is a very subtle psychological line between the two.

How do you see the role of Spanish immigration in Catalonia and the country's capacity for integration?

Political correctness makes that question the most difficult one to address. It is the one to which people are most attuned when they hear the wrong message coming through. There's the cliché about immigrants being impervious to Catalan and spending all day listening to COPE.[5] Well, I think that's oversimplifying things. The only Spanish students I have come across who regularly listen to COPE do so just for fun (or at least, that's what they say to me). Who can believe what they say on COPE? There is a long history of people from other parts of Spain settling in Catalonia, and while they often carry cultural baggage that doesn't help them understand that Catalonia is different there isn't a simple cause-and-effect relationship that means they will recoil into their own little worlds. As I suggested before, it all depends on there being the grounds for an encounter. That is why Catalan language classes are so important, for instance; they help to make dialogue possible, to ensure that voices on all sides can be heard and respected. Anyhow, even in situations where you would think it was impossible, there are always opportunities for immigrants to learn Catalan. What is also very important is that

immigration is taken notice of and talked about. It is vital that the languages that people who come to Catalonia speak and value are recognized and respected too. The more contact there is, with initiatives like *Voluntariat per la Llengua*,[6] the better. Professor Carme Junyent's work, showing just how many languages are spoken in Barcelona, is magnificent. These are lines of research that fascinate me, as a person from a bilingual background who went through an education system in which other languages were dealt with in a less than helpful way. I think what would really help Catalan sociolinguistically would be more openness to other languages. For that reason I am not convinced that the proposed reduction of three hours of Spanish to two at school is a good idea.[7] It may not make too much of a difference educationally. Yet, symbolically, it plays into the hands of politicians who claim that Castilian is being eradicated, which is absolute rubbish. Newcomers from Spanish-speaking areas should be made to feel as much at home as possible. That can be done perfectly easily by just saying we'll support family languages, whatever they may be.

How do you see the development of the social usage of Catalan?

My impression is that things have changed a lot in the past five or ten years. I learnt Catalan in the 'ideal period'—1989–90—when bilingual conversation practice was actually working. If, as a foreigner, you tried to use Catalan in conversation, people would actually answer you in Catalan. Now it's very difficult to use Catalan if you're a foreign learner. I have even found myself in situations in which I'm happily chatting away to someone in Catalan, then I'll hand them my passport, and they'll immediately switch to Castilian. I suppose they are trying to be nice to me, but it's patronizing, really. This is just the tip of the iceberg of what seems to be happening in Barcelona. You hear less and less Catalan in large areas of the city now. My perception is that the level of usage has gone down, even though the level of knowledge has gone up. Apart from that, when I learned Catalan—a very positive experience—what I did find bizarre, considering that a lot of the people in the class were effectively Catalan-speakers, was that much too much emphasis was put on the need to eliminate *barbarismes*,[8] which made you feel that you were 'wrong' and 'foreign' if you used Castilian-sounding words. On the other hand, in the anti-Catalan camp, there's also plenty of bloody-mindedness, with people interpreting the use of terms such as *barbarisme* or *immersió lingüística* (linguistic immersion) as proof of the Catalans' innate perversity! The important thing is that people ought to be prepared to see what really lies behind words and concepts such as these; that in a situation of language contact some degree of negotiation of the boundaries between the languages in contact is not only inevitable but necessary in order to encourage mutual recognition and respect. The really distressing thing is the lack of good will.

What perception do foreigners get of Catalonia when they visit the country? Do they get an idea of the cultural reality?

On offer for tourists there are visits to the Gaudí buildings that appear in one of Woody Allen's latest films—which didn't really tell you anything about Catalan culture either—or to go and see bullfights or flamenco, and other practices more associated with clichéd notions of Spanish culture rather than being Catalan as such. Although there is information available on Catalan culture, I suppose a lot of the tourists are not really interested. But if they go to museums, they do find that Catalan culture is explained to them. I find there are enough events and services on offer for me to show Catalan culture to my children, and that is quite a good litmus test. However, there is a tendency for city-bound tourism to centre on monuments, rather than on people. If tourists have no wish to get to know the country, to choose rural tourism over city-based tourism, to mix with the locals, then there seems to be no alternative. As regards Barcelona, I would say the situation is unsustainable at the moment. The way tourism is evolving there has radically changed the day-to-day reality of the city centre. I have lots of friends who have lived in Barcelona at different periods, and when they go back there now they see the Rambla as a no-go area. Not simply for security reasons, but because it's turned into a beer-swilling playground, with constant reports in the papers about prostitution. And, of course, it's now comparatively rare to hear the Catalan language spoken there, so a key aspect of Catalan cultural reality is hidden from view.

Have you noticed any changes as regards the expression of pro-independence sentiments in recent times?

I'd say that the signs of support for independence are more visible now. You see lots more *estelades*[9] around, sometimes linked to particular events, such as the great success of FC Barcelona in recent years. The phenomenon certainly seems to go hand in glove with some kind of resurgence of national self-esteem.

I think the repudiation of the *Estatut* by lots of Spaniards and Spanish media is quite horrifying. I have been shocked to see the language adopted with regard to the Education Law that was recently passed in the Catalan Parliament, presenting it as some kind of coup against the Spanish State. It just seems recklessly over the top. But when that is the mirror image Catalans are getting of their own cultural reality, it's hardly surprising that they don't feel very comfortable about forming part of the Spanish State. I don't know to what extent it actually means that the majority of Catalans overtly favour independence. But there are certainly signs that support for independence seems to be growing, and I do think it is positive that people are now openly talking about the issue.

Susan DiGiacomo
An American anthropologist who teaches in Catalan

Susan M. DiGiacomo came to Catalonia for the first time in 1972. She was then studying in France. However, she fell in love with Barcelona at first sight. 'It looked nothing like what I had imagined a "Spanish city" might be,' she remembers today. DiGiacomo was later to be a graduate student in anthropology, and did her dissertation in Barcelona on Catalan national politics during the transition to democracy. She has published works on class and identity, historical memory, and the politics and ideology of language in Catalonia.

She is now a teacher of anthropology at the Universitat Rovira i Virgili in Tarragona, in southern Catalonia, where she teaches her classes in Catalan. She complains that, in order to travel to Tarragona every day, she has to take dirty moth-eaten trains which clatter 'along railway tracks that were laid donkey's years ago', a situation that she considers to present 'a stark contrast with the excellent railway services in many parts of Spain'. Although born a citizen of the United States, she identifies so much with the Catalan cause that she speaks in the first person about the issues involved. On July 27, 2010 she wrote a letter to President Barack Obama informing him about the use she considers Spain to be making of its Constitution, as a 'weapon to crush the legitimate national aspirations of a people', the Catalan people.[1]

Why do you think there is not so much international sympathy for the Catalan 'cause'?

I think it's partly due to the question of exoticism. Tibet is mythical and exotic, and so it appeals to people. The Catalans are Europeans and they dress in western clothes. We don't wear funny hats or stand out physically. Catalans are not ethnically singular. Having said that, the truth is that the struggles the Tibetans and Catalans are engaged in have a surprising number of points in common. Both of them, like so many indigenous peoples, are forced to campaign more or less permanently to save their language and culture. But the issue is not limited to the question of the way others see us. It also has to do with our own vision of ourselves. Some Catalans often fail to identify with this kind of struggle and, instead, see themselves as a sophisticated European people with a history and a literature of our own. All that is perfectly true. But that does not mean that the language isn't in serious danger, or that it doesn't need to be supported. There seems to be too little awareness of the dramatic consequences of the situation.

Why do you think that is the case?

For lots of reasons. Habit is an important one. Habits which took root during the Franco dictatorship. But it also depends on the region we are talking about. Take Vic,[2] for example. There everyone addresses you in Catalan. The problem is the Barcelona area. And it is a problem here because this is where 75% of the population is concentrated. It's here that the battle must be won. Another factor is, of course, immigration. It's no fault of the immigrants, mind you. It's no-one's but ours. Apart from that, I do not think the language normalization campaigns that the Catalan institutions carry out are effective. The last one, *Dóna corda al català* ('Keep Catalan Going!'), linked to an image of some chattering plastic teeth, looked more like a dental fixative commercial than a message to keep Catalan going! In any case, I think Catalans tend to trust too much in the law. People say, 'Oh, but there's a law to protect Catalan...' OK. That's all very well. But that hasn't solved things, so far. People all too often tend to shirk their personal responsibility and rely on politicians who often know nothing about the state of the language, or who do not even care! We need to find more efficient ways of making sure Catalan is brought back.

What makes the Catalan issue important for you as an American-born anthropologist?

I think the world was fascinated by what happened at Arenys de Munt when the first referendums on independence were held there in September 2009.[3] I reckon there are a great many people out there who know there is a small country called Catalonia that lives under the heel of Spain, and that many of its inhabitants want it to become an independent country.

Do you think independence is justified in the case of Catalonia?

Yes, without a shadow of a doubt. It is a question of human rights. If a country freely decides that it wants to be independent, and wants to decide its own future, it must have the right to do so. And that is the case in Catalonia.

What sort of a perception do you think people are getting of this question in Spain?

Well, I think they get a very distorted view of things. Even liberal mass media, such as the famous *El País* newspaper—a newspaper of record—have a clearly nationalistic, pro-Spanish editorial line. That means that it is quite anti-Catalan. One cannot really say that the Spanish are necessarily to blame for being anti-Catalan. If you are constantly exposed to such media, and only come into contact with papers such as *El Mundo* or *ABC* and radio stations such as COPE,[4] then it's hardly surprising if you end up with a pretty warped idea of what is going on in Catalonia.

Do you think the Spanish authorities do enough to counter anti-Catalan feeling in Spain?

To tell you the truth, I cannot see that they do anything at all! They have absolutely no wish to do so. After thirty years of democracy and so many initiatives of an educational nature conducted from Catalonia, with a willingness to open up debates on the

subject, as far as I can see there is absolutely no interest on the part of Spain to engage in dialogue with us. In this regard, I do not really see a lot of difference between the Partido Popular and the PSOE. At the end of the day, they are both guided by a strong Spanish-nationalist impulse.

When you speak, you include yourself in the Catalan collective 'we'. Why do few foreign-born residents adopt the same practice?

The Catalans themselves are partly to blame for this. Foreigners are not exactly helped to take that step. It often happens to me. Although Catalan is the language I speak to everyone all the time, if someone detects that I was born abroad, they quickly change language and speak to me in Spanish. I keep on in Catalan and sometimes they switch back. We Catalans must change our attitude and use our language in a normal way all the time. Thirty years of supposed 'Language Normalization' still has not achieved that.

President Montilla[5] twice spoke, in speeches given in Madrid, about the 'disaffection' Catalans increasingly feel towards Spain. What do you think about that?

The disaffection is definitely there. Lately there has been a lot of talk about the figure of the 'perplexed' and 'angry' Catalan that the press has conjured up. Now, after Arenys de Munt, I think that it's the Spanish who are perplexed and angry. They don't know what's hit them! It has come quite out of the blue to them. For us, on the contrary, the whole Arenys de Munt affair has underlined to what extent we live in a highly controlled and limited democracy. I have lived in Catalonia since the time of the *Transición* and I have thought from the very start that the State placed immense restrictions on democracy. My feelings are that, in many ways, things have got worse, rather than better. There is less of a willingness now to let the Catalans and the Basques do their own thing.

Yet some international media suggest that the Catalans and Basques are asking for too much...

Some of these media are very conservative, and so their position should not surprise us too much. They are media that always talk in terms of states and state economies. They see things from the point of view of Madrid, and that's it. For them we are just stroppy or ungrateful regional Spaniards. They do not share our view that Spain prevents Catalans making decisions, or that Madrid is strangling our economy by way of exorbitant taxation, which is what is happening.

You wrote your doctoral thesis on the *Transición* period. And you are critical of it.

Yes. I think the results are very limited. I believe the Constitution was drawn up at a time of fear. And I think that fear does not provide a suitable climate for agreeing on constitutional affairs, here or anywhere in the world for that matter. The fear that existed severely conditioned the idea of what was democratically possible and what was not. However, I think the present moment is interesting, because Catalans are beginning to shake off their age-old fear. This is proved by events such as the Arenys de Munt referendum, despite the pressure applied. It is a sign that a process of mental 'decolonisation' is under way among Catalans, despite the huge pressures applied by the State to halt it.

What pressure was applied in the case of Arenys de Munt?

Incredible though it may seem, on the very day of the referendum the State allowed Franco's old Falangist Party to hold a demonstration in the town. Seventy-odd Falangists were escorted in and allowed to make their fascist salutes, insult the locals and wave Spanish flags furiously at them. Then the State Advocate who was appointed to advise whether the referendum was to be prevented or not was revealed to have been a candidate of the Falangist party himself not long earlier. Yet no attempt was made to replace him.

Can anyone image a notorious ex-Nazi party member being asked to monitor public events in post-1945 Germany? This is the sort of episode that politics in Spain regularly produces. Despite all that, in Arenys and other towns, lots of Catalans turned out to vote publicly in favour of independence. So big changes are indeed occurring. People are showing that they are no longer afraid, and that's a very hopeful sign for the future. But I think it will be Catalan society that makes the breakthrough towards a more democratic society, and not so much the political parties.

What do you make of the June 28th Constitutional Court ruling against the Catalan Statute?

It was an assault on democracy. That Court has no legitimacy whatever. I went to the July 10th rally and it reminded me of the huge demonstrations of the seventies. The same broad social mix, the same enthusiasm, the same feeling that the future is in our hands. Now we need leaders that can transform the July 10th spirit into a programme for the future. I hope that a new candidature will emerge that will introduce a new way of doing politics and lead this country towards independence. I think that the Court ruling has opened people's eyes, and I think we are nearer that goal than ever.

You wrote a letter to US President Obama in July 2010. Why?

I thought I had to do my bit. I wanted to warn him about the situation in Catalonia and the constrictions there were to democracy here. I wrote to him not only as president but as a former professor of constitutional law and author of *The Audacity of Hope*, in which he warns against 'any tyrannical consistency that might lock future generations into a single unalterable course…'. This is clearly what Spain intends to do with Catalonia, with a ruling issued by an entirely politicized Court. I told him that despite being an American passport-holder, the ruling affected me—amongst other things—because the status of the language I teach in (Catalan) is now openly threatened by the Court's decision. I also wanted to remind him that there is nothing in international law that prevents the democratically elected representatives of a people from unilaterally declaring independence, as the International Human Rights Court in The Hague has just ruled for Kosovo. I also offered President Obama my services—as did former President Jimmy Carter recently—because international interlocutors and international visibility are badly needed at a time when the rights of the Catalan people are being so overtly challenged.

Dr. Henry Ettinghausen
A Catalanist by marriage and research

When called upon to tell his story, Henry Ettinghausen will often ask inquirers if they remember Victor Kiam, the man who liked the razor so much that he bought the company. 'Well, that's more or less my story', he tells them. His first contact with Catalonia was over half a century ago, when, as an undergraduate, he spent a memorable day and night in Barcelona, hitchhiking from Santiago de Compostela to Oxford. Just a few months later, a friend introduced him to a marvellous girl he had just met who turned out to be from Barcelona. Within a short time she started teaching him Catalan as they cycled around Oxford, and the rest is history. When Franco finally died, they started up Catalan studies at the University of Southampton, where he taught for thirty-six years and became Professor of Spanish.

Over forty years ago they bought a tumble-down house in La Pera, a tiny village in the Empordà region, which is where they now live, next door to their son, daughter-in-law and grandson. Proof of the family's complete integration into rural Catalonia is the publication, by his son Dídac, of the oldest known collection of photographs of Andorra, taken by the Englishman H.F. Deverell in the 1880s, and of his translation into Catalan of Through the High Pyrenees *by Harold Spender, the poet Stephen Spender's father. Henry's wife, Mercè, has also published her memoirs of the end of the Civil War and her childhood exile in a French Pyrenean village,* Ombres sota un cel radiant [Shadows under a Brilliant Sky].

As for Henry—now an Emeritus Professor much dedicated to his vegetable garden and orchard—his multi-volume facsimile edition of pamphlets produced during the War of the Reapers (1640–1659)[1] and his eight-year commitment to the Comissió de la Dignitat,[2] for whom he acts as international spokesman, are, among other things, what led him to be distinguished with the Creu de Sant Jordi (Saint George's Cross) by the Catalan Government in 2003. In April 2010, he and Dídac helped to organise the popular referendum on independence for Catalonia in La Pera, for which there was a 60% turnout, with 93% voting in favour. That's about as integrated as you can get.

You have publicly given support to various 'Catalanist' initiatives in the last few years. Why?

I have enjoyed an increasingly close relationship with Catalonia over the past half century, having been married to a Catalan lady for the past forty-eight years, spent part of every one of those years in Catalonia, and retired to a village in the Empordà nearly a decade ago. The 'Catalanist' initiative I have supported with the greatest enthusiasm is the campaign, led by the *Comissió de la Dignitat* (the Catalan Dignity Commission), to obtain the return of the millions of Catalan documents that were seized by Franco's troops at the end of the Civil War and sent to the police archive in Salamanca to be used to identify, incriminate and sentence to death, imprisonment or forced labour those who opposed the Fascist regime. In time, those Catalan documents have become known as the 'Salamanca Papers', and the vast majority of them are still in Salamanca, over four years after the Spanish parliament finally passed a law that decreed their return to Catalonia. My support for the campaign for their return springs primarily from a simple desire to help reverse a gross injustice, one of the very few committed by the Franco regime—as the historian Paul Preston likes to point out—'that can still be undone'. At the same time, I have a personal interest in the matter, since my wife's parents—like nearly half a million other refugees—went into exile abroad in order to avoid the reprisals wreaked by Franco upon defenders of the Republic.

Do you think enough has been done to put Francoism into the past?

Spain's transition to democracy, which began shortly after Franco's death in 1975, was hailed by a lot of people as a model of peaceful change. However, it was achieved at the cost of drawing a very thick veil over the nearly forty years of Franco's dictatorship. Not a single member or agent of that brutal regime has ever been put on trial or even officially censored, nor is there the slightest prospect of that occurring. (Indeed, with grim irony, Judge Baltasar Garzón's attempt to give legal support to people wishing to find their relatives who were shot and buried in unmarked graves by Franco's troops has landed him in the Supreme Court, accused by the Falange of perverting of the course of justice!)[3]

While the vast majority of the fascist trappings of the Franco regime have been removed, some have not. Let me give you a couple of examples. The Bishop's Palace in Salamanca, which was Franco's headquarters during the Civil War, still vaunts a plaque that reads, 'The Caudillo Franco resided here when he led our National Crusade', *Caudillo* being the Spanish equivalent of *Duce* or *Führer*, and *National Crusade* being the pseudo-religious euphemism with which Franco baptized his annihilation of the Spanish Republic. And a large inscription, done in tiles on a wall in the main square next to Seville cathedral, still proffers thanks to the Virgin Mary for her hand in the military uprising of 18 July 1936 that sparked off the Civil War and brought Franco to power.

However, perhaps the most scandalous sense in which Francoism still persists is in the refusal of successive Spanish governments to declare illegal the vicious retribution exacted by the Franco regime's kangaroo courts, most notably the tens of thousands of executions carried out, from the very beginning of the Civil War until very shortly before Franco's death. One such act of vengeance involved Lluís Companys, the President of the Catalan Government during the war, who was kidnapped by the Gestapo from his exile in France and handed over to Franco as a trophy.[4] President Companys' death by firing squad in Barcelona in October 1940 was not just a vindictive reprisal against a democratically elected national leader; it also represented the ruthless obliteration of the aspirations of Catalonia that had been fulfilled under his leadership during the Republic. The campaign to obtain the annulment of all the sentences passed by the Franco regime against its perceived opponents has also been led by the Dignity Commission, and naturally I have given it my support.

In the epilogue you recently wrote for a book called *Hasta aquí hemos llegado*,[5] **you were particularly critical of the Catalan Socialists. Why?**

In that epilogue, regarding their dealings with Catalonia, I referred to the Spanish Socialists (the PSOE) as the 'nice' policemen, and the Spanish Conservatives (the Partido Popular) as the 'nasty' ones. The trouble with the Catalan Socialists is that, in the last resort, they go along with the Spanish Socialists, and the latter very often demonstrate that either they do not have the courage of their convictions or else they simply lie. However, the Catalan Socialists are not the only Catalan party that, to put it politely, shows remarkable patience in the face of successive Spanish governments' intransigence and insensitivity. To take just one instance, the Catalan conservatives (CiU), who were in power in the Generalitat for nearly a quarter of a century, never actively campaigned for the return of the Salamanca Papers.

The greater or lesser timidity of all the Catalan parties has recently been highlighted by their response to the fate of the Centelles archive. In autumn 2009, the Spanish Ministry of Culture announced that it had bought the unique collection of over twelve thousand negatives taken by the Catalan photographer Agustí Centelles—the single most important visual testimony to Catalonia's resistance during the Civil War and to the sufferings of the hundreds of thousands of refugees who fled to France. The Spanish Socialist Minister of Culture clinched the purchase of the collection for her Ministry by secretly outbidding the Catalan Government. And she then had the gall to decide that the collection would be housed in the very same archive in Salamanca in which the Salamanca Papers have been held for seventy years. Just for once, the ultra-conservative Partido Popular had nothing to say in criticism of the Spanish Socialist government: both the conservatives and the Socialists were clearly perfectly happy with this act of utter callousness towards Catalonia. Meanwhile, the Socialist President of Catalonia and his government, as well as the Catalan Opposition parties, accepted the *fait accompli* with what strikes me as astonishing restraint.

Do you think European and English historians and politicians are supportive enough of the Catalan cause?

Well, a significant number of European and US academics have given their support to the Dignity Commission over the famous 'Salamanca Papers' issue. Likewise, many politicians in other stateless nations, such as Scotland and Quebec, support Catalan aspirations to greater autonomy or independence. However, support from other States, including some full members of the EU that are much smaller than Catalonia, has been far less in evidence. Some British historians have gone out of their way to support Catalonia; others, especially some who butter up to the Spanish Establishment, tend to distinguish themselves by their silence in this respect.

What is your view regarding the Catalan language and Catalan identity? Some say promoting them is a thing of the past…

Whether the Catalan language and Catalan national identity are things of the past depends, primarily, upon the Catalans. Catalan, which is as old as any of the other Romance languages, has been having to compete with Spanish since at least the 16th century. It has survived numerous attempts to kill it off—not least under the Franco regime—and it is still going strong. The main challenges now to the Catalan language are no doubt globalization and immigration, especially the massive immigration over the past decade on the part of Latin Americans, who can get by in Catalonia speaking only Spanish.

You have written extensively about the conflict between Catalonia and Spain in the 17th century. Have things changed that much?

The Catalan political cause is as old as the hills. In the Middle Ages, before Spain was Spain, and long before Spain had an empire, the Catalans and the Castilians were competing in the reconquest of the Iberian peninsula from the Moors, and Catalonia was colonizing parts of the Mediterranean—Sardinia, Sicily, southern Italy, Athens… When, in the 15th century, Catalonia was linked to Castile by the marriage of Ferdinand and Isabella, Catalonia's traditional rights and autonomy were preserved. Then, in the first half of the 17th century, when Castile sought to override those rights, the Catalans revolted and, between 1640 and 1652, fought, unsuccessfully, to shake off Spain's yoke. Catalonia was to attempt to break free from Spain on many subsequent occasions, not least during the War of the Spanish Succession, at the beginning of the 18th century.

In 2009 and 2010 hundreds of Catalan villages, towns and cities have carried out unofficial polls on independence. What do you think about that?

What with the Catalan political parties being so obsessed with trying to score points off one another, and the Spanish parties (and Spaniards in general) firmly opposed to any further devolution for Catalonia, let alone independence, once again—as with the creation of the Dignity Commission in 2002—the Catalans have taken the initiative of organizing themselves unofficially, at grassroots level, this time to further the cause of independence. The outcome, so far, suggests that there is a powerful groundswell in favour, though it's too early to tell how strong that feeling is in the larger cities.

As for the principle, for lots and lots of Spaniards—and certainly for the Partido Popular and the PSOE—the unity of Spain is still a quasi-religious dogma. Which is why I think it is important to stress how, throughout history, scores of nations have joined together, or been colonized, and have then separated again or achieved independence. People need to hear that independence is not, as Spain would have it, the dirtiest word in the book, but that states and empires have come and gone—not least the Spanish and the British empires. The referendum across Catalonia is providing a very useful opportunity to ponder how, in 1640, when the Catalans revolted against Spain, the Portuguese did likewise, achieving their independence in 1668 and maintaining it to the present day. When given the chance to think seriously about it, lots of Catalans realize they have got plenty of reasons to want to express their views on the question of independence for their country. And the vast majority of those who vote express their wish to see Catalonia independent.

Alex Rietman
A Dutch journalist's view

For all its size and ebullience, and its power to attract tourists in their hundreds of thousands, Barcelona is the headquarters of fewer foreign journalists than many reckon it deserves. Dutchman Alex Rietman is one of them. Since he works freelance, he has been able to indulge his love of Barcelona and resist the temptation to move on to media-clustered Madrid, with its 'Central' government and its massive accumulation of corporate headquarters that pour their taxes into the State capital. With the merest touch of disdain, he points out that Madrid-based foreign journalists 'rarely have a clue what's going on in Catalonia', and tend to dismiss the country as 'provincial'.

Rietman has got a lot of the virtues of the critical journalist. He reports for *De Groene Amsterdamme*, as well as for *Radio 1 and for Dutch public TV*. He is daring when selecting his stories, and conservatives no doubt find some of his work off-beat and provocative. He may never win a Pulitzer, but he certainly pokes his microphone into interesting nooks. The Basque peace process and the less savoury corners of Spanish politics are his favourite haunts. This is not always appreciated in northern climes, where the official line—at least until the 2010 Spanish EU Presidency—was that Spain was the place to invest, and Juan Carlos the monarch to be photographed with. In fact, until recently, it has not been easy to sell views of Spain expressing anything short of drooling wonder over the Bourbon royal family and "Spain's Economic Miracle". Now that the bubble of Spain's economic miracle has burst, Rietman and other journalists are finding it easier to report about Spain's less savoury issues.

Writing for readers and listeners 700 miles away from Amsterdam is a bit of a bind for Alex. For one thing, he isn't always certain about the effect his keen portraits of things Spanish will have on his audience. While he fears some may see them as 'radical', he recalls how one of his most pungent reports on the ultra-right-wing COPE radio station—in which the Spanish bishops are major shareholders—elicited the ardent praise of one listener in The Hague. 'He actually phoned to thank me for the report, saying it was "about time someone talked about the media in Spain that lie all the time". He just kept saying "Thank you!" over and over again,' recalls Alex, not without a tinge of pride.

He and his Galician girlfriend, Lola, are great FC Barcelona fans. They watch the matches in bars in the Poble Sec district, where they don't have to put up with the comments of Real Madrid fifth-columnists if Barça doesn't win—something that almost never happens since Pep Guardiola has been appointed coach, giving the club a record six trophies on the trot in the 2009–10 season. One of their favourite locals has an elderly anarchist waiter who, Alex hopes, will illustrate a forthcoming report with lesser-known aspects of the Franco years. Lola and Alex are great fans of old Barcelona—the bits that survived, unpolished, the 1992 Olympic spruce-up.

Why does the foreign press in Spain take more interest in the Catalans and the Basques than in other provinces?

Probably because they are so different. The Catalans and the Basques express themselves in their own ways. In the other autonomous regions, people just see themselves as Spanish, and justifiably take pride in that. Andalusians also have a strong personality of their own and the Galicians, like the Catalans and Basques, have a language of their own. The Canary Islands once had their own separatist movement, but that was back in the seventies. So it's only the Catalans and the Basques who are seen as national communities with distinct and permanent political identities. In that sense they are clearly different, and they are often looked down on for it.

Does this kind of nationalism make sense in the age of globalization? Isn't it outdated?

It is the long-established states that regard regional nationalism as 'bad', while regarding their own brand of nationalism as perfectly natural. In Spain, the term 'nationalism' often has negative implications when it is applied to the Basques and the Catalans. Things relating to Spain are never referred to in this way. In fact, in our apparently united Europe there may well be more nationalists than ever. This is obvious when it comes to sport. As I see it, the aversion towards the Catalans and the Basques expressed in many of Madrid's mass media is inspired by a very strong brand of centralism.

You have been a front-line witness to the process whereby Catalonia recently tried to upgrade its Statute of Autonomy.

Yes. It has been a very unpleasant period. There have been lots of completely unjustifiable attacks against Catalonia, often led by a supposedly 'serious' press. Most of the Madrid press is clearly right-wing, and in the case of *ABC*, *La Razón* and *El Mundo*, extreme right-wing. But it is particularly shocking to see *El País*—allegedly a liberal paper with a better understanding of the autonomous regions—joining in the hostilities.[1] Between these four major papers, they have conducted what can only be termed an all-out campaign against the Catalans. Everybody accuses them of being uncooperative, of wanting everything for themselves and leaving nothing for the others. Oddly enough, the statistics say just the opposite. Few autonomous regions show more solidarity than Catalonia does.

What do you make of the Spanish Church's position regarding the Catalan issue?

The amazing thing is that the Spanish bishops should have felt justified in pontificating on the matter of the Statute at all. The reason they gave is that the unity of Spain is a 'moral' issue. What is the bottom line in this? Does it mean that what Catalans want is immoral? It makes me wonder what kind of country and what century we are living in. That is just one example of their constant sallies into politics. The crusade against abortion is another. The bishops keep on telling Spaniards what they ought to do and think—even what party to vote for! I reckon that, as Spanish society matures, people will eventually stop taking any notice of them. If that has not happened before now, it's because so much of the press supports the radical right.

You did a radio program, on Holland's Radio 1, denouncing COPE, the Spanish bishops' official radio station.

That's right. COPE is a station in which the Spanish Episcopal Conference is a major shareholder. Nowadays one might expect the Church not to take such a clear political line. It shocks lots of people to see how the leadership of the Spanish Church doesn't think twice about taking sides in favour of the right—often the extreme right. The message COPE gives out goes well beyond that of normal European right-wing parties such as you would find in England or Holland. The Dutch *Bilders*, who are just as right wing, concentrate on the Islamic issue. But COPE's line is that of a fully-fledged extremist party. Indeed, the Spanish Church hasn't changed much since the Civil War, when it gave its blessing to Franco's military coup. In the heat of the Statute battle, the Bishop of Jerez went to far as to say that Jesus Christ had been a staunch advocate of Spanish unity!

You have often expressed concern about Spain's inability to put Franco, and what he represented, into the past.

Yes, indeed. Spain's 'model' transition from Francoism to democracy was really little more than a makeshift propaganda exercise. The fact that for years Spain's transition to democracy has been sold as flawless shows the complete ignorance there is regarding the reality of Spain today. No Truth Commission was set up to lay bare what had happened under Franco—unlike in South Africa and other countries, where democracy could be regarded as flimsier than in Spain, yet where a catharsis of sorts has been achieved. Some people justify that by saying, 'well, there was brutality in equal measure on both sides'. That is an absolute lie. You just cannot compare the two scores, either in terms of figures or moral responsibility. It is just a way of enabling the victors to bend history their way and keep on winning. Some so-called historians, such as Pío Moa or César Vidal, with easy access to the media, have no qualms about falsifying history in such a way as to blame the democratically-elected Republican government for a war which cost a million dead.[2] They are also experts at whitewashing Franco's brutal post-war repression. That would be unviable if more had been done to lay bare the truth.

What do you think about the presence of ex-Francoists in posts of international prestige today?

For me, the case of the late Sr. Samaranch, Honorary President of the International Olympic Committee, is particularly awe-inspiring. Should that post have been held by someone who was still making the fascist salute in public as recently as 1974, especially given that no regrets or apology were ever forthcoming from him? Again, I think it is only possible because people do not know the truth about what happened. It has all been carefully concealed from them. No common version of history was established in which each party could recognize its mistakes and the harm it inflicted on the other side. I know it is still very painful for the victims of Francoism and their families today, because they have never had any proper recognition. We do not even know where many of those who were executed were buried. Yet honours of all kinds have been poured on the other side.

Don't you think the Historic Memory Law of 2007 put things right?

Quite honestly, I think it has added insult to injury. It did not even set aside funds for the proper burial of the Republican dead. Why should families and private associations have to pay to have their dead recovered and decently buried? We are talking about the victims of a military dictatorship who were slaughtered for defending a legally established government! About tens of thousands of people out there, unidentified, in unmarked mass graves. It just goes to show what an enormous influence Franco's ideological heirs still wield today. They accuse the victims of wanting to 'stir up the past'. But I ask: If a society cannot face up to its past, how can it face up to its future?

Foreign public opinion seems oblivious to these issues... Do Dutch residents and tourists in Catalonia share your views?

Unfortunately, I cannot say they do. I don't think they really get a chance to see the truth. As regards Catalonia, most of those who come here are not aware of the fact that Catalonia has an identity of its own, different from the rest of Spain. But I do think that, if there has been any progress on this front, football has made a major contribution to it. Since the arrival of Johan Cruyff, the presence of Dutch players in Catalonia has not gone unnoticed in Holland. Cruyff named his son Jordi—Catalan for George—a very special gesture, because in those days it was semi-illegal to give a child a Catalan name. The Dutch know that Catalonia has a different language. Nevertheless, they still largely see things through the filter of Madrid.

In 2009-10, the international press took considerable interest in developments in Catalonia. Yet sometimes it gives a negative picture of Catalan politics.

Yes, indeed. And to accuse Catalonia of 'lacking solidarity' with Spain, as it has done, is to ignore the truth. It took ages to get the balance of payments between the Spanish State and the regions published.[3] But, now it has been made public, it still doesn't seem to have made any difference. It is clear that the State invests very much less in education and health in Catalonia than, say, in Extremadura or Andalusia. How can you explain why a richer community, which generates more revenue, should be punished with lower investment per inhabitant in such basic areas? Even so, lots of Spaniards continue to accuse Catalans of 'lacking solidarity'. I cannot think of any rich country helping development in another with the result that the recipient country actually becomes richer than the donor. It doesn't make sense. But that is what is happening today in Catalonia, and it is damaging an economically dynamic region. It is a case of cutting your nose off to spite your face.

The question of the Catalan language has also caused complaints…

To claim that there is a linguistic dictatorship, or any kind of language discrimination against Castilian speakers in Catalonia, is rubbish. But some people seem to have no other purpose in life than to spread that kind of lie. I have been living here for twelve years, and my Catalan is pitiful—much to my shame!—but I have never had the slightest problem.

Things may be a little different in areas where Catalan is the predominant language. What Catalonia's very reasonable language policy is aiming for is the protection and promotion of the Catalan language in areas where the predominance of Spanish is overwhelming. You can learn Spanish in the street. Not so Catalan. To encourage Catalan in schools in order to reinforce bilingualism seems logical to me. I find it grotesque that the Madrid press has portrayed children as terrorized victims, 'forced' to speak Catalan even in the playground. That is an absolutely false image fostered by sectarian communications media and anti-Catalan activists close to the extreme right.

I gather you're a keen FC Barcelona fan. Is the club motto 'More than a club' true, or is it just a catchy slogan?

No-one who loves good football could dislike Barça! Some people try to ridicule the motto. But then you can ridicule anything, can't you? I must say people are very tolerant here. In some bars you get desperate Madrid supporters making nasty comments about Barça. People just ignore them. I don't know what would happen if you went into a bar in Madrid and made the same kind of comments there about Real Madrid. You would probably get clobbered. I remember a waiter once who was anti-Barça. When in the bar anyone said 'More than a club', he would come back with the quip 'More than a club, a club and a half'. He thought he was very funny. Of course it's more than a club! Barça is still as much a symbol of resistance as it was in Franco's time.

Matthew Tree
An author transplanted into Catalan

Matthew Tree is something of a cult figure in Catalonia, though he may well prefer to think of himself as more like a freak. When you walk down the street with him, heads turn. His regular appearances on television and radio have helped make 'Matthew Tree' a household name throughout the land. He even had his own very entertaining TV series, which featured him travelling by rail up and down the country, indulging in spontaneous (and perhaps not so spontaneous) conversations with other travellers. They were always intriguing and sometimes hilarious. The programme went into a second series, and would doubtless have lasted longer had so many of the country's railway lines not been axed over the years. In a few months he had been everywhere you could possibly go by rail in Catalonia!

Matthew Tree seduces his audience with his direct, bold language. He says things, both grammatical and ideological, that certain Catalans would probably need a few glasses of Penedès wine to come out with. His use of loose language on TV might not have gone down too well if he had made Poland his new home. But with Catalans, this is not a problem.[1] There probably is no other country in the whole of Europe where people are more trigger-happy about religious blasphemy than Catalonia, where terrible things are done to and said about God and his family at the drop of a hat. What makes heads turn in Barcelona when Matthew is spotted is mainly his down-to-earth language, which captivates people, along with his complete lack of prudery when talking about things blue and his openness when talking about the trials of being, or trying to be, Catalan. He is also increasingly popular as one of Catalonia's leading writers, having won several hefty literary prizes, although he insists he is just one among a lot of foreign writers who are adopting Catalan as a literary language. His latest book, La vida després de Déu [Life after God], *Ara Llibres, 2007*), has rapidly run to three editions. But it is undoubtedly as an outspoken defender of things Catalan that Matthew Tree stands out most. We met him at the northern end of Barcelona's Eixample district, near the vast Doric-style temple that Ricardo Bofill raised to house Barcelona's thriving National Theatre.

Why did you settle in Catalonia, Matthew?

I came to Catalonia when I was 26, to get away from London, where I was in danger of going under. I was afraid I'd end up drinking too much and writing even worse than I did. I came to Barcelona to give myself a second chance. I learnt Catalan in the seventies, and it got under my skin. In 1989 a publisher friend suggested I started writing in Catalan. And it worked from word one. Now I write in both languages.

Did you know what to expect before you settled here?

Yes, I'd been here before, in 1978. On that first occasion I could have written all I knew about Catalonia on half a postage stamp. Most English people are the same when they first arrive. The sad thing is that they are often still the same after living here for donkey's years! Lots of them don't just choose to ignore what Catalonia is, but actually reject it. When you find out that the real situation is quite the opposite, I think it is time to change. But, to my great surprise, lots of English people seem to feel more comfortable living with clichés. The least they could do is acknowledge Catalan reality, whether they sympathise with it or not. I've lived in Barcelona for 25 years, and I have never thought I was living in Spain. I do not mean it in a political way, and I'm not waving a flag. It just is another country. It has everything it needs to be a country: its own history, social structure, economic system, cultural past and language. All it needs now is a State.

Don't you think the Catalans are to blame for not stating their case more clearly and coming across better?

It's hard to generalize, but I see two positions among Catalans. Either they just shut up every time they are called Spanish or told to change language, because these English people don't understand, pretending they don't really exist. Or else they make a point of explaining, in which case they are branded as obstreperous trouble-makers. They cannot win either way.

Have there been any changes on this front since you arrived?

There has been one huge change in the attitude towards people who are not Catalan, or whose parents were not born here. I remember reading a book about non-Catalan-born Catalans[2] who, right up to the 1970s, were still considered foreign bodies. By the eighties, with self-government, they were seen as fellow Catalans. This positive shift is being applied to the massive wave of immigrants coming to Catalonia now—1,200,000 in fifteen years, on top of a base population of six million. What I like about Catalans is that they have completely cut out the ethnic element from their sense of identity: a first step towards eliminating racism and assimilating people from outside. The exceptions are some English, American and other affluent groups, who have no need to assimilate and continue to live in their mental shells. Those who want their kids to get on in Catalonia want them to learn Catalan.

Does that make Catalonia a model for integration that other nations could learn from?

The Catalan case is interesting for a good many reasons. Firstly, because it is a huge small culture! This isn't Brittany, or the Basque Country, or even Wales. In linguistic terms, it is a very large small European culture which has been treated like a tiny region of no importance whatsoever. And that is interesting in itself. People who get interested in it and start reading translations of Catalan books—as happens more and more in countries like Holland, Germany, France, and so on—discover that Catalan literature is world class, not something local or regional. But another significant thing is to see how much the Spanish hate Catalans. That is a big story in itself. Whenever I explain the boycott of Catalan goods in Spain to people in Britain or Holland, they get very upset. They ask you when it happens, and you have to tell them that, actually, it happens all the time, although it is not reported and the background to the conflict remains largely unexplained. I think that is news in itself. It's man bites dog, really.

So can Europeans be sensitive to what's going on in Catalonia?

I think the reaction I got at a talk I gave at the London School of Economics is significant.[3] I thought it would be interesting to give a summary of the history of Spanish prejudice against Catalans, from the end of the 18th century to the present. It was all based on fact, not propaganda, I gave plenty of examples, and I added my own perceptions at the end. I think that was particularly interesting for the audience, because it was all news to them. I was able to get across the fact that it wasn't just Franco, but at least two and a half centuries of institutionalized popular rejection, in very large areas of Spain, of the very existence of something called Catalonia, not to mention its language. At question time, the issue of the Andalusian 'immigrants' came up, and I was able to assure people that the then President of Catalonia is himself Andalusian-born. They asked about racism, and I told them that one of the most prestigious writers in Catalan today is a woman born in Morocco. Catalonia is probably more broad-minded than Britain. The proof, at that talk, is the fact that someone subsequently protested that the LSE was being used for 'separatist propaganda' and that funding should be discontinued. So it seems it isn't only in Madrid that Catalonia is misunderstood!

What do you mean when you talk about discrimination and racism against Catalans?

Let me give you a couple of examples in the context of the language issue. A TV cameraman I know was in Burgos, in northern Spain, in 2006, and went into a bar with his crew, ordered something in Spanish and sat down to discuss the day's shoot. They were talking in Catalan. The owner came up to them from behind the bar and told them that, if they wanted to speak in Catalan, they had better go somewhere else. You hear stories like that almost every day. The last time I read about anything like that happening in England was when a couple of Welsh women, on holiday on the Isle of Wight, were thrown out of a shop for speaking Welsh. They went to the press, and it caused such a stir that the Isle of Wight authorities invited them back for a free holiday because they felt so embarrassed. The Catalan camera crew, four years after the incident in Burgos, are still waiting for an apology. Another case that springs to mind is what happened to writer Empar Moliner when she was talking in Catalan on her mobile phone in a Madrid taxi. She was asked to get out, but managed to avoid being evicted when she claimed she was speaking in Italian, at which the driver told her, 'well, that's OK, then'.

Why do some international media go on about Catalonia being 'selfish', 'turned in on herself' and so on?

Journalists tend to go along with the information that's dished out to them. A lot of what they write is plain bullshit. They have no idea of the context in which the Catalan language is taught, and no idea about the use of Castilian in Catalonia. The journalist Carles Puigdemont, today an MP in the Catalan parliament, once looked into the situation of English correspondents in Madrid and found that they only read two newspapers: the Madrid editions of *El País* and *El Mundo*. Well, if that's what they do, they are not going to get a positive idea of Catalonia, because these papers either aren't interested in Catalonia, or are totally opposed to Catalan ideas and thinking.

Apart from that, Catalonia finds it hard to project its culture and identity beyond its frontiers...

Yes. And, after years dithering between different options, I now feel the only way Catalonia is going to get recognized at a cultural level is through political independence. What they used to see as an option—'asymmetrical federalism'—just isn't on. It is more difficult to conceive of than independence itself. What I notice is that people fly over Catalonia without seeing it, so to speak. And this is never going to change unless it is put on the map. If you don't have your little State and your little flag, they are not going to read books by your writers, or watch films by your film-makers. They are not going to treat you like a serious culture. They will not even understand that phenomena like Salvador Dalí or Joan Miró are incomprehensible outside a Catalan context, let alone the poet Foix or the philosopher Francesc Pujols. The

Catalan administration may be partly to blame for some of this. When my Dutch girlfriend wanted to learn Catalan some years back, she actually found it hard to find a place where she could learn the language at a reasonable price. The Catalan government was putting on Spanish lessons, but not Catalan ones.

Despite that, the general feeling seems to be that support for independence is growing…

Definitely! In the late 1970s people who wanted independence tended to keep quiet about it, because they were afraid of another coup d'état. In the eighties independence became a fad among some young people: visible, yes, but only stuff for kids. And then in the nineties things began to change for lots of reasons, especially because people came to realize that Catalonia had been ripped off for decades, and there was a general lack of respect for people in Catalonia, whatever language they spoke. In that sense it is interesting to learn that 30% of those favouring independence actually come from Spanish-speaking families. This should mean that the Catalans have won. There is no rift between the Catalan and Spanish-speaking population, though various agencies—including State ones—have been trying to create one for years.

Do you think Spain has got over Franco? Has Catalonia?

I find it extraordinarily offensive that there are still monuments to Franco all over Spain. Most of them have been torn down in Catalonia. There is also a rather moth-eaten Francisco Franco Foundation which has been getting considerable Spanish government funding until quite recently. Whereas in places like Argentina that sort of aberration was done away with relatively soon after the dictatorship, issues such as looking for the mass graves left by Franco are still controversial matters in Spain. We are talking about 150,000 to 200,000 people put to death after the end of the Civil War. My perception is that things are radically different, depending on the part of Spain you visit. In Central Spain and Castile, and in some parts of Galicia and Aragon, you get the feeling that they really wouldn't mind if Franco were still in power, whereas in Catalonia you get the impression that almost everyone abhors him.

What do you think about those who say that there were also Catalan Francoists and that Catalonia benefitted from Franco?

The fact that there were Catalans who collaborated with Franco means exactly nothing. Whenever there is a dictatorial regime, in any country, there is always that small percentage of opportunists, usually among the wealthiest classes. You need only look at the extraordinary level of collaboration there was with the Nazis in France. Three-quarters of the population was either with them or didn't mind them.

British historians often identify with the romantic view of Republican Spain and the war. But would you say the Catalan cause is treated with the same degree of enthusiasm?

I'm not sure about British historians in general, but I think Paul Preston does his bit here, especially as regards his personal commitment to things Catalan, having acquired a very reasonable level of spoken Catalan. Here people tell you that Franco rebelled against the Republic largely because he and others reckoned Catalonia had 'gone foreign', or 'gone Catalan', so that one of the main reasons for starting the war was to get Catalonia back into the Castilian fold. I have never actually seen a major British historian include that as one of the reasons for the uprising. Yes, they go on about the Anarchists, economic issues, violence, etc., but I think they always underplay what it meant to a clique of Spanish generals that Catalonia had achieved a degree of autonomy. I think it is significant that, when Franco's army entered Catalan territory, it adopted a different name to the one it had sported when rampaging through the rest of Spain. Here it was to sign its decrees as 'Army of Occupation', whereas elsewhere it had been the 'Army of Liberation'. Quite significant, I feel, but no British historian I know seems to have picked it up.

Notes

Introduction

1. Initially signed by MPs Hywel Williams, Elfyn Llwyd, Jonathan Edwards, Pete Wishart, Angus Brendan MacNeil, Mike Wier, Caroline Lucas, Stewart Hosie, and Eilidh Whiteford.
2. *El Periódico*, *La Vanguardia*, *Avui*, *El Punt*, *Segre*, *La Mañana*, *Diari de Tarragona*, *Diari de Girona*, *Regió 7*, *El Nou 9*, *Diari de Terrassa*, and *Diari de Sabadell*.
3. *Independentista* is the word generally used in Catalan and Spanish for supporters of Catalan national independence and separation from Spain (the corresponding movement in Catalan is *Independentisme*). These terms have no natural equivalent in English, so *Independentist* and *Independentism* are used where necessary in this book.
4. February 18, 2006 and December 1, 2007. Former presidents of the Catalan government Jordi Pujol and Pasqual Maragall both took part in the latter march.
5. By giving it entirely the same status as Spanish as an official language in Catalonia.
6. One Socialist former deputy prime minister of Spain spoke of the need to 'cut the text down beyond recognition'.
7. The Zapatero government has only published hitherto secret interregional fiscal balances since 2008.
8. As seen at the final match of Spain's King's Cup (Copa del Rey) between FC Barcelona and Athletic de Bilbao, on May 13, 2009, when the King's arrival at the stadium was met with widespread disapproval by both Catalan and Basque supporters.

Carles Boix

1. Carles Boix and his wife Alícia Adserà—also an academic at Princeton—received us at their Palamós holiday apartment in mid-August. That morning one of their three sons had cut his leg on a glass-topped table. The emergency rush to the hospital, stitches included, did not prevent the interview being conducted.
2. 'El fracàs estatutari', July 6, 2010.
3. The moderate nationalist coalition Convergència i Unió (CiU) is made up of two parties, Convergència Democràtica de Catalunya and Unió Democràtica de Catalunya, and was led for many years by Jordi Pujol *(see page 54)*. CiU formed the ruling party in the autonomous Catalan government or Generalitat for 23 years from the first elections after its restoration in 1980 until 2003, and has again been in power since the elections of November 28, 2010.
4. The association Òmnium Cultural (20,000 members) founded in 1961 but for periods outlawed by Franco.
5. A poem which Catalan cult singer Lluís Llach set to music in the record 'Ítaca'.
6. The conservative leader of the Catalanist Lliga Regionalista party from 1917 to 1936.

Salvador Cardús

1. He argues that by publishing in a more conservative and Spanish-language paper he will be read by more people than he would be in Catalan-language papers. *La Vanguardia* has since begun publishing a Catalan edition.
2. The Partido Popular (PP) is the leading conservative party in Spain as a whole, and was in power in the central government from 1996 to 2004 under Prime Minister José María Aznar. Its current leader is Mariano Rajoy. The Partido Socialista Obrero Español (PSOE) is the Spanish socialist party, founded in 1879. Since Spain's transition to democracy it was in power in the central government from 1982 to 1996, under Felipe González, and has again held power since 2004 under Prime Minister José Luis Rodríguez Zapatero. The Catalan Socialist Party (Partit dels Socialistes de Catalunya, PSC) is affiliated to the PSOE and its deputies form part of the Socialist group in the Madrid Cortes or parliament.
3. The 'Organic Law for the Harmonization of the Process of Autonomy', of June 30, 1982, known as the LOHPA in Catalan or LOAPA in Spanish, sought to limit, regulate and standardize Spain's regional home rule model, almost certainly in response to the attempted military coup of February 23, 1981.
4. In March 2000 the Partido Popular under José María Aznar won an absolute majority in the Spanish Cortes. This allowed it to pursue a much more independent policy than his previous government, which had been obliged to rely on agreements with the Catalan CiU and other nationalist parties.
5. Argentine-born writer Patrícia Gabancho calls this 'the price of being Spanish'.
6. This refers to the proposal put forward in the early 1990s for the creation of a Catalan Bishops' Conference within the Catholic Church, separate from the Spanish Bishops' Conference.
7. This interview was carried out in the summer of 2010, before the Tripartit or three-way coalition headed by the Socialists lost power in the Catalan Generalitat government to CiU in the elections of November 28, 2010.

Eliseu Climent

1. A 3,500-square metre, dynamic four-storey cultural centre designed by Carles Dolç, with the aid of the prestigious Barcelona architect Oriol Bohigas, on the site of the El Siglo department store in central Valencia, hosting a whole range of state-of-the-art cultural amenities.
2. In Spanish, *Alicante*.
3. Dates of the battle of Almansa in 1707, which led to the fall of Valencia to the forces of the Bourbon King Philip V of Spain, and the fall of Barcelona in 1714, both during the War of the Spanish Succession.
4. Namely, to make Catalan voluntary in schools and to place the province of Alacant in a new region with other non-Catalan-speaking territories.

Joan Laporta

1. See interview, page 194.
2. Joan (originally Hans) Gamper was a Swiss resident of Barcelona who founded FC Barcelona in 1899, played for the club for several years, and served as club president on five different occasions before his death in 1930.
3. 'Sport and Citizenship', regularly published in his Barcelona newspaper *La Rambla*.
4. In 1996, after the Partido Popular under José María Aznar emerged as the largest single party in the Spain-wide general election, but without an overall majority, Convergència i Unió agreed to provide the support necessary for the PP to

take office in return for a range of promised concessions on the powers of the Catalan government and other matters, in an agreement negotiated in Barcelona's Majestic Hotel.

5. The party referred to is Esquerra Republicana de Catalunya (Republican Left of Catalonia, ERC), a historic leftist, republican and pro-independence Catalan party that, following the Generalitat elections of 2003, formed a three-party leftist coalition or *Tripartit* with the Catalan Socialist Party (PSC), the largest and thus leading party in the coalition, and Iniciativa per Catalunya-Verds, a leftist-green alliance. The Tripartit coalition formed the successive Catalan governments from 2003 until losing power in the elections of November 28, 2010.

6. In the elections of November 28th, the coalition Solidaritat Catalana per la Independència headed by Joan Laporta and including his Democràcia Catalana party gained four seats in the 135-member Catalan parliament, including that of Laporta himself.

Alfons López Tena

1. '*Catalonia under Spain. National oppression in democracy*'. Barcelona, La Magrana, 2007.
2. On April 23, 2001, at the award-giving ceremony for the annual Premio Cervantes literary prize for writers in Spanish, King Juan Carlos said: 'Never was our language an imposed one, but rather one of encounter; no one was ever forced to learn Castilian', a statement that caused a major upset in the Catalan media.
3. 'The Valley of the Fallen', the giant monument in the hills outside Madrid that contains Franco's tomb.

José Montilla

1. *Generalitat* has been the name given to the Catalan Government since the 14th century. Sr. Montilla lead the Generalitat government of 2006–10 at the head of a Tripartit or three-party coalition, of his own Catalan Socialist Party (the largest partner), the Esquerra Republicana de Catalunya (Republican Left of Catalonia, ERC) and the leftist-environmentalist Iniciativa per Catalunya-Verds (Initiative for Catalonia-Greens, ICV). The different parties stood separately in the Generalitat elections of November 28, 2010, when the Catalan Socialists and ERC in particular lost heavily. The conservative, moderately nationalist Convergència i Unió (CiU) emerged as the largest party and on December 27 formed a new government under Artur Mas as President of the Generalitat. The following interview took place during the summer of 2010, when Sr. Montilla was still President of the Generalitat.
2. The Independence referendums, the suspense over the Statute of Autonomy, the language controversy and the ban on bullfighting are the major issues referred to here.

Jordi Pujol

1. The *Fets del Palau* or 'Palau Events' took place in May 1960, when the centenary of the birth of the Catalan poet Joan Maragall was due to be marked at a ceremony in the Palau de la Música concert hall with the attendance of ministers in Franco's government. Protesters interrupted by singing the 'Cant de la Senyera', a song with words by Maragall that has become one of Catalonia's national anthems, but which had been specifically prohibited by the authorities. Jordi Pujol was not actually present but was rapidly arrested as one of the organizers of the protest.

2. During the Republic, the main Catalan bank, the Banc de Catalunya, failed in the financial crisis of 1931 and, denied support by the state authorities, was bought by the Banco de Vizcaya, one of the leading Spanish banks. [Previous note was factually inaccurate]
3. For example, former Catalan Justice Minister Agustí Bassols and Alfons López Tena *(see page 42)*.
4. An ex-Justice Minister in Jordi Pujol's Generalitat government.
5. He was actually born in the province of Cordoba in Andalusia *(see page 48)*
6. A prominent Catalan politician during the Republic and the Civil War, Josep Tarradellas (1899–1988) was elected President of the Generalitat in Exile in France in 1954. He returned from exile in October 1977 and headed a provisional government of the restored Generalitat until 1980, when the first full elections were held.
7. Spanish poet Antonio Machado wrote, 'Castilla miserable, ayer dominadora envuelta en sus andrajos, desprecia cuanto ignora'. (Miserable Castile, yesterday all-powerful, [today] wrapped in rags, despises what it does not know about).

Joan Ramon Resina

1. According to Barcelona municipal police.
2. A reference to the participation by Esquerra Republicana de Catalunya (Republican Left of Catalonia, ERC) with the Socialists in the Tripartit three-party coalition government of the Generalitat headed by President José Montilla from 2006–10.
3. Following the November 28, 2010 Catalan elections Artur Mas became President of the Generalitat at the head of a CiU administration.
4. In 1640 Catalonia revolted against the Spanish Crown and the Generalitat offered sovereignty over Catalonia to Louis XIII of France, then at war with Spain, in return for military aid. After a bloody war most of Catalonia was conquered by Spanish armies by 1652, and the war formally ended in 1659 with the Treaty of the Pyrenees between Spain and France, under which the latter acquired the Catalan territory of Roussillon.
5. A prominent leader of the conservative nationalist Catalan Lliga Regionalista party in the early 20th century.

Germà Bel

1. For more information, see www.germabel.cat
2. The T1 Terminal at Barcelona airport, designed by Ricard Bofill, was inaugurated on June 17, 2009.
3. The High Speed Train system, known as the TGV or, in Spain, the AVE (Alta Velocidad Española). Most rail lines in Spain (and Portugal) have been built on a broader gauge than that of the rest of Europe, so direct freight trains into France have been impossible to run. In December 2010 the first-ever European-gauge freight rail line opened between Barcelona and Lyon, allowing the transfer of containers from the Port of Barcelona onto trains connecting directly with the European rail network, but still with only a limited capacity. The TGV/AVE high-speed lines are passenger-only.

4. Rodalies (or Cercanías in Spanish) is the name for the main local train network in the Barcelona area. Since the 2007 collapse it has come under Catalan government control.
5. Formerly owned by Scandinavian Airlines, the airline Spanair was acquired by a group of Catalan investors in January 2009, with SAS retaining a minority interest.
6. A reference to the large-scale collapse in the local railway system and the electricity grid that severely affected the Catalan economy a few months later, in mid-2007.
7. The governments of the Basque Country and Navarre enjoy special fiscal regimes under which they contribute less proportionately to central government than other autonomous regions.

Joaquim Boixareu
1. He is on the board of prestigious organizations such as the Unió Patronal Metal·lúrgica, Foment del Treball Nacional and the Barcelona Graduate School of Economics.
2. Which is in fact a Catalan adaptation of the name of the Irish party Sinn Feín, or 'Ourselves Alone'.
3. The vast majority of rail lines in Spain and Portugal were built with a broader gauge than those in the rest of Europe, and there remain very few direct connections with the international network despite many calls for the building of European-gauge freight lines.
4. In the summer and autumn of 2007 cumulative deficiencies in local infrastructure were reflected in large-scale power cuts in many parts of Catalonia lasting several days, a paralysis of the local rail network and service interruptions in flights and other transport links.

Xavier Sala-i-Martin
1. He gave the entire $95,000 prize to the Umbele Foundation, which promotes education and development in Africa.

Elisenda Paluzie
1. Though both are socialists, Pasqual Maragall left the PSC after being prevented from standing again in 2007 by the more Madrid-oriented wing of the party and a press campaign against his 'excessive Catalanism'.
2. Coordinadora Nacional de les Consultes sobre la Independència.
3. Convergència i Unió, the moderate nationalist coalition long led by Jordi Pujol *(see page 54)*, and which headed the Catalan government from 1980–2003 and again since December 2010.
4. The historic Catalan Caixa Laietana savings bank agreed a 'cold merger', under which each element will retain its corporate identity, with the large Madrid-based Caja Madrid and four other savings banks in September 2010.

Dr. Moisès Broggi
1. Rodolfo Martín Villa, who held various posts under the Franco regime and was Interior Minister in the transition government of Adolfo Suárez from 1976 to 1979, has been chairman of Sogecable, one of Spain's largest pay-TV providers, since 2006; Juan Antonio Samaranch (1920–2010), famous as the President of the International Olympic Committee from 1980 to 2001, had previously been one of the leading figures of the Franco regime in Catalonia from the 1950s to the 1970s.
2. The Federación Anarquista Ibérica (Iberian Anarchist Federation), a radical and violent anarchist group linked to the anarchosyndicalist union the CNT before and during the Civil War.
3. Lluís Companys (1882–1940), President of the Catalan Generalitat from 1933 and throughout the Civil War, went into exile in France at the end of the war. In August 1940 he was arrested by the German Gestapo with the assistance of the French Pétain government, and handed over to the Franco regime. He was tried by court-martial and executed in October 1940.
4. A reference to three of the most distinguished Catalan exiles who played prominent roles in international cultural life after the Civil War: the celebrated cellist Pau Casals (1876–1973; often known internationally as Pablo, the Spanish form) worked tirelessly to publicize the cause of Catalonia and democracy from his exile in France and Puerto Rico; the historian and anthropologist Josep Maria Batista i Roca (1895–1978) also went into exile and taught for many years at Cambridge University, founding various institutions to promote awareness of Catalan culture; and Doctor Josep Trueta (1897–1977), Professor of Orthopaedics at Oxford from 1949 to 1965 and one of the creators of the Nuffield Orthopaedic Centre, also published a short book in 1940 on *The Spirit of Catalonia*.

Josep Cruanyes
1. That of Peiró in 2006, and that of Puig Antich in 2007.
2. Original title: *Das Leben der Anderen* (2006).
3. President of the Catalan Government from 1933–1940, and executed by the Franco regime in October 1940.
4. Rodolfo Martín Villa, a former Francoist official who was Interior Minister in the post-Franco government of Adolfo Suárez and is now chairman of the Sogecable media group.
5. Manuel Fraga Iribarne, born in 1922, served as Information Minister for several years under Franco in the 1960s, and in 1975–76 was Interior Minister in the first government after Franco's death. During the transition to democracy he became the leader of the conservative Alianza Popular, precursor of the current Partido Popular, but gave way to a younger leadership at the end of the 1980s since it was felt his image was too reactionary to win a general election. Subsequently he headed the Partido Popular government of his home region of Galicia from 1990–2005. He remains Honorary President of the Partido Popular.
6. As denounced in a series of books and documentaries by former Sunday Times and BBC journalist Andrew Jennings, among others.
7. Judge Baltasar Garzón first came to prominence as an investigating magistrate in the late 1980s through his investigations into the GAL, a shadowy state-sponsored group that had carried on a 'dirty war' against the Basque revolutionaries of ETA. However, he has also investigated ETA itself, and is famed for his involvement in many other high-profile cases, many involving the extension of legal investigations into previously-untouched areas. In 1998 he issued the order for the arrest of former Chilean dictator General Pinochet

that led to his being arrested and held for prolonged extradition hearings in Britain. In 2008 Garzón began to investigate unresolved cases of executions, mass killings and other incidents possibly committed by the Franco regime and its agents during and since the Civil War. This met with intense opposition, and in April 2010, following a complaint by two extreme-right organizations, Spain's Supreme Court, which has a conservative majority, indicted Garzón for exceeding his authority and perverting the course of justice, which led to his suspension from the Audiencia Nacional. This led to massive protests across Spain, and was criticized by many international jurists and human rights organizations. Garzón has appealed the decision, but partly as a way of avoiding the issue for some months he has been appointed a consultant to the International Criminal Court. The fierce controversy over the politicisation of the Spanish justice system is ongoing.
8. In the Basque Country and Catalonia, particularly, many cannot forget moments in which his proceedings turned a blind eye to the possible police torture of detainees.
9. A town in the Empordà, in northern Catalonia.
10. During the War of the Spanish Succession (1701–1714) Catalonia, Valencia and other former territories of the Crown of Aragon supported the Austrian candidate to the Spanish throne, Archduke Charles, who had promised to maintain their historic rights, against the French Bourbon candidate Philip V. Initially they were also supported by Britain, Austria and the Netherlands. The other powers made a separate peace and recognized Philip V as King of Spain in 1713, but the Catalans fought on alone, until Barcelona fell after a ten-month siege on September 11, 1714. This led directly to the decrees of *Nova Planta* of 1716, which abolished the traditional Catalan institutions, extended a uniform State administration and established Spanish as the sole language of government. September 11 is now Catalan National Day.

Hilari Raguer
1. The 'little brown one'.
2. It was on this rock that Catalan activists hung an enormous Catalan flag during a ceremony to enthrone Our Lady of Montserrat on April 27, 1947, in the presence of 100,000 Catalan Catholics, much to the fury of the Francoist authorities.
3. Hilari is 'a man's name in Catalan, although—as he points out—he regularly suffers 'gender crises' at English-speaking venues.
4. Jacint Verdaguer (1945–1902) was one of the foremost poets of the 19th-century Renaixença or 'rebirth' of Catalan literature, and also a priest known for his dedication to the poor.
5. A progressive Republican school created in 1932 with advanced educational methods.
6. Josep Benet (1920–2008) was a distinguished historian of contemporary Catalonia and a leading figure in the opposition to Francoism.
7. José Calvo Sotelo (1893–1936) was a minister under the Primo de Rivera Dictatorship in the 1920s and the most prominent political leader of the far-right in Spain in the years prior to the Civil War, intransigently opposed to any concession of autonomy to Catalonia. He was assassinated just before the outbreak of the war in July 1936.
8. Josep Pla (1897–1981) was a prolific novelist, essayist and journalist.
9. Santos Juliá, Professor of Social History and Political Thought of the UNED university in Madrid, is one of Spain's leading contemporary historians and the biographer of President Manuel Azaña.
10. Manuel Azaña (1880–1940) was Prime Minister of the Republican central government from 1931–33 and again after the election victory of the Popular Front in February 1936, and President of the Republic from May 1936 to the end of the Civil War.
11. Ramón Serrano Súñer (1901–2003) was Franco's brother-in-law and served under him as Interior Minister, Foreign Minister and head of the Falange movement, and was the most enthusiastic proponent of closer links with Hitler and Mussolini during the first years of the regime. His mother was from Gandesa in southern Catalonia and had used the Catalan spelling of her name Sunyer, but he always used the Castilianised version Súñer.
12. Professor Paul Preston of the London School of Economics has written several books on the Spanish Civil War and an authoritative biography of Franco; Dr. Enrique Moradiellos of the Universidad Complutense in Madrid has carried out the most extensive study yet undertaken of the Non-Intervention Policy imposed by France and Britain during the Civil War, published in books such as *La Perfidia de Albión: El Gobierno Británico y la Guerra Civil Española* (1996).
13. The key double agent working for the British, known as 'Garbo', who in Operation Fortitude led Hitler to disregard the likelihood of a Normandy landing.
14. Francesc Bosch, who smuggled large quantities of photographs out of the notorious concentration camp, which were to provide vital evidence at the Nuremburg trials.
15. This ceremony, much played down by the media, was held in the Generalitat Palace on September 29, 2008. See also interview with Dr. Moisès Broggi, page 100.
16. Doctor Josep Trueta, Professor of Orthopaedics in Oxford for many years.
17. Especially the Christian Democrat group around Maurici Serrahima.
18. See interview with Josep Cruanyes, page 106.
19. Signed by Mitford Crowe, representative of Queen Anne, and Catalan ambassadors Domènec Perera and Antoni de Peguera.

Empar Salvador
1. The 'Pacts of the Moncloa' were a series of agreements reached in October 1977 between the government of Adolfo Suárez, the various parties that had achieved parliamentary representation in Spain's first post-Franco election the previous June, and the main trade unions, on the way in which the transition to democracy was to proceed. They included political and social elements, and a stability pact to ensure immediate economic stability. The Palacio de la Moncloa is the Prime Minister's official residence in Madrid.

2 The former, President-Emeritus of the Italian Republic, and the latter, a distinguished academic and expert on international law, originally from Valencia, who was an adviser to Salvador Allende's government in Chile and later that of François Mitterand in France.

3 *El genocidi franquista de València. Les fosses comunes silenciades del cementiri*, Editorial Icaria, Barcelona, 2008

4 Among them the ex-Director General of UNESCO, Federico Mayor Zaragoza, and Danielle Mitterand, of France Libertés. Video messages sent by Desmond Tutu and Francesco Cossiga were also shown.

5 See interview with Josep Cruanyes, page 106.

Eugeni Casanova and Jordi Llisterri

1 The general concern has been that this operation could cause a disaster similar to that in Barcelona's Carmel district, where the collapse of a new tunnel for Barcelona's underground rail network affected the homes of over 1,000 people in January 2005.

2 This dispute concerns an area along the western border of Catalonia known to Catalans as the Franja de Ponent ('Western Fringe'), which despite being Catalan-speaking was included in the Aragonese provinces of Huesca and Zaragoza in the provincial division of Spain established in the 1830s. In ecclesiastical terms, however, these communities had always formed part of the diocese of Lleida, in Catalonia, until in 1995–98 they were transferred by a Vatican decree to the diocese of Barbastro-Monzón in Aragon. A further controversy arose when the Aragonese authorities demanded the transfer of religious artefacts from the Franja held in Lleida's diocesan museum (now part of the Museu de Lleida Diocesà i Comarcal), leading to a prolonged legal dispute that is still unresolved.

3 On the cover of this book one can see a group of Christian demonstrators appearing to brandish Catalan flags and banners with the slogan 'The Catalan Church exists' at the Archbishop of Barcelona during a procession.

4 Jordi Llisterri (JL).

5 Eugeni Casanova (EC).

6 The 'rebirth', the movement that brought about the literary re-emergence of Catalan in the 19th Century.

7 Isabella of Castile married Ferdinand of Aragon in 1469, leading to the union of the different Spanish crowns in their heirs.

8 See interview, page 54.

9 The Spanish Cardinal Eduardo Martínez Somalo was Chamberlain of the Holy See from 1993–2007.

10 The conservative Catholic organization Opus Dei, founded in Spain in 1928 by Monsignor José María Escrivá, has long been controversial for the allegedly excessive covert influence it is often said to wield in the country. Internationally it was especially favoured by Pope John Paul II, who initiated the 'fast-track' canonisation of Mgr. Escrivá, declared a Saint in 2002.

11 Cardinal Vicente Enrique y Tarancón (1907–1994) was head of the Spanish Church during the last years of the transition to democracy and the transition to democracy, and associated with an openness to social dialogue and liberal ideas.

12 Cardinal Antonio Suquía (1916–2006) succeeded Tarancón as Archbishop of Madrid and was a much more conservative figure.

13 Historically, the Archbishops of Tarragona had been considered the principal figures in the Catalan Church. In 2004, however, the see of Barcelona was also elevated to the status of Metropolitan Archdiocese by the Vatican.

14 Barbastro was the birthplace of the Opus Dei's founder Mgr. Escrivá, and nearby is one of the organization's principal centres at Torreciudad.

Jennifer Berengueras

1 An *Iniciativa Legislativa Popular (ILP)* is a provision under Catalan law through which any measure presented with the support of at least 50,000 signatures of Catalan residents collected within a 120-day period has to be considered by the Catalan Parliament.

2 This is a reference to the Faroe Islands, not Denmark itself.

3 Bullfighting enthusiasts.

4 An international cultural festival promoted by the City Council that was a notorious flop. One critical journalist remarked that, in contrast, the anti-bullfighting motion had been 'rather more successful'.

5 Barcelona's Monumental bullring had been an increasingly secondary venue in the bullfighting calendar, with a continuous decline in audiences, until charismatic bullfighter José Tomás chose to make his return from a five-year retirement there, in a series of highly-publicized fights that, as the text indicates, were heralded as a demonstration of a continuing enthusiasm for bullfighting in the city.

6 Catalan actor, writer and theatre director Albert Boadella became prominent for his radical productions in the 1970s, when he was arrested by the Spanish authorities. Since the 1980s however he has moved towards a position ever-more critical of most currents of Catalan nationalism, and in particular has been an enthusiastic supporter of bullfighting.

7 Spikes that are stabbed into the bulls' back, and the red capes used for bullfighting.

Bernat Joan

1 This interview was conducted in mid-2010, before the Catalan elections of November 28, 2010, after which CiU returned to power.

2 The 'Law on Linguistic Policy' of 1998, following on from the 'Law of Linguistic Normalization' of 1983, has been the keystone of Catalan government measures intended to re-establish the public role of Catalan. Among other things it established a set of incentives for Catalan learners, and requirements of a certain level of Catalan for access to some areas of public employment.

3 French or north Catalonia consists of the area of Roussillon, around Perpignan, and the Cerdagne valley in the Pyrenees. Catalan has also been spoken in the city of L'Alguer (Alghero) in Sardinia, and in the 'Western Fringe' or Franja de Ponent on the border with Aragon.

4 The use of minority languages in full sessions of the Spanish Senate in Madrid was in fact permitted in January 2011. The measure has been heavily attacked, especially on the

grounds of translation costs. Using languages other than Spanish is still not permitted in the more important lower house, the Cortes.

5 A term invented by Ortega y Gasset, suggesting 'coexisting with', but also a much more grudging 'putting up with', a connotation of tolerating an unavoidable burden.

Jordi Portabella
1 Founded in 1931, Esquerra Republicana de Catalunya or the Catalan Republican Left was the leading political party in Catalonia through the Republic and the Civil War, and re-emerged after the death of Franco.

Oleguer Presas
1 Oleguer Presas is known as a player only by his first name, as is common in Spain.
2 Since singer Lluís Llach's 1975 LP *Viatge a Itaca [Journey to Ithaca]*, the Greek myth of Ithaca has been a favourite reference for Catalanists.
3 A requirement the recent Constitutional Court sentence has ruled out, making Spanish the only obligatory language in Catalonia.
4 A Catalan national football team has existed since the 1900s, with a parenthesis during the Franco regime, and has been put on a more regular basis since the late 1990s. Since 2009 its coach has been the legendary former Barcelona and Netherlands player, and Barcelona manager, Johan Cruyff. However, it is not recognized by FIFA or UEFA and so can only play friendly matches.
5 Referred to, by many Catalans, as *partits de costellada*, or 'barbecue-picnic matches'.
6 The popular Barcelona newspaper *El Periódico*, launched in Spanish in 1978, has since the mid-1990s been published daily in two parallel editions, in Spanish and Catalan. There are two additional papers published in Catalan: *Ara*, which began in November, 2010, and the Catalan edition of *La Vanguardia*, whose first issue hit the stands in May, 2011.

Joan Solà
1 Professor Solà died of cancer on October 27, 2010, only a few weeks after this interview took place. The word *homenot*—literally 'big man'—was coined by author Josep Pla in reference to the leading figures of Catalan society.
2 Gemination is a linguistic term referring to the use of extended consonants in some languages, such of Catalan. The Catalan double-l has a distinctly prolonged sound.
3 The anonymous epic *Poema del Mío Cid (Poem of my Cid)*, dating from the late 12th century, is one of the foundation works of literature in Castilian Spanish. *L'Atlàntida* (1876) was the greatest work of Jacint Verdaguer (1845–1902), the foremost poet of the 19th-century Catalan literary Renaixença or 'rebirth'. It also takes the form of an epic, in ten cantos, evoking the travels of Heracles in Iberia and the legend of Atlantis.
4 La Molina is a popular ski resort in the Catalan Pyrenees.
5 Baltasar Porcel (1937–2009), born in Mallorca, was one of the most popular and prolific of modern Catalan novelists, who also produced theatrical works, non-fiction and a great deal of journalism.

6 This interview took place when José Montilla *(see page 40)* was still President of the Generalitat, before the Catalan Elections of November 28, 2010.

Xavier Vinyals
1 See interview, page 54.
2 See interview, page 150.

Montserrat Armengou
1 Televisió de Catalunya is Catalonia's public broadcasting network, established by the Generalitat government in 1983, and TV3 is its main channel.
2 The Fundación Pablo Iglesias is a cultural and historical foundation linked to the Spanish socialist party, the PSOE, named after the party's founder and first leader from 1879 to 1925. The exhibition Exilio (Exile) was presented in the Palacio de Cristal in the Retiro park in Madrid in autumn 2002, and a documentary film was produced with the same title.
3 King Juan Carlos was born in 1938 in Rome, where the Spanish royal family had taken refuge after the proclamation of the Republic in 1931, and lived there and in Switzerland before going to Spain for the first time at the age of ten.

Josep Gifreu
1 Founded in 1907 by Enric Prat de la Riba, the first theorist of modern Catalan nationalism and the first President of the Barcelona Provincial Council to see the need to promote the Catalan language and Catalan culture
2 The division into Spanish provinces in force since the 1830s is widely unpopular in Catalonia, where smaller districts called *comarques* are seen as a more realistic territorial division.
3 TV broadcasting in Catalan began in 1983 with the establishment of Televisió de Catalunya by the Generalitat government. Roughly half its funding comes from public sources, and the rest from advertising, programme sales and other sources. It now has a total of eight channels, of which TV3 and Canal 33 are the main conventional channels.
4 Its major shareholder is the Godó group, which also own *La Vanguardia* newspaper.
5 The popular newspaper *El Periódico* has been published in Barcelona in Spanish since 1978, but since the mid-1990s has also had a simultaneous edition in Catalan, and both versions are available online. *La Vanguardia* has traditionally been Barcelona's principal newspaper, published since 1881. However, it too began a Catalan edition in May, 2011. A new Catalan newspaper, *Ara*, began publishing in November, 2010.

Pedro Morón de la Fuente
1 The *Diada* or Catalan National Day on September 11th commemorates the date of the fall of Barcelona after the siege of 1713–14, in the War of the Spanish Succession (see notes to interview with Josep Cruanyes). Rafael Casanova was the chief councillor or mayor of Barcelona and the leader of Catalan resistance. Marking September 11th was prohibited during the Franco regime.

2. Pedro Morón's other books include *Catalònia Acord, Yo, catalán de Granada, Historias de la inmigración, Naturalezas del amor azul* and *Ràdio Sant Boi, història d'una il·lusió*.
3. Alejandro Lerroux rose to prominence in Barcelona in the early 1900s as the demagogical leader of the Radical Republican Party, and his name is associated with a policy of gaining electoral support among immigrant workers in Catalonia through opposition to Catalanism, appeals to Spanish patriotism, and the feeding of fears of being marginalised in a Catalonia with greater national rights.
4. José Bono is currently Speaker of the Spanish Parliament (the Cortes) and was previously Defence Minister in the Socialist government of José Luis Rodríguez Zapatero and head of the regional government of Castilla-La Mancha; Juan Carlos Rodríguez Ibarra, now semi-retired, was head of the Junta de Extremadura, the autonomous government of Extremadura, from 1982–2007; Alfonso Guerra was deputy prime minister during most of Spain's first socialist government under Felipe González, from 1982 to 1991, and remains an MP and an influential if polemical figure in the party; Manuel Chaves has served as a minister in socialist governments under Felipe González and again today under Rodríguez Zapatero, was head of the Andalusian regional government (1990–2009) and is Chairman of the PSOE. All, especially Bono, Guerra and Rodríguez Ibarra, are known for their antagonistic stance towards Catalan demands.
5. Josep Maria Sala was Secretary for Organization of the Catalan Socialist Party (PSC) for several years in the 1980s and 1990s and also a member of the Executive Committee of the Spain-wide PSOE. With a controversial reputation as a 'power behind the scenes' in the party apparatus of the PSC, he is particularly associated with a policy of building up voting support among immigrants to Catalonia through establishing connections with and fostering separate organizations based on regional and, in the case of non-Spanish immigrants, ethnic origin, such as Andalusian, Galician and, lately, Moroccan and Latin American associations. In 1997 Sala served a prison sentence in connection with the Filesa case, which involved illegal funding of the PSOE. However, after his release (most of his sentence was suspended) he has been rehabilitated by the party, and is again a member of the PSOE executive.
6. A cultural organization set up by the PSC that undertakes to assist the maintenance of the separate 'original cultures' of immigrant groups by assisting individual organizations for each one, rather than pursuing any kind of integrational model. This has been accused of creating 'greenhouses' for the preservation of each culture in isolation.
7. Raimon Obiols was the unsuccessful PSC candidate to be President of the Generalitat in several elections in the 1980s and 1990s, and is now an MEP. He is seen as one of the most Catalanist figures within the PSC.
8. A flamenco club typical of Andalusia, associated particularly with El Rocío, a pilgrimage to the hermitage of the same name in Huelva province made each year on the Pentecost (Whit Sunday) weekend that is one of the largest and most famous of Andalusia's fiestas.
9. A *Feria de Abril* (or *Fira d'Abril*) based on the famous April Fair in Seville has been held in the Barcelona area since 1971, as a celebration of Andalusian culture. Since the 1980s it has had increasing official support and has grown ever-larger in size.
10. This interview took place when José Montilla *(see page 48)*, was still President of the Generalitat, before Convergència i Unió regained power following the elections of November 28, 2010.

Vicent Partal
1. The Internet Corporation for Assigned Names and Numbers, which regulates domain names worldwide.
2. Dubbing of foreign films and programmes predominates today both on TV and in the cinema.
3. Francesc Cambó (1876-1947), the most prominent conservative Catalanist politician prior to the Civil War and the leader of the Lliga Regionalista party from 1917 to 1936.

Vicent Sanchis
1. Other examples would be ex-Generalitat universities minister Carles Solà, VilaWeb online newspaper editor Vicent Partal *(see page 188)*, and writer Isabel-Clara Simó.
2. *La Vanguardia* began publishing a Catalan edition, parallel to and otherwise the same as its Spanish one, in May 2011.
3. **Telefónica** is Spain's largest telecommunications and internet provider and a continuation of the former state telephone monopoly, which was privatized in the 1990s. It owns a wide range of operations and subsidiaries especially in Europe and the Americas (including the O2 mobile phone network) but since 2007 it has been obliged to relinquish some of the sectors in which it still had an effective monopoly in Spain after being penalized and fined under European competition law. **Prisa** is a major Madrid-based Spanish media group which among other interests owns El País newspaper, several radio stations, publishing houses and the Sogecable digital TV service. Since 2008 it has had serious financial problems caused by huge debts. **Grupo Planeta**, based in Barcelona, is one of Spain's largest publishing companies, in Spanish and Catalan, and has also diversified into TV. **MediaPro**, founded in Barcelona only in 1994, is a multi-aspect media services and production company with operations worldwide. **Prensa Ibérica** is a group that owns many local newspapers around Catalonia and in other parts of Spain.
4. The 'half' Catalan channel is a reference to 8TV, a channel with limited coverage owned by the Godó media group.
5. In the *Guerra dels Segadors* or War of the Reapers, a peasant revolt in 1640 led to a wider war in which Catalonia first declared its independence and then placed itself under the authority of Louis XIII of France as an alternative to the Spanish crown. However, France and Spain eventually made a separate peace, Barcelona was taken by the Spanish in 1652 and in 1659 under the Treaty of the Pyrenees the Catalan territory of Roussillon was given to France. In the War of the Spanish Succession, all the former territories of the Crown of Aragon (Catalonia, Valencia, the Balearics and Aragon) gave their support to the Austrian candidate to the Spanish crown Archduke Charles, who had promised to respect their historic rights, in opposition to the

French Bourbon candidate the Duke of Anjo, later Philip V of Spain. The defeat of the Aragonese territories after the withdrawal of their allies (principally Britain and the Netherlands) from the war led to their absorption into a unitary Spanish state. See also interview with Josep Cruanyes, *(see page 106).*

6 Fuster supplied solid ideas, and a much more dignified national outlook as the ideal for the future of Valencia, under the motto 'Being Valencian is our way of being Catalan'. See also interview with Eliseu Climent, *(see page 30).*

7 La Caixa is Catalonia's largest financial institution, and the largest savings bank in Europe.

8 The first all-Catalan newspaper of the post-Franco era, founded with a broad shareholder base in 1976. The Godó media group also own Barcelona's historic principal newspaper *La Vanguardia*.

9 A priceless sketch on the hugely popular TV3 satirical program Polònia portrayed an official interview between the Catalan and Valencian presidents 'communicating' by way of interpreters.

Helena Buffery

1 Literally, *What bollocks!*, but really an expression of surprise or anger.

2 Mercè Rodoreda (1908–1983) is widely considered the finest Catalan novelist of the post-Civil War years, and was also a prolific writer of short stories.

3 'Our old classics…', a reference to the reverence with which some Catalans regard their historic literature, mainly from the medieval period.

4 Catalanists are often accused of playing the victim and complaining at excessive length about their lot.

5 A very right-wing, pro-Spanish radio station, partly run by the Catholic Church.

6 Catalan language volunteers, a programme for Catalan-speakers to offer free language practice to learners of the language.

7 An issue under debate in the 2009–2010 period.

8 A term used to refer to words borrowed from other languages, especially Spanish, which are shunned by preceptive lexicologists.

9 Pro-independence Catalan flags, with a white star on a blue triangle next to the mast added to the historic Catalan flag of four red horizontal stripes on yellow.

Susan DiGiacomo

1 The full version of this letter may be found at http://emma-col-cat.blogspot.com/2010/07/letter-to-president-obama.html

2 Vic is a small city and capital of the Osona district, north Barcelona towards the Pyrenees.

3 The first local referendum on Catalan independence was held on September 13, 2009 in the small town of Arenys de Munt, near the coast north-east of Barcelona, initially as the result of an entirely local initiative. Out of a 41% turnout, 96.2% voted in favour of independence. This has since developed into a broad movement, with similar consultations in many towns and districts.

4 *El Mundo* and *ABC* are two of Spain's leading right-wing newspapers; COPE is a chain of radio stations also known for right-wing views, partly owned by the Catholic Church.

5 This interview took place when José Montilla *(see page 48)* was still President of the Generalitat, before the Catalan elections of November 28, 2010.

Dr. Henry Ettinghausen

1 One of two major revolts in the 17th and 18th centuries in which Catalonia sought greater independence from the Spanish crown. See also notes to interview with Vicent Sanchis.

2 The organization that has campaigned to recover the archives confiscated from Catalonia by the Franco regime in 1939, and held in Salamanca. See also interview with Josep Cruanyes, page 106.

3 On Garzón see interview with Josep Cruanyes, page 106.

4 See also interview with Dr. Moisès Broggi, page 100.

5 *Hasta aquí hemos llegado. Claves para entender el hartazgo de Catalunya con España (We're up to here. Key points for understanding Catalonia's frustration with Spain)*, Toni Strubell i Trueta (also the author of this book), Ttarttalo, 2009.

Alex Rietman

1 *ABC*, *La Razón* and *El Mundo* are Spain's principal right-wing newspapers, based in Madrid but with editions in some other parts of the country. *El País*, Spain's most prestigious daily newspaper and normally considered sympathetic to the Socialists, is also based in Madrid but has many regional editions.

2 Pío Moa and César Vidal are the foremost representatives of what have been called the 'neo-Francoist' historians of 20th-century Spain, who place the blame for the crisis of the 1930s and the Civil War on a violent, totalitarian left, which, in this account, gave the right and the army officers around Franco legitimate cause to fight back in self-defence. Following on from this is a defence of the subsequent Franco dictatorship. Deliberately polemical, in a way that has aided their media profile, they have been criticized by most academic historians for inadequate methodology and for simplifying and distorting many issues, but their books have had huge sales in Spain. Vidal in particular also writes for many right-wing newspapers, appears frequently on TV and has a regular programme on the COPE radio network.

3 A major Catalan demand only accepted by the Spanish Government in 2008.

Matthew Tree

1 Funnily enough, Bernard Loughlin, the first Irishman to regularly use four-letter words on Irish TV, first rose to fame shortly after his return from some years living in Barcelona, some of them in the house of the author of this book.

2 *Els altres Catalans* by Francesc Candel, first published in 1964.

3 Tree's lecture, "Life on the Receiving End", (November 5, 2008), is well worth a read: *http://cataloniathenextstate.blogspot.com/2009/06/life-on-receiving-end-matthew-tree.html*

About the Author

Toni Strubell has written several books about Catalonia. History, sport, travel, and politics are his favourite subjects. Born and brought up in Oxford (1952), he is the son of a Second World War RAF pilot and the grandson of an Oxford Orthopaedics professor, Josep Trueta, a Catalan surgeon who went into exile from Franco's Spain in 1939. Upset that the allies tolerated the Franco regime, in 1947 Trueta published the famous treatise on Catalonia, *The Spirit of Catalonia*, a book aimed at convincing western leaders that 1945 had not seen the end of all fascist dictatorships in Europe. His intention was to spell out what it meant for democratic Catalans to suffer Franco.

Strubell's book today is like a sequel to his grandfather's book in that it, too, tries to describe the country through its people. But whereas *The Spirit of Catalonia* spoke of historical figures, *What Catalans Want* interviews today's Catalans, and, even a handful of foreign residents living in Catalonia. He weaves the hidden story behind one of Europe's small "forbidden" countries, one which so many British tourists visit without getting much of an idea about what is going on. Strubell's Oxford education (Pembroke College) helps him discern just what things about Catalans and their country will appeal to, intrigue, and maybe even scandalize English speakers.

In recent years, the author has worked as a teacher in the Tourism department of Deusto University in the Basque Country. However, living four hundred miles from Catalonia has not prevented him being active in the Catalan civil rights movement. Indeed, from 2002 he has coordinated the *Comissió de la Dignitat*, an independent body which strives to recover the historical memory and, indeed, the archives pillaged from Catalonia by the Francoists at the end of the Civil War. Strubell was granted the *Creu de Sant Jordi* (Saint George's Cross) in 2002, one of Catalonia's most esteemed awards. He is currently an MP in the Catalan Parliament.

About the Photographer

Lluís Brunet i Palou was born in Sabadell, near Barcelona, in 1954. He began working as a freelance photographer in 1969. While pursuing academic studies, he apprenticed in graphic design and photography studios and laboratories.

In 1974, Lluís became exclusively freelance, with such clients as *La Vanguardia, Oriflama, El Correo Catalán, Destino, Diari Sabadell, Avui*, and many others. He opened his first independent photography studio in 1976.

Lluís began studying digital imagery in 1987 and in 1989, he developed a system, together with Josep Brunet i Llobet, that allowed clients to preview projects in colour, long-distance, via modem.

Between 1995 and 2003, Lluís taught classes, consulted, and participated in the creation of the curriculum for the Image Processing and Multimedia Technology Centre of the Polytechnic University of Catalonia.

During the same period—with the job title "trafficking in images and ethics"—he led photography and digital imagery seminars, conferences, radio shows, and workshops, while also doing consulting and visual design work.

In 2005, Lluís opened a new studio where he continued to work with creative imagery, publicity, and new multimedia communication technologies. He also opened a store where he could attend to beginners and more advanced amateur photographers, together with Maria Navarro i Francès (Maru). Together their goal is to put people before business.

Lluís' work has appeared in publicity campaigns, technical books, and in specialized magazines and yearbooks both locally and internationally, including "Photographs" and "Visual", among many others. He has also exhibited extensively throughout Catalonia, France, Spain, Germany, and Brazil.

Lightning Source UK Ltd.
Milton Keynes UK
UKOW021415240412

191377UK00007B/67/P